FROM THE HOOD
TO THE HOLLER

FROM THE HOOD to the HOLLER

A STORY OF SEPARATE WORLDS, SHARED DREAMS, AND THE FIGHT FOR AMERICA'S FUTURE

CHARLES BOOKER

CROWN
NEW YORK

Published in the United States by Crown, an imprint of Random House,
a division of Penguin Random House LLC, New York.

CROWN and the Crown colophon are registered trademarks of
Penguin Random House LLC.

Library of Congress Cataloging-in-Publication Data
Names: Booker, Charles, author.
Title: From the hood to the holler: a story of separate worlds, shared dreams, and
the fight for America's future / Charles Booker.
Description: First edition. | New York: Crown, [2022]
Identifiers: LCCN 2021050696 (print) | LCCN 2021050697 (ebook) |
ISBN 9780593240342 (hardcover) | ISBN 9780593240359 (ebook)
Subjects: LCSH: Booker, Charles, 1984– | Legislators—Kentucky—Biography. |
African American politicians—Kentucky—Louisville—Biography. | Kentucky—
Politics and government—1951– | Kentucky—Race relations—History—
21st century. | Louisville (Ky.)—Biography.
Classification: LCC F456.26.B66 A3 2022 (print) | LCC F456.26.B66 (ebook) |
DDC 976.9/044092 [B]—dc23/eng/20211025
LC record available at lccn.loc.gov/2021050696
LC ebook record available at lccn.loc.gov/2021050697

PRINTED IN THE UNITED STATES OF AMERICA ON ACID-FREE PAPER

CrownPublishing.com

RandomHouseBooks.com

2 4 6 8 9 7 5 3 1

First Edition

*I dedicate this book to my mom, my grandparents,
and every single person in my huge family.*

To Tanesha and my angels—Kaylin, Prestyn, and Justyce.

Kentucky, I pray this book honors you justly.

To the West End, thank you for making me who I am. This is for you.

CONTENTS

PART III

FROM THE HOOD
TO THE HOLLER

PROLOGUE

I KNEW I had to say something. I couldn't stay seated. I couldn't stay quiet.

It was March 14, 2019. We were in the final days of the year's legislative session, and it was nearly 10 P.M. We'd been in a marathon session since two that afternoon, and at the stroke of midnight we would adjourn for the governor's veto period; beyond last-minute efforts to override vetoes or rush through surprise bills, this would be the last day new laws would be passed this year. The bill up for debate was Senate Bill 9, a deceptive piece of political theater known as the Fetal Heartbeat Bill that would ban abortions as early as six weeks into a pregnancy—except that it was unlikely to ever become law, because similar bills had been passed by Republican legislatures that year and they'd all been caught up in court battles or struck down outright as unconstitutional for violating the protections of *Roe v. Wade*. This bill was likely to suffer the same fate, a fact the legislators behind it knew all too well, but they were driving its passage anyway to further fan the flames of a wedge issue that would bring their supporters out to the polls. It was a tiresome exercise for everyone, the more so for me since I hadn't eaten dinner and my glucose was running low—an always-present danger of living with type 1 diabetes.

Everyone in the Kentucky State Legislature knew the bill was a farce, a political statement masquerading as legislation. Even some of my Republican colleagues had no desire to waste time voting on it. Still, the debate droned on. Some Republicans got up and made passionate statements about faith and the sanctity of life. Others got up and accidentally said the quiet part loud: They opposed reproductive choice because they believed women should still be treated as property. Meanwhile, the rest of them stayed silent even as they planned to support the bill for craven political reasons. The previous day, an amendment had been offered by a Republican that would provide an exception for abortion in cases where the pregnancy would threaten the life of the mother. It was emphatically voted down by the majority, which tells you pretty much everything you need to know about the value these legislators placed on the sanctity of a woman's life.

As it happened, just a few days earlier we had debated another piece of legislation that, to my mind, pertained every bit as much to the sanctity of life: a bill to allow concealed carry of weapons without a permit. If passed, it would put police officers in dangerous situations and increase the likelihood that more innocent people, particularly Black and brown Kentuckians, would be shot by police. It was a contentious piece of legislation that united an unlikely coalition, as it was opposed by activists demanding justice reform, gun safety groups, and law enforcement. Its only real supporter was the NRA. It was framed as a gun rights bill, but like the Fetal Heartbeat Bill, it had nothing to do with protecting rights. It was about scoring political points at the expense of Kentuckians.

With Republicans holding a supermajority in the Kentucky House and Senate, the outcome of the debate was a foregone conclusion. That didn't stop me from fighting it. As the only legislator present who had seen police pull their firearms for a rolling-stop traffic violation and the only legislator present who recently lost multiple loved ones to gun violence, I poured my heart out against that bill. In what was likely a first in the Kentucky legislature, I acted out a scene of what this law could mean to a young Black man pulling a wallet out of his pocket. I even reenacted gunshots piercing the bodies of innocent people. I cast my vote and sat in my seat fuming while the bill passed. Now, instead of addressing poverty, homelessness, cannabis legalization, or the health of coal miners suffering from black lung, I was stuck listening to a bunch of misguided and dishonest sermonizing about abortion.

I decided I'd had enough.

I don't have time for people who twist the truth. I can't tolerate liars. We all knew the bill wasn't really about reproductive health. We all knew an issue of faith was being weaponized to divide people against each other. But nobody was standing up to say that, and I felt I had to call it to attention. If my colleagues on the right wanted to preach about this bill, I felt a charge to do some preaching myself. I pushed the white button that alerted the speaker pro tem, David Meade, that I was requesting time to speak. Several of my colleagues looked over at me, wondering if I was going to stand up and give a sermonette, as I was known to do. I looked back at them and slowly nodded. My faith wouldn't let me hold my tongue. As Kentucky State Representative for the 43rd District, I had a job to do. As one of only six Black legislators in the House, I felt the weight of that responsibility multiplied a thousandfold. As heavy as it was to carry that obligation, I did it with pride.

The 43rd District sits inside Louisville, the largest city and metropolitan area in Kentucky. With the rest of the state being largely rural—from its fertile farmland to the rolling bluegrass to the beautiful hills of Appalachia—a chasm has formed in the state legislature, and that chasm regularly pits Louisville against the rest of the state. I see that dynamic from a different perspective than most, because I don't just come from Louisville, I come from the West End of Louisville, a place so isolated and segregated that in many ways it has more in common with the hollers up in coal country than it has with the rest of the "big city." That often-ignored reality gave me a unique responsibility: to shine a light on our common struggle and bridge the divide between the urban and rural communities, to tell the stories that too often don't get told inside rooms like the Kentucky State Capitol.

Sitting there with my "request to speak" button glowing, mentally exhausted from hours of debate, my palms sweating slightly from anxiety, I thought about all the women in my life this bill would affect. I thought about my mom, my wife, my daughters. I thought about Grandma, the matriarch of my huge family on my mom's side. I thought about Maw Maw, the hardworking woman who gave birth to my dad and taught me how to use a rotary saw—all the incredible, strong Black women in my life who got up every day to stake their place in a society that didn't always acknowledge their humanity.

But they weren't the only ones on my mind. I also thought about everyone in Kentucky whose lives had been long neglected and forgotten by the people in that chamber. I thought about Appalachian coal miners like my friend Scott, who does all he can to earn a livelihood, even if it means working three different jobs in three different states. I thought about immigrant community leaders I know, like Karina, the Guatemalan native who works with families every day at La Casita Center in Louisville to help them to get counseling, legal support, and resources to survive. I thought about my cousin T.J., a young man with big dreams, wrongly arrested and thrown into the system, only to be released, awarded a settlement, and then murdered on Easter Sunday in his new Dodge Charger. I knew when I rose to speak, I'd be speaking for all of them.

Finally, it was time. The speaker pro tem acknowledged my request. I said a prayer of thanks for the charge on my heart, asked God to give me the words to say, and rose to address the chamber. I began my remarks by expressing my appreciation for my Republican colleague who'd put forth the amendment granting an exception when the life of the mother was in danger. I thanked him for the grace that he offered in his remarks.

"But," I said, "I wanted to stand and explain my vote, because I'm not here looking for your grace. See, God's grace is sufficient. And the reality of the matter is—because there are a lot of preachers in this room—we are not God. We can't be God. We don't understand—our capacity is not large enough to even grapple with what God can be and what God does. He set the whole universe into definition and reality, gentlemen. We don't know what that's about! We can't comprehend that! So why are we still trying to be God?" Because that's what these men were trying to do: sit in judgment of women and the decisions they made for their own bodies in their own lives. "We're ignoring the woman in this conversation," I said. "Every. Single. Doggone. Time."

I was preaching now. My voice boomed throughout the chamber as I pivoted to call out the larger hypocrisy going on: folks claiming to be "pro-life" on abortion legislation while simultaneously voting for gun legislation that would threaten my life. I walked my fellow legislators through what it means to be a Black man in Kentucky, the pain of having cousins murdered every year for each of the last four years. I could tell my remarks were unexpected; they brought a nuance to the debate that regularly got left out. I wasn't going to let that happen this night. I made everyone listen as I laid out the fallacy of backing the Fetal Heartbeat Bill while also supporting a permitless concealed-carry bill that would increase my chances of getting shot. "And the same folks that have the audacity to vote yes now," I said, "voted for that legislation!"

At that moment, the speaker pro tem cut in, tapping his gavel three times. "Gentlemen, I apologize," he said to the other members, as if calling out their hypocrisy were something to be sorry for. So I turned my attention to him.

"My life matters, too, Speaker!"

"Your three minutes is up."

I didn't care. I said it again. "My life matters, too, Speaker!"

"You are out of order!" he said, now pounding the gavel.

"My life matters, too, Speaker!"

"Your three minutes is up."

This time he dispensed with the gavel and simply cut off my mic. So I shouted, lifting my voice the way my mom used to do when she preached at church.

My life matters, too!!

Tears fell from my eyes as the words echoed across the room. My voice was filled with pain because, when I speak, I always visualize what I'm saying. As I said those words, I was thinking of all the people in the streets shouting them out, having to declare that their lives mattered. It was also a pain born of the desperation of being the only young Black man in that whole building, screaming in the middle of this political hurricane. No one could hear me, no one was listening, and so I had to scream it out. It was the pain of even having to scream. It hurt me that I even had to open up in that way. It hurts me now. But I wanted everyone there to understand that my truth would not be silenced even if they took my microphone away. I wanted my voice to make it to the stained glass in the ceiling forty feet above my head. I wanted my voice, *our* voice, to be heard in every room and every hallway and every corner of the Commonwealth.

A few members applauded, but they were quickly cut off by another voice yelling from across the room.

"Sit down!"

The shout came from Representative Randy Bridges, a legislator from Paducah, the largest city in McCracken County in the Purchase Region of Western Kentucky. And he hadn't just yelled it; he'd jumped to his feet, turned on me, and screamed it at the top of his lungs, his face twisted with anger.

Bridges was a short, middle-aged, mostly unassuming white man who'd used his successful real-estate business to ride into office on a wave led by Donald Trump. Prior to that moment, Rep. Bridges and I had never spoken. We voted differently most of the time, including on the abortion bill and the concealed-carry bill. But when I was growing up, I was taught that you treat everyone the way you want to be treated. Intentionally, I greeted every person in that chamber as my sister or brother. I knew that my presence was a challenge to some of my colleagues, and it was my way of helping them see me as a Kentuckian, just like them. But my kind gestures and respect clearly hadn't meant much to the man now yelling at me in defiance of House rules.

Being told to "sit down" bothered me because it reminded me of the way my grandad told me white folks used to talk to him. A short man with dark skin growing up in Mississippi, he'd been called "Boy" and "Darkie" and "Nigger." He refused to tolerate it and would fight any person who called him anything but his name: Lindsay Eugene Hearn. Grandad was also a man who dressed like a million bucks.

Grandma kept him in nice suits, and he always had shoes, socks, and a top hat to match. He wore big gold rings on his fingers and shiny cuff links on his sleeves. Most of the men in our church dressed like that on Easter Sunday. For Grandad, that look was all the time. He wanted to look his best because he didn't want anyone to doubt him; he knew he was smart, strong, and able to do whatever he wanted. When he passed, I took a lot of his dress ties, and I was wearing one of them at that marathon legislative session because I wanted to make a statement, too. Like my grandad, nobody was going to tell me to sit down.

My colleague's anger shocked me, frankly. But in that moment, Bridges was more than just angry. It was like my words had struck a chord in him. Grandad had always told me about certain types of people who fought against desegregation—not the ones who were simply ignorant or naïve about America's history but the ones who held on to Jim Crow for dear life. There's a certain tone of voice those people would use. It's the tone that you hear anytime you threaten to disturb the false reality that someone has created for themselves.

Which I understood. Facing truth isn't easy. People fight it. They turn away from it. I understood that about Randy Bridges because I could see his humanity in a way he could not see mine. He was mad, but he didn't even understand *why* he was mad. He'd grown up so ensconced in his own world that he had no understanding of mine, no understanding of why people like me keep rising up to demand that he open his eyes and see our humanity as equal to his.

When you're a young Black man in the hood, you see the cops cracking down on folks and you think you know what racism is. But you don't. Not really. Because the further you go in life, the closer you get to the center of power and the closer you get to challenging that power. That's when you see the lengths that power will go to in order to preserve itself. That night I wasn't silenced by a beat cop or a schoolteacher but by the House leadership in the center of democracy for the Commonwealth of Kentucky. It was an eye-opening moment, one that I'll never forget.

People like me are always told to sit down, get back, or shut up. No one listens to us . . . until we take a stand. Kentuckians who look like me may have been relegated to cleaning the Capitol Building in past generations, but this is a new day. I'd been elected to my office to represent my community and the entire Commonwealth, and the events of that night left me more determined than ever to do exactly that. When I walked out of that marathon session at midnight, as tired and weary as I was, I truly understood the challenge that I faced, and I knew I would never sit down again.

PART I

CHAPTER 1

GRANDMA'S HOUSE

O N COLD WINTER nights, my childhood bedroom would get well below freezing. The furnace in our old house worked, but the cracks around the windows let air in, and the holes in the roof where the squirrels gathered made sure any heat we did generate quickly escaped. Since the only heat vents were on the main level, by the time you made it to the bedrooms on the second floor it felt like you were walking around outside. The floors were made from skinny wooden planks that creaked when you walked. When it was that cold it was like walking on ice, but wearing my socks inside the house would get me in trouble, because my mom didn't want to deal with dirty socks. "C.J.!" she'd holler up the stairs. "You know better than to have those white socks on in the house. You're gonna have sock feet!"

To avoid "sock feet" I would quickly run from room to room, hurrying to get to the warmest place in the house: my bed. It was covered with big, beautiful quilts my mom used to sew from the scraps from her old work suits and blue jeans and wool coats. I had four or five of them layered one on top of another, creating a mountain of covers on my bed. They were so heavy I had to slide my feet in near my pillow and burrow my way under.

Eventually I got a space heater, too, courtesy of Mr. Eugene, my mom's second husband. I wasn't a fan of Mr. Eugene. They'd gotten married about a year before, and in all the pictures from their wedding I'm this grumpy seven-year-old hanging around in the back of the frame, a big frown on my face. My new stepfather was a fast-talking preacher who always kept a Bible close by and usually walked everywhere he went. I liked that he made my mom laugh, but I didn't trust him.

Mr. Eugene was always looking for a way to save a dollar—or "cut corners," as my grandad would say. Whether it was tattered clothes from a thrift store or junk from a back alley, Mr. Eugene would snatch things up and bring them home for us to use. One day Mr. Eugene walked through the door carrying this busted-up floor heater with a frayed power cord that he must have pulled out of the trash. "I'm sure this still works," he said, as he lugged the old thing into the house. "We can use it in Charlie's room." He pulled out some electrical tape and wrapped it around the hole in the cord. Then he hauled it up the stairs and down the hallway and set it up near the foot of my bed.

When he plugged it in, sparks flew and there was a loud *POP!* Then the power went out. My mother stared at him, worried, but Mr. Eugene waved her off. "Ain't nothing wrong with this heater!" he huffed as he went down to the basement to throw the circuit breaker and put the power back on. When he did, the floor heater slowly hummed to life, eventually getting so hot that my skin burned if I got too close to it. I was grateful for the heat, but I didn't trust that thing. I couldn't forget the pop of that spark. The way it was always buzzing and cutting out was not reassuring. The fact that my old bedroom door always jammed and got stuck, that wasn't great, either.

Mr. Eugene was the whole reason we were living in a run-down old house with squirrels in the roof in the first place. My mom and dad had split up when I was a couple years old. After their divorce, my mom and I moved around a lot, eventually settling in a little apartment in South Louisville for a few years. I loved that apartment. It was just the two of us playing endless games of Uno and her watching me ride my Big Wheel around the parking lot. It was home. All that changed the day she met Mr. Eugene. He started coming around more and more, and so did his older son and two daughters. Then my baby cousin Bianca moved in with us while her mom, one of my older cousins, got on her feet. So my mom and Mr. Eugene went house hunting, and pretty soon we were moving into this ancient wooden house from the 1920s at 35th and Market in the West End.

The first time I saw it, my heart sank. It was big—big enough that it had been carved up into three apartments that now needed to be converted back into a single-family home. But it had been abandoned, left to the squatters and the elements. There was junk all over the lawn, broken appliances, rotted wood and shattered glass, pieces of furniture left behind by the previous tenants or squatters. Inside, every couple steps you'd come across a roach or a mouse dropping. Off the living room was a huge closet filled to the ceiling with old tires, pieces of chairs, bricks, and dirty mops. A rank odor followed you from room to room.

But my mom is a visionary. She sees only the potential in things, so we moved in, and she rolled up her sleeves and put on some gloves and set to work making a home. With every step through that dilapidated house, her smile grew. Everywhere I saw a problem, Mom saw an opportunity. She'd walk to a corner, wave her arm across the room, and describe everything she could do with it. Everywhere there was blight, she saw the chance to turn it into something beautiful. And when I looked at the house through her eyes, she was right. Every room had original hardwood floors. Underneath the dust and debris, the dining room had wood trim and brass finishes that looked like something you'd see in the movies. Out on the front porch there was this old, rotted, rickety swing hanging from rusted chains. My mom took one look and blurted out with joy, "We can sit out here and watch the sun set!"

After we moved in, weeds were pulled, mops were pushed, paint was rolled, and piles of trash were loaded up and carried out. It took some time, but in the end we had a place that felt like home. Mom even restored the old wooden floors throughout the house. By the time she was done they shined like new. It wasn't perfect, but it was ours.

Then, one week before Christmas, not long after I turned eight, I'd crawled up under my mountain of covers and drifted off to sleep with the orange glow of Mr. Eugene's heater flickering at the foot of my bed next to the closet. It was toasty, but as the night went on it got hotter than it had ever been, so much so that the heat wrenched me out of my sleep. As I opened my eyes, everything was blurry, but I could sense a thick haze in the room, like a cloud glowing orange. I scratched my head and started rubbing my eyes. Then the smell hit me. This wasn't a dream. I bolted upright, and the whole room snapped into focus. Sparks had leapt from the heater into my closet, sending my clothes up in a tower of flames that stood between me and the door. A sheet of fire was slowly creeping its way to the edge of the mountain of blankets that covered me.

I screamed, *"Mama! Mama! My room is on fire!"* I screamed it over and over again, sweat pouring down my face, but no one responded. No one could hear me. I looked over at my window but realized right away that jumping from the second story wasn't an option. I turned and looked back through the flames to the door. It was closed tight, which meant it was surely stuck. I knew I didn't have any choice. My survival instincts kicked in. I threw off the covers, stood up on the bed, got my balance, and jumped for it.

And I made it, crashing into the door on the far side of the flames. I didn't even stop to see if I'd been burned. Petrified that the door would be jammed shut like it always was, I grabbed the doorknob with both hands and yanked on it with all my might. Miraculously, it swung right open, as if there were angels looking out for me.

I ran down the hall and into Mom's room, screaming the whole way. Mr. Eugene woke up first, groggy and rubbing his eyes. "What's going on, Charlie?" he said. I tried to tell him my room was on fire, but, agitated from being woken up, he didn't hear a word I was saying. He cut me off and told me to go back to bed.

I kept screaming at my mom that there was a fire and she needed to get up. Her eyes flew open, and it was like she understood me in her sleep, because she woke up screaming, *"Jesus, Jesus, Jesus!"* as she jumped out of bed and burst out of the room to grab little Bianca out of her crib.

Mr. Eugene finally got up as well. Completely misreading the peril of the situation, he took his little cup from his nightstand to get some water from the bathroom to try and put the fire out. My mom wasn't about to stop and debate him on the matter. She yelled at me from Bianca's room down the hall, *C.J.! Get downstairs! Right! Now!*

She didn't have to tell me twice. I ran down the hallway and all the way down the stairs, and as I got to the bottom I could hear my mother coming right behind me. I turned and looked up and she came flying through the air. She'd jumped the last ten steps, cradling Bianca in her arms as she glided to the landing, falling to the floor and twisting her body to avoid landing on Bianca before rolling up to her feet by the front door. The whole thing seemed like it had happened in slow motion. Neither of them even got a scratch.

Running to the kitchen, Mom grabbed the phone and made two calls, the first to 911 and the second to my grandad. Then we ran outside and stood in the street and watched our house burn.

I hadn't had time to get any shoes, so I stood barefoot on the asphalt, my feet all scraped up from running out of the house. It must have been freezing that night, given how cold it was in the house, but my adrenaline was running so high I don't remember it as being cold at all. As I watched the orange glow engulf the roof and the top floor, I started to cry. It was like watching an episode of *The Twilight Zone.* "This can't be happening," I thought. All my clothes were gone. Every award I ever got from school was going up in flames. Even the presents Mom had bought for Christmas were in there. How would we fix this? What would we do? I felt empty and numb.

After a few minutes that felt like an eternity, fire trucks and ambulances came roaring up the street, and I watched as the firefighters jumped off the truck and ran into the house. Soon after they ran in, having failed in his heroic attempt to put out the fire caused by his prized heater, Mr. Eugene came out. One by one, our neighbors walked out into the street to watch the fire. They asked us if we were okay. Still speechless, we nodded yes.

Then, out of the darkness, I saw a set of headlights turning onto our street. It was Grandad in his big burgundy Chevy Astro conversion van, coming to pick us up. Seeing his van gave me the first feeling of peace I'd had since jolting out of bed. Mr. Eugene stayed behind as my mother, Bianca, and I climbed in. Mom put her arms around me as Grandad drove off. I couldn't believe everything was gone. I couldn't believe I'd actually made it out of that room. As we rode along in silence, I said a prayer quietly to myself, grateful to be alive and grateful to know we were going to the one place we'd be safe: Grandma's house.

GROWING UP IN the West End, much of my life revolved around Grandma's house, which is what everyone called it even though Grandad lived there, too. It was the mothership, command central, the place where we all gathered, which given the size of the family meant it was always cramped. If we all have a ministry, Grandma's was family. She always wanted a big one, and she loved babies. After raising eleven of her own, as they started to leave the house, she and Grandad decided to open their home to foster children, too, to provide a home to children who didn't have one. Over time, Grandma and Grandad formally adopted seven of them.

Anyone who'd ever lived at Grandma's house even for a little while was considered family. They were always welcome at Christmas and Thanksgiving. So by the time my generation came along, there had to be at least seventy siblings and step-siblings and cousins from all the different families. You couldn't walk through the hallway without bumping into someone, and the minute you walked into that house you knew you were home.

Grandma's house sat in the middle of a small, congested street, surrounded by houses that looked just like it. When I came down 38th Street and turned onto Parker Avenue, my eyes would get big and I'd stretch my neck to see who was outside. Before we even parked and got out of the car, friends and relatives would be waving on the street. A ball would be in the air. A hula hoop would be spinning. A few of my uncles would be in the driveway talking sports and I could hear them calling out my name.

"C.J.!"

"What's going on, Chuck?"

"What's going on, Uncle?" I would shout back as I got out of the car and hugged each one, with big smiles all around. Uncle Tony would be flexing his muscles and talking about his workout regimen. Uncle Terrance would be leaning up against his car, with music playing and a beer hidden out of view so Grandma couldn't see it. I marveled at them all.

Then it was time for my entrance. I'd make sure my shoes were clean and my fit was straight, and I'd walk through the sea of cousins. I was one of the oldest, and everyone would yell my name and run to give me a hug; there would be at least ten hugs before I got to the porch.

The porch was small but always packed. Each step up the front stairs was a dap or a handshake, as each step was a seat for two or three more cousins. Navigating around them was like running an obstacle course. The front door would be opening and closing as people went in and out, fanning the smell of Grandma's cooking into the yard, and it always smelled so good. Even though Grandad worked several jobs from sunup to sundown, there was never a lot of money to go around, but Grandma was a magician in the kitchen. Between a garden in the backyard and the food commodities and WIC we got from the government, no one ever went without a meal, and that included neighbors, church members, extended family, even passersby on a Sunday afternoon. Every Sunday felt like the story from the Bible about Jesus and the two fish and the five loaves of bread. The only difference is that we also had cakes and pies.

When I hit that last step and made it to the porch, if she wasn't in the kitchen, Grandma would be sitting in her long jean skirt and Christ Temple Choir T-shirt, hair pulled back in a bun, her rolled-up crossword puzzle beside her. "Hey, C.J.!" she'd say, letting out a joyous laugh as I leaned down to hug her. Then she'd smile her radiant smile, the light sparkling off her gold teeth.

"How was school?" she'd say. "You still getting all *A*s?"

"Yes, ma'am."

Grandad would be to her left, his cup of lemonade resting on the rail, his Louisville Cardinals cap on tight. His right hand, short a few fingers from an accident at the aluminum factory, would be reaching out for a handshake.

"Hey Charlie! You doing all right? What you think about the Cardinals? They sure were turning that ball over, but they pulled it out!"

I would shake my head and laugh. It was always good to see him, but I knew if I didn't keep moving, a story would soon begin and a line of cousins would soon be forming trying to get in the house. Right inside the front door, I'd usually find a few more cousins singing and dancing and cutting up—that is, until Grandma yelled for the kids to go to the basement, at which point, one after the other, we'd all line up and rumble down the stairs.

The adults had the upstairs, but the basement was ours. There were so many of us and the house was so small, every day something was spilled on the floor or broken. Sending the children to the basement was Grandma's way of keeping the house from being completely destroyed. The basement was a wide-open concrete floor, perfect for doing cartwheels, with couches lined around the sides. After school, we'd all head down there for what was, in effect, free daycare for our working parents. On Friday nights we would all huddle on the couches to watch movies, or pile the couch cushions on the floor to make forts and have huge pillow fights. It was like a nonstop party.

As full as Grandma's house was with people, it was filled even more with love. Not the simple kind of love that always makes you smile but the kind of love that pushes you, inspires you, calls you out, makes you sing and, sometimes, makes you cry. There was always a story being told, a gospel song being played, an eruption of loud laughter, a heated argument, or an all-out fight.

A core value in our family is that we fought for one another. We always had one another's backs. We helped one another with homework. When you had a major victory, everyone would show up to support you. When you fell down, everyone would be there to pick you up. No one necessarily talked about the troubles they faced at home, but as kids, we could always tell if someone was having a tough time. If you missed a meal, got in trouble at school, or were bothered by seeing the street taped off from a shooting, you didn't really need to say anything. Everyone else just knew.

Even when there was drama or disagreement in the family, when someone was hurt, all of that was put aside. When you are raised with such a deep connection to family, you understand the importance of selflessness, communication, loyalty, and love. These things are a type of wealth that money can never buy. We didn't have money, make no mistake about it. But you could never have convinced me that *poor* was a term that remotely applied to us. Our love was too deep, our faith was too great, and our hardworking spirit was too strong. The struggles we faced didn't seem like struggles. We may have experienced times where we didn't have the things other children did, but we never went without, and because of that I knew that even when we didn't have a house, we always had a home.

WHEN GRANDAD PULLED up to Grandma's house on the night of the fire, it was pitch-black out. There were no hula hoops in the street, no cousins playing ball or sitting on the steps up to the porch. Bone-tired and shivering from the cold, we walked into the living room to a rare quiet scene. All the aunts and uncles and cousins were fast asleep. There was no empty bed for me and my mom. There were no empty couches and no empty chairs, either.

"C.J.," Mom calmly urged. "Go get one of your Grandma's T-shirts to sleep in and get some blankets out of the closet."

"Where am I going to sleep?"

"Just find a spot downstairs on the floor."

I got the T-shirt and blanket and went downstairs. I wasn't a fan of sleeping on the basement floor. Most of it was bare concrete except for the area near the TV, where there was a thin green carpet. Grandma's house always had roaches, too, and I was always afraid one would crawl on me, like the time one crawled in my big cousin Geno's mouth. But I found a bare spot on the carpet, curled up, and did my best to get to sleep.

For the next few weeks, the routine was pretty much the same.

Mom slept on the couch upstairs most nights, but sometimes she slept with me on the floor. The bigger challenge was school. In the beginning, I hoped this whole "my house burned down" excuse might get me out of class for a while. My mother, always prioritizing education as she did, quickly disabused me of that notion. "Just because our house caught fire doesn't mean you get to miss class," she said, but the idea of going to school and taking tests when my whole life was upside down seemed unbearable. I didn't even have any clothes to wear. They'd all burned up in the fire. For a young kid, it was a lot to process.

My mom's faith never wavered. She assured me we'd be okay no matter what. "Son," she said, "if the Lord sees you to it, He will see you through it." And we didn't have to rely on faith alone, because we had family.

Everyone showed up. My aunts, my uncles, my cousins. They helped us get clothes, kept us fed, and even helped fix up the house on 35th and Market. The fire had taken a huge chunk of the second floor, but the building itself was still salvageable. I was too young to understand what insurance was, but I overheard Mom and Mr. Eugene talking about it, and while we had some coverage for the major repairs, it wasn't enough to fix everything. It didn't matter. For everything else, we had Grandad.

Grandad had moved up to Louisville from Mississippi as a teenager. There weren't many good-paying jobs for Black folks back then, but since he was good with his hands, he used that to build a career. Like a lot of people of the West End, Grandad was a hustler, meaning he always figured out a way to keep the lights on and put food on the table. It made him a jack of all trades. He'd get up early to work at the factory, then spend his off hours fixing cars, repairing appliances, doing electrical work, and raising crops in the yard to feed his family. To me, he seemed as strong as twenty men. Even with his missing fingers, he still had the powerful handshake of a man half his age. I was convinced he could do anything.

When it came time to fix up our house, Grandad took over the project. He had shifts of people coming into the house—my uncles, all of the people he did odd jobs with over the years. Even the neighbors would wander in and pick up a hammer. He had them doing plumbing repairs, rewiring the electrical, putting up cabinets, painting the walls. Even though they were all volunteers, he was still hard on them. "Wayne, don't move that nail!" "Archie, that's the wrong drill!" It was like a comedy routine, but I never let them know I thought that. I would quietly do the tasks Grandad asked me to do, making sure to keep a straight face as Grandad gave everyone a hard time.

The house wasn't perfect when we moved back in. It was still old. It still had creaks and leaks. But seeing the smile on my mom's face as she walked through each room was amazing. I loved my new bedroom. Now I had carpet, so there were no more cold wooden floors at night. The door to my room had been fixed so it didn't get stuck anymore. We even had vents that reached all the way upstairs, bringing heat straight up from the basement, so I was done with Mr. Eugene's space heaters, too. Walking through the house was exciting and weird. It was like watching our lives being put back together. It felt like much more than a home repair project. It felt like we mattered.

That first night back, with my mom by my side, I kneeled next to my bed and folded my hands. Together we asked God for the grace we prayed for every day. "May the angels be encamped around and about us, keeping us safe." As we said, "Amen," I smiled to myself: Our prayer had been answered. I got up, gave Mom a hug, and then slid under the mound of covers, pulling them up to my chin.

Mom leaned down and kissed me on my forehead.

"Sweet dreams."

CHAPTER 2

EARL

"*C*.J., IT'S TIME *to come in and eat! Put the basketball away! Say bye to your friends and get ready for dinner!*"

On long summer evenings, my mom always had to call me in for dinner, because every night I was out in the street playing basketball—and by "basketball" I mean shooting baskets on the milk crate we had nailed up to the utility pole. Hearing her voice hollerin' through the screen door was the start of our nightly ritual. I'd dap up my friends, throw the basketball into our old rickety garage, and run to the house, using my shirt to wipe the sweat off my face as I called into the kitchen, "What are we going to eat, Mama?" Then the delicious smell would hit me, answering my question before she could. I'd hurry to change my shirt and we'd sit down for our family dinner, me and Mama and Bianca, and sometimes Mr. Eugene. We would all pray and dig in, and I wasted no time scarfing it down.

I loved my mom's cooking. It didn't matter if it was fried Spam, frozen fish sticks from the Save-a-Lot, canned Glory greens, doctored ramen noodles, or instant mac and cheese, I always ate it as if it were a gourmet meal. As far as I was concerned, she was the best cook in the world, because I could tell that every time she set down my plate for me to eat, she was telling me she loved me. Nothing had to be said. She would smile and gently put her hand on my head as she sat down next to me. I'd smile back and say my prayers so we could eat. There wasn't a lot of talking during dinner—Mom made sure I didn't talk with food in my mouth—but it was our time to be together and have some peace. I looked forward to that time each day.

Then, one evening, we were going through the whole routine—the holler through the screen door, the sweaty shirt, me bowing my head to pray—but my mom didn't sit down next to me.

"Hurry up and eat, baby," she said as she set down my plate and walked out of the room.

"Aren't you going to eat too, Mama?"

"You just eat, son. I'll be okay."

"Yes, ma'am."

Something was wrong.

"Why aren't you eatin', Mama? It's dinnertime. You're supposed to be eating with me."

"Son, don't worry about Mama," she said breezily. "Everything's fine. Quit asking questions and eat your food before it gets cold."

I shrugged it off and kept eating, figuring she had her reasons. Then the next day it happened again. Then the next, and the next. Our whole afternoon routine would go as normal, but she would skip sitting down to dinner. It started to agitate me. That peace I felt when Mom sat down with me was gone, and I didn't know why.

I started peppering her with questions, and every night she gave me the same hand wave and the same dismissive answer. "Everything's fine, son. Go ahead and eat so your food doesn't get cold." None of it felt right. This was our time together, and I wanted that. Besides, I was hungry and Bianca was hungry, so Mom had to be hungry, too.

On the fourth or fifth night of this, she brought my plate out and set it down, and as she started her walk back to the kitchen I asked again, "Mama, why don't you eat with me anymore? I'm confused."

She stopped at the doorway and turned to look at me.

"Son, Mama's not eating because there's only enough food for you and Bianca. But that's okay. I'll be fine. Mama just needs you to eat so you can get ready for school."

Growing up, I never really knew how hard life was for my mother. Most of the time she protected me from the burdens she carried. But in that moment she pulled the curtain back and showed me a side of her life that I've only glimpsed a handful of times since. I was stunned, and I was grateful. She wasn't eating because of me, because of her love for me. More than that, she was letting me know I was worthy of that kind of love and that kind of sacrifice.

As she walked away, tears started to fall down my face. I wiped them on my sleeve and finished eating my dinner. I didn't want Mom to go without to take care of me. I didn't want her to be hungry, and I felt a deep determination to make sure she never had to do that again.

MY MOM ALWAYS sacrificed for family. For her, there was never really any other option. Out of eleven kids, she was the oldest. She was named Earletta after my great-great-aunt, but everyone called her Earl for short. With Grandad working over twelve hours a day, by junior year of high school my mom had to stop going to class so that she could help out more at home, the same thing Grandma had done for her siblings when she was a teenager.

My mom was struck from the same mold as her mother, and Grandma was a rock. JoAnn C. Hearn was her name, and despite the fact that she'd never finished high school, she was the expert in every room she was in. Mom was the same, stepping in and all but raising some of her younger brothers and sisters, my aunts and uncles. And she didn't just raise them. She fought for them and protected them, too. One of my favorite stories about my mom is one my aunties Lisa and Linda would tell, about the time one of them got jumped. "So listen, C.J.," they'd say. "We were fighting in the street. It was a group of girls ganging on us. Your mama was back at the house, so we didn't think she knew what was going on. Then, out of nowhere, here she comes. She starts grabbing the girls and tossing them off of us. All we could see were arms and legs flying, because your mom was tossing them girls in the air!" Every time they told the story, they'd act out the parts, impersonating my mom as she beat up all the girls, and whenever they did Mom would listen and smile and shrug, like it was nothing. She's a sweet woman, but don't ever mess with family.

My mom's sacrifice for her siblings paid dividends. All the kids grew up right and soon they were all working, too. Uncle Tony and Uncle Alonzo learned to cut hair, which meant I hardly ever had to go to a barbershop when I was little. Uncle Terrance and Uncle Lamont performed in a dance group, traveling the country to show off their incredible break-dancing skills. My aunts all became hustlers in their own right, working multiple jobs in hospitals and factories and schools while raising children of their own, some of them as single parents. Hearing them talk about what my mother means to them is always humbling; it's like everybody knows she's special, but I'm the lucky one that gets to be her son.

I was born on October 20, 1984, and my mom always called me her miracle baby. I'm an only child not because she didn't want more children but because of health complications. I remember her having several miscarriages when I was little. Besides me, the one time she did carry a baby to term was my little sister, Ebony, who lived only a few moments after being born. We both cried for a while after this, but I know I can never fully understand what my mom went through. All I know is that she made sure to always tell me how much she loved me, and her hugs always told me that I meant the world to her.

Mom and I had each other, but most months we didn't have much else. I didn't understand what it meant to be poor, but no matter what hardship we endured, Mom always taught me to see our challenges as opportunities to grow. Given everything my mom had done for my aunts and uncles, they would never hesitate to help out when things were tight, but she rarely let on that we needed the help. She just juggled as many jobs and side hustles as she could, from working at TJ Maxx to serving pizza at Mr. Gatti's, from putting in long hours at a fabricating warehouse to spending years in a distribution center for Natural Wonders, a science and nature company. Mom did it all.

She never told me how much money she made, but like any kid I often went snooping around. I would regularly bring the mail into the house, and one time I snuck a look at her pay stub and it shocked me. I didn't understand what minimum wage was, but even then I knew that six dollars an hour wasn't a lot of money.

The pay stubs always came in the mail alongside a stack of bills. I learned how to read a Louisville Gas & Electric statement pretty early on, and we were always months behind. The bill in the brown envelope was always the last one to come before the lights were cut off. Those came far too often.

I had no idea how she did all the things she did for us with so little money. I was convinced she worked miracles, and, in her own way, she did. She'd done some modeling in her earlier years. She never left the house without a pair of high heels, and she always wore elegant suits and dresses. To look at them, you'd think they cost hundreds of dollars. She would pin a beautiful brooch to her collar, place a large hat on her head that matched her outfit (we called them church hats), and step out like the star of the show. Her secret was that, like Grandma, she's a seamstress. Everything she wore she made herself. She even made my clothes, creating from scratch polyester and linen shorts with matching shirts that I loved.

In church we always used to say, "We don't look like what we've been through!" That was especially true when it came to my mom. I always got anxious when I saw that brown bill from LG&E, but then I'd look to my mom and she never showed a hint of worry, so I concluded that everything must be okay. "Don't let anything steal your joy," she would always say. Even in the dark, we knew God would make a way. If she was able to walk around singing after she saw the same brown envelope that I saw, surely I could keep it together and support her. Inevitably, the lights would end up getting cut off. The water, too. But Mom never stopped singing. She would regularly quote 1 Corinthians, chapter 10, verse 13, reminding me that God never puts more on us than we can bear.

THE MAIN REASON we were able to survive the toughest of times was our strong foundation of faith. I was born and raised as a member of Christ Temple Christian Life Center. My grandparents were one of the founding families, and all my aunts, uncles, and cousins went there. Christ Temple Apostolic church was our spiritual home and a haven from the trauma that existed in the streets of the West End; the ride from our house to church would take us past several liquor stores, abandoned houses, drug corners, and people wandering the streets looking to sober up or find a place to sleep.

Our lives revolved around the church. We often spent five or six days of the week there for prayer meetings, Bible class, Friday night worship, choir practice, revivals, and, of course, morning and evening services on Sundays. Since there were so many of us, Grandad ended up getting a couple of used church vans to transport us. Many times, we would all meet over at Grandma's house, and Grandad would have the vans running like shuttles to get us all to church in time for Sunday school. We never missed Sunday school.

My family was deeply involved in every aspect of the church. Grandad was the senior deacon for the church, officiating the offerings, handling church administration, and counting all the money. Grandma and my mom were ushers, passing out the fans and helping people find a seat.

Mom was one of the lead singers in the choir. She sings an opera soprano, and when she hit those glass-shattering high notes, everyone would jump up and start shouting. Pastor loved Mom's singing so much that he would randomly call her to come up during service to sing a solo. I'd watch with pride as she held her choir robe and did a Holy Ghost dance across the stage. In my head I was shouting, "That's my mama!"

I come from a family of bishops, pastors, evangelists, deacons, ushers, choir directors, gospel singers, musicians, praise team leaders, Sunday school teachers, and church janitors, so there was rarely a moment where our conversations didn't revolve around church in some way. As the song would say, we were part of a "hand-clapping, foot-stomping, tongue-talking, Pentecostal, Apostolic church." It shaped everything in our lives. We prayed regularly throughout the week. We weren't allowed to listen to worldly music, weren't allowed to wear shorts above our knees or pants that sagged below our waists, and we were strongly discouraged from doing things like going to the movies.

Strict though it was, the message from Christ Temple was always rooted in grace and love, and it directed us to understand that mistakes don't have to mean life is over. In every service, there would be an altar call, where we could confess our sins and shortcomings and ask God for healing and forgiveness.

I went to the altar often.

I was baptized when I was nine years old. Once you repented and dedicated your life to Christ, you would get baptized to wash away your sins. That process is called being "born again." It was a dedication to being rooted and guided in faith, to live upright, and to make sure every action or word we said was directed toward loving one another, helping our neighbors, and lifting up the word of God.

After you were baptized, ministers in the church would counsel you. We would learn more about the teachings of the Bible and take a more active role in church, and after showing that we were ready, we would tarry to receive the Holy Ghost. Tarrying was a process of praying, crying out to God, and waiting to receive the Holy Spirit. We would go into a back room of the church and cry out for the Holy Ghost. There were several small rooms down a hallway behind the pulpit. Each room had a curtain for privacy and benches for the saints to kneel on. Ministers would sit with us, praying as well, and encourage us to cry out to God.

In the Apostolic faith, we believe that receiving the gift of the Holy Ghost is evidenced by speaking in tongues. We would have to tarry until that happened, which could take several hours. It truly was an exercise of faith. It was an exercise of incredible focus on something bigger than you. You had to believe with everything in you that this deep elevation in the spirit was possible. Those aspects of personal commitment and unlimited faith meant as much to me as the idea of speaking in other languages. There is power in finding that place where nothing will stop you from fighting for what you believe in. When I came out of the tarrying room, the church shouted and danced in celebration.

I felt like a new person after that night. Faith became the foundation to everything I did. The power of the Holy Spirit taught me that no matter how hard the night may be, joy will come in the morning.

That every single step I take, and every word I speak, is to be intentional in giving God glory. Still, as strong as my faith was, I had questions. At night, I would sit on Mom's bed and ask her about everything under the sun. "Why does God allow bad things to happen? Why did God allow our house to catch on fire? Why do we always learn about how to get through tough times?"

She would take time to answer all of my questions, even admitting when she didn't have an answer. Although there were strict practices in our faith, Mom never got upset when I questioned them or wrestled with their inconsistencies. Like everyone, she faced her own struggles with the earthly failings of the church, but she never let them disconnect her from her own relationship with God. Because of that, her faith sustained her through the crucible she was called on to bear.

TRAUMA ECHOES DOWN through the generations, and when I was a child the trauma of my father's childhood reverberated throughout my mother's life and my own. In many ways, it still does to this day. When my dad was eleven years old, his father was shot and killed during a domestic altercation with my dad's mother, my Maw Maw. The man was an abusive husband, and one fateful day he forced Maw Maw to defend herself. Afterward, she immediately went right down to the police station and turned herself in, letting the authorities know what had happened. She was initially charged with his murder, but once all the facts were in they ruled it self-defense and she was free to go.

In the wake of that trauma, my father struggled with mental health issues his whole life. It caused problems in my parents' marriage, and they divorced before I was two, a stigma my mother had to carry in a church where divorce is seen as a great sin. I never knew my mom and dad as a married couple. I knew my father only on weekends, and there was a lot about his life of which I knew nothing at all. I do know that my father coped with his trauma by blocking it out and never speaking of it again. I know that as the oldest of four he was very protective of his siblings. I know that he was a soft-spoken boy who learned to laugh and keep things light to avoid dealing with the drama at home, and as a result he struggled in school and eventually dropped out to join the Army.

I also know that for the rest of his life he'd go through times of being quiet and melancholy and withdrawn for reasons that he never explained to me. He had a hard time being vulnerable or expressing himself or dealing with pain. He did confide in me a lot when I was little. When I was still in elementary school, we would sit in his car for hours, and he'd talk to me about his past relationships and ask for my advice. I can't say I necessarily knew what we were talking about or what I should say to him, but it always seemed like my advice helped.

My mom and dad actually had a lot in common. Both of them were born in 1960 and were raised in the West End. Both were the oldest in their families; both dropped out of high school to work and support their families. They met not long after he'd returned from a deployment in Germany. He was still in the Reserves and working at KFC, where he met my Uncle Terrance, who introduced him to my mother, and a few months later they were married. Once they learned that I was on the way, Dad left the service and found a full-time job working the third shift at the post office, and they settled on the East End of Louisville in an area called Jeffersontown, or J-Town. But by the time I was old enough to comprehend the world and ask questions about it, Mom and I were already living in our little apartment, and I only saw my dad once a week after school, every other weekend, and holidays.

But, man, what incredible weekends they were.

My dad had a shiny black Honda CR-X. It had low-profile rims with spinners, two subwoofers in the back that made it sound like a concert on wheels, and neon lights underneath that lit up the street. We called it the Batmobile. He told me it was the fastest car in the world, unbeatable in a race. Because he was my dad and my hero, I believed him.

In my mom's Apostolic household, we weren't allowed to listen to anything other than gospel music. Things were different with Dad.

When he came to pick me up, before the Batmobile even pulled into sight I could hear his music blasting from down the block: Michael Jackson, Dr. Dre, Mint Condition, Tupac, the Isley Brothers, Keith Sweat, House of Pain, A Tribe Called Quest. Through him I learned about rap and R&B, even some rock and roll, and seeing his appreciation for all different types of music helped me come to love them too. The rides in his car were the best, especially if he'd just bought a new tape. Whenever a cussword would play, he'd immediately apologize, but he wouldn't stop the tape.

Climbing into the Batmobile with him was like going on an adventure. He'd have his driving gloves on and his hat on backward, sunglasses hanging in the neck of his sleeveless T-shirt and a fanny pack clipped around his waist, which was where he'd keep the money to get milkshakes later on. I knew we were going to have a great time, even if we just hung around his apartment. One of my favorite parts of going over to Dad's house was the food. He'd become an exceptional cook during his time overseas in the Army, and I knew that whatever he made for me would be delicious. If he didn't cook, we would order pizza, rent a movie from Blockbuster, and lie on the floor with our shirts off like bachelors. He even bought me a Nintendo, and we often played long into the night, way past my bedtime.

Dad and I would go to church, too. For years he was a member of Hill Street Baptist Church, which was the spiritual home for his side of the family. He was such a smooth guy, it always surprised me to see him sing and worship in service, but faith was a centerpiece for him, same as it was for Mom. For a man who kept many of his emotions to himself, he found joy in church. It was a haven for him, and it gave him a source of meaning and clarity; he needed a connection to something that could protect him, and the word of God gave him that protection. Though not as outspoken as my mom, he too found himself in ministry, eventually leaving Hill Street and finding a more permanent spiritual home at St. Stephen Church, the largest Black church in Kentucky.

As he sought a new church home, Dad and a friend from the Army started a drill team to engage and uplift young Black teenagers in the city. He called them the Disciples for Christ, and taught them to step with military precision and perform drills and dance routines. Then he'd bring it all together with a gospel rap.

"Check this out, Buddy," he'd say. "I have a new rap. It's called 'Shake the Dust Off Your Feet.' When I say my lines, you and the team will come in and yell out, 'Shake the dust off your feet!' It comes from the Book of Matthew. It's Jesus's way of saying we need to shake the haters off."

I wouldn't say it was corny, but he definitely rapped like a dad in my eyes, like a mixture between Kurtis Blow and Will Smith. However, the words were powerful, and he delivered them just right.

Every church he moved to, he continued with this step team, bringing young men from the other churches and welcoming more young men from the new church he joined. As his son, I was automatically on the team as well. I started when I was around eleven, and I was definitely the smallest person on the squad, as the rest of the team was in high school. Dad got us all matching white sweat suits and matching shoes. The sweat suits had DISCIPLES FOR CHRIST airbrushed on them in black-and-gold letters, both on the sweatshirt and running down the legs of the pants. We would perform during service as well as at events and programs around the city.

I was always a little nervous. Singing in the choir at Mom's church helped prepare me for being in front of an audience; I was a natural in front of a crowd. But performing in a step team/gospel rap group was not something I ever saw myself doing. We would start the show by standing at parade rest. Dad would bark out formation commands like he was back in the service: "Left face! Right face! Forward march!" We would line up and march down the center aisle of the church and head to the stage, singing as we marched: "That's the sound of the men, working for the Lord!"

When we made it to the front of the church, we would line up facing the congregation. The claps and cheers would get louder when they saw me, this little kid with a big baggy sweat suit standing with these tall, muscular teenagers and adults. The step leader would pop out of line, start the step, and then we would go at it, clapping our hands behind our backs, on our chests, and under our knees, performing the intricate steps. Then we would finish and hold our position, and the music would kick in, and Dad would grab the mic and perform his rap like he was Jay-Z rocking the crowd, quoting Bible verses and mixing in positive messages about loving and being kind to your neighbors.

I enjoyed stepping with my dad, but more than that, it made me proud of him. I saw my dad's confidence the most during the times when he led those drill teams. It bonded us together. In everything my dad did, I felt as if he was doing all he could to be there for me, in part to make sure I didn't have the painful experiences he'd had when he was little. "Your grandfather never really spent time with me, Buddy," he'd say as we were getting ready to play basketball or ride bikes. That was the most he ever spoke about his childhood. Whenever we were together I would try to hug him and tell him I loved him, and he would always respond, "Me too, buddy." But it was enough, because I knew through his actions that he loved me.

The only thing I didn't love about being with my dad was having to leave Mom. But when the weekend was over, it was equally hard to leave him and go home. I missed Mom when I was with Dad, and I missed Dad while I was with Mom. They seemed to have a good relationship. They never really argued, at least not around me. Still, children can sense things, and I always knew something wasn't quite right. It was in the way Dad avoided Mom. His words were kind, but he kept them short. He didn't really make eye contact, and for most of my childhood the cause for their separation was a mystery. I knew both of them loved me, but I'm sure every child of divorce wonders at some point if it was their fault, and I asked my mother that many times. She was always adamant that that wasn't the case, so I continued to ask and investigate, which is how I learned about his melancholy quiet spells. "Your dad always felt distant when we moved to J-Town," Mom told me eventually. "There were times he would just sit and stare out of the window in silence. I would try to talk to him, but he wouldn't respond. I never knew what was wrong, but I knew he wasn't happy."

I saw some of what she was talking about. On our weekends to-gether, we always had fun if we were out doing something, but if we didn't have anything planned, he'd be in the house, lying down or moping around, piles of clothes everywhere and dirty dishes in the sink. Some weekends he'd sleep the whole time. The blinds would be closed, it would be dark in the house, and I would just be sitting in the living room playing the Nintendo.

Then came the time when he was gone for two weeks. I was never really told why, and Mom didn't seem to know either. Maw Maw let us know that he was in the hospital for a little while. "Sometimes peo-ple have breakdowns," she told me. I never asked him about it when he got back. My dad was like Batman to me. He was my superhero. You don't want to think that Batman has a weakness or is hurting. He seemed fine, and I just wanted him to be fine.

But on the issue of the divorce itself, I was still getting nowhere. Eventually, Mom flatly told me to ask my dad—only he could give me the answer. So I asked him, over and over. He'd deflect and change the subject until, finally, one day when we were over Maw Maw's house, he sat me down and told me. There'd been another woman, a woman he'd known before he met my mom, and he'd been unfaithful with her before leaving my mom. He kept saying, "C.J., I am sorry," over and over again, because what else could he really say?

I walked away from that conversation prepared to never forgive him. I finally understood why his absence hurt my mom, and I couldn't ignore the fact that he'd caused her so much pain. My dad let me be mad at him for as long as I needed to be, and eventually I learned how to be okay with it, which I was able to do because of Mom. "Your dad didn't want me," she said, "but he loves you. He made a bad decision, son, but you need to forgive him. I have already forgiven him. You need to forgive him, too."

Over time, I did. But even though I was able to forgive my dad for hurting my mom, there was still the reality that my mother deserved companionship. She deserved to be loved. She'd sacrificed her teenage years to look after her siblings, sacrificed her young adulthood to look after me, but who was there to look after her? My mother was a magician in so many ways, somehow pulling us through and making a home despite the formal education she missed and the little money she made. It was nothing short of amazing that she was able to shoulder so much pain and forgive my father in order to make our family work as well as it did. It was even more amazing that she survived Mr. Eugene.

MY EARLIEST MEMORIES of Mr. Eugene weren't all bad. I first met him over the course of a few evenings when Mom and I would go over to his house. "I'll be right back, baby," she would say as she hopped out of the car and walked up to his house, leaving me to sit in the car and do my homework, waiting for the door to finally open and Mom to come back to the car. Then, as the sun started to go down, Mom would be walking back down the steps toward me, and she always had a smile on her face. I noticed that he made her laugh, too, which certainly won him some points with me.

Mr. Eugene was short in stature, maybe five-eight. He had a gap in his teeth and a small afro that was thinning on top, and he used this old-school shaving paste that stank so bad. At the time, he had a temp job making computer parts at a plant up the street from his mom's house in the West End. Mr. Eugene also occasionally preached sermons at our church, which is how he was first introduced to our family. I was raised to admire preachers, but I was suspicious of him from the start. Mr. Eugene was a fiery preacher. It was as if his preaching was a way to vent about things he was dealing with, like he was in his own world in the pulpit, talking to or even arguing with himself. He would yell at the top of his lungs, make the volume crackle in the microphone. He'd pound the podium with his fist or slam the Bible down as he delivered his sermon with sweat pouring down his face. His sermons were a little scary.

Mr. Eugene spoke really fast, which I didn't care for, but the bigger problem was that he rarely spoke to me at all. For someone who was marrying my mom, he mostly seemed happy to ignore me—unless he was putting me to work. When we moved into the house at 35th and

Market, there were plenty of odd jobs that needed to be done, and Mr. Eugene was always enlisting me in some little project. "You see that hole in the ceiling?" he'd say, pointing up at some crumbling drywall. "Let's get a piece of wood to cover it up."

His attempts at home improvement rarely improved anything, but that never stopped him from starting up a new one, and pretty soon after he started a project, he would usually stop and begin another one. One day, he noticed our sidewalk was cracking, so he decided the way to fix a cracking sidewalk was to paint it. "Charlie," he said, "get some of the paint out of the house."

I ran in and got the paint and brought it back out. "But Mr. Eugene," I said, "the can says it's house paint, for inside. Is this gonna work on the sidewalk?"

"Ain't nothing wrong with this paint, Charlie."

He took his shirt off, kneeled down, started painting, ran out of paint about halfway through, and gave up. Then, a few weeks later, he came back and finished with a different color.

Any kind of real repairs or renovations that took place were always done by Grandad and Mom, and as far as the yard work and the housecleaning went, Mr. Eugene left all that to me. I was only nine years old at the time, but I did what I was told. Mom would speak up and tell him she didn't like it, but ultimately she deferred to him as the head of the household. Grandad, on the other hand, made it very clear that he was not happy with a man having a little kid doing all the work at the house while he lay around, and he gave Mom an earful about it. "If that man sends my grandson out in that hot sun one more time while he sits on his butt, I am going to hit him with my tire rod!"

Mowing the lawn was the worst. When we moved in and it came time to tackle the overgrown jungle of a backyard, Mr. Eugene sent me out there to deal with it alone while he tinkered with junk in the garage. Growing up in a small apartment, I'd never really used a lawnmower before, and he didn't really show me how to handle it or what to look out for. So I put a towel over my head to block out the sun, pulled the string on the lawnmower, and started pushing it through the tall grass and weeds.

"Get closer to the bushes, Charlie!" he hollered from the garage. I did what he told me, pushing as hard as I could into the bushes, but buried behind them was a rusty metal box, and when I rammed into it a swarm of bees poured out, buzzing loudly. I started running frantically in circles, hollering and yelling and swatting them away as they attacked and stung me. Then one of them landed in the middle of my face and stung me in the eye. It was excruciating. I screamed and ran into the house to get my mom, and she came down and got some ice for me.

My eye was swollen shut, but when Mr. Eugene saw me, he promptly dismissed it. "There's nothing wrong with him. He'll be fine."

"Why did you have him doing the yard work by himself, Eugene?" Mom demanded.

"The boy needs to learn," he said. "He'll be fine."

One trip to the hospital later, the swelling eventually went down, and when it did, I was right back to cutting the grass.

It was strange that Mr. Eugene reacted so indifferently to seeing a nine-year-old boy screaming in agony after getting attacked by bees. Even stranger was when he abandoned my dog.

As an only child, I often felt alone, so Maw Maw got me a friend that I could always have by my side: a dark-brown dachshund that I named Rocky. That little weenie dog was my partner. I'd come home and he'd be shaking with excitement, his little tail wagging a million miles an hour. He'd jump in my arms and we'd run around the yard together. In the evenings, I used to sit with him on our rickety old porch swing. Rocky loved sitting on that swing; he'd let the breeze hit his little face as he lay in my lap. Then, when it was time to go to bed, he'd snuggle up in a box on the floor beside me.

Everyone in the house adored Rocky. Except Mr. Eugene. He talked all the time about how he'd love to get rid of the dog. I ignored him. Since Maw Maw had gotten Rocky for me, I never thought Mr. Eugene would actually do it. Still, I made sure Rocky stayed in my room whenever I left the house so that Mr. Eugene wouldn't be upset.

Then one day Mom, Bianca, and I went out, and when we got

home Rocky was gone. Mr. Eugene told us he'd run away. I couldn't believe it. I sat down on the porch and cried. Rocky was my best friend. He loved us. There was no way he would run away. I refused to believe it, and I was right not to, because pretty soon the truth came out. My mom got it out of him. Mr. Eugene had scooped Rocky up, driven him a few miles from the house, and let him out of the car.

Now, if you supposed Mr. Eugene couldn't stoop lower than abandoning a little boy's dog, you would be wrong. That same year, after several attempts and several miscarriages, my mom beamed with joy as she prepared to give birth to my baby sister, Ebony, but in those final weeks she was worried that she might be having problems with the pregnancy and couldn't drive herself to the hospital anymore. Not wanting to worry Grandad, Mom pleaded with Mr. Eugene to take her to the hospital to get checked out. The doctors even called the house to tell him he needed to take her, but he downplayed the urgency and wouldn't do it.

Since Mom couldn't get to the hospital, she ended up having major complications while she was in labor. Ebony passed moments after she was born. Mom was crushed, and I felt so powerless. There was nothing I could do to ease her pain, nor could I make Mr. Eugene treat Mom better. I had a gutting, empty feeling that stayed with me right up until Mom finally left him.

With everything that had happened in the first two years of their marriage, I have to imagine she thought of leaving him, but as a religious family, we were raised on the importance of staying married, and I know she didn't want to get divorced again. Mr. Eugene took advantage of that. My mother was so strong and so independent, but since the time she was a girl she'd been sacrificing and doing for others nonstop. She wanted to be loved herself. She wanted someone to do for her what she spent so much time doing for everyone else. She deserved that. Mr. Eugene offered companionship, and although he was abusive, Mom put up with him and fought to avoid losing her marriage. We both cried when he got rid of Rocky, but I don't remember Mom doing anything in response. I think she was at a point where she was trying to manage everything and keep the peace, hoping that things would get better. So she stuck it out. But Ebony's death drove a major wedge between them, and then came the beginning of the end.

One day Mr. Eugene came home and announced that God had instructed him to quit his job at the factory. He never really kept another job after that. He started collecting aluminum cans to redeem for cash instead. He'd make me go with him, and we'd walk up and down the streets with trash bags, picking up pop and beer cans and shaking out the remaining liquid in them. If he wasn't out collecting cans Mr. Eugene mostly just lay around, listening to sermons on tape or watching the Christian ministry channel on TV—and that was if he was home at all. He started disappearing for long stretches of time.

When Mr. Eugene was at the house, he was erratic and angry, and it wouldn't be long before he and my mother got into an argument. They'd send Bianca and me upstairs, but the old house had vents that carried the sound, and you could pretty much hear any room in the house if you knew the right spot to listen. When the fights started, I'd lie on the floor outside my door and listen to him hurling insults at Mom. I'd hear her cry and yell back at him. I'd never heard Mom scream that loud at anyone else in my entire life, and I hated it. Afterward, she would come upstairs and hug us, always with a smile on her face, but we both knew she was hiding something. Seeing myself as her protector, I despised every moment I saw her hurt.

Then, just as it seemed my mom might come to her breaking point, Mr. Eugene was arrested for walking up and down the street and staring in the windows of people's homes with a knife and binoculars in his hand. Several months later, we learned what had been driving his behavior all along: He suffered from bipolar schizophrenia and had been battling it for years without any treatment. Without sustained employment, he hadn't been able to access quality mental health coverage. On top of that, in church we were never taught about mental health. Inexplicable behaviors and mental impairments were called "demons" that needed to be "cast out." Mom later explained that this was one of the reasons so many people kept their mental issues secret; no one wanted to be accused of having a demon in them. But it wasn't like folks at church hadn't noticed. I discovered later that some of the deacons had pulled Mom aside to ask whether Mr. Eugene was abusive, because they were concerned for our safety.

With Mr. Eugene in jail, we were left at home trying to figure out what to do. In the end, my mom chose her peace. She chose her sanity. As much as she wanted to honor the church's teaching on marriage, she knew she had a higher duty to keep us safe. She filed for divorce and told Mr. Eugene's family he was no longer welcome in our home. Once he was gone, it was like a cloud had lifted. The arguments stopped. The tension went away. Mom started singing around the house again. I learned a lot from seeing her poise and patience in the face of great pain. More than anything, though, I learned about the strength it takes to walk away from an abusive relationship. I learned that eventually you have to know that you deserve to be cared for, because you can only sacrifice so much.

One day Mom and I were at the bus stop on the way home from the grocery store. Mr. Eugene was gone, money was tight, and we'd lost the car and had started riding the bus again. It always took several transfers to get to the store and back home, and if we missed our transfer we'd be stuck waiting thirty minutes or more before the next one came along. That happened a few times, and on this one day we were stuck there on the bench for what felt like hours, grocery bags piled up all around us. As we sat there, she didn't say anything or tell me she was upset. She dropped her head a bit. Tears started to form in her eyes and slowly run down her face. I didn't notice at first, but when I went to lie on her lap like I normally would, I felt the wetness from her tears. Instead of lying down, I scooched over and put my arms around her and she put her head on my shoulder and cried and cried and cried. I kept holding her while we waited for the bus. When it finally arrived, she wiped her tears, gathered the groceries, and got on with the day.

I never asked her what was wrong.

CHAPTER 3

THE BEST END

I COULD ALWAYS hear the crickets at the bus stop. It was early, not yet six, and still pitch-black outside but for the flickering of the yellowish street lamp. The stop itself was at a utility pole on a slight hill near the curb. There was no sidewalk to stand on, but the hill made for a good seat. It was quiet and lonely waiting to see the light from the bus make its way up the street to pick up all the other kids and me for the two-hour ride. It felt less like we were going to school and more like we were taking a trip out of town in the dead of night.

In some ways, that's exactly what it was.

The day would actually begin while I was still in bed. Around 3:30 in the morning, my Auntie Lisa would come by on her way to work at the hospital, dropping off my cousin Lindsay so that he could catch the bus with me.

Before we'd head out, Mom would always stop us both and pray. Then she would stand in the door waving goodbye in her robe with her hair wrapped, the light from the house casting a shadow on the street as we set off on a dangerous mission. Which is only a slight exaggeration. I never felt like my life was in danger, but I definitely felt like we were doing something significant.

The bus stop was a couple streets up from my house. We'd hustle along the busted sidewalks, skipping over the gaps between the concrete slabs pushed up by tree roots, always making sure not to scuff our shoes and running double-time past the house with the big angry black dog that always barked and looked like it was going to jump the fence and get us but never did.

Out of the dark shadows up the street, we'd see the bright headlights of our school bus cutting through the fog as the rumble of its engine filled the street. The bus was yellow, but it often had a cast of gray on it from dirt; it didn't look shiny and new like the buses coming from the East End.

The bus would roll to a stop, and we'd pick up our backpacks, brush ourselves off, and climb on. Our driver was a middle-aged white lady who looked as sleepy as we were and who always smelled like cigarettes. She never said much unless a fight broke out.

By the time Lindsay and I got on the bus, the seats in the back would be taken already, but that was fine with me because there was one seat by the wheel well that had a heater underneath. It was the toastiest seat on the whole bus, and I always made a beeline for it. If my backpack was empty enough, I would sit on that, because the seats were old and dirty and there were always rips in the vinyl that cut your hand if you rubbed them the wrong way. When the radio wasn't on, there would be complete silence and everyone on the bus would sleep. Most of the time, Lindsay would sit with me, and we would rest our heads against the seat in front of us.

Once we were settled, the doors of the bus would close, and the lights would cut off and the engine would roar as we took off on our way to Louisville Male High School. Male was one of the highest-performing schools in the city, and it took a two-hour bus ride to get there because nothing like it was allowed to exist in the world in which I grew up.

"THE WEST END is the best end!" we used to shout when I was younger. We had so much pride in our community. The West End was filled with hardworking families who'd fought the indignities of segregation, who'd been deprived of places to sit down in restaurants and blocked from voting in elections. But that never stole our joy or broke our spirit, and the streets were rich with places to commune and celebrate and show love.

The bonds we developed living in the midst of poverty, crumbling buildings, police sirens, and constant gunshots were a true testament to the power of family and the resilience of community. All the elders like my grandparents used to sit on their front porches like lighthouses, and you could hardly go anywhere in the West End without someone knowing you, especially with my big family. I used to hear "You Deacon Hearn's grandson?" at least once a week.

Riding down Broadway or Market Street, you were likely to see either a music-filled block party spilling out of a church or a tent revival with folks singing, clapping, and playing the tambourine into the night. Every weekend, folks would make their way to Shawnee Park or Chickasaw Park, two historic parks within minutes of each other. There would be BBQs, cards and domino tournaments, small concerts. There would be races, little league games, football games, basketball tournaments like the Dirt Bowl. My cousins and I would go to the corner store and get the 69-cent bag of Grippo's and the Faygo orange cream soda. And every Sunday in the summer: cruising. Everyone would clean up their cars and file in to cruise the road that circled around the park.

The neighborhood associations were active, too, with people coming together to bring resources to the community, to block the continued expansion of liquor stores, to report concerns of crime. They'd host events to help families and give children productive things to do. They'd sponsor community festivals, parades, choir concerts, and resource fairs, giving adults the opportunity to sign up for an exercise class and providing the kids in the area the chance to ride a small Ferris wheel or get some cotton candy. It always felt special to go to neighborhood fairs like the big one on the parkway in the Portland neighborhood close to our house. Things like that were much more common across town, but when it happened in our neighborhood, we absolutely loved it.

Other than a few fast food places and dollar stores, the major business chains wouldn't invest in the West End, but residents in the area worked to create local businesses and infrastructure. From Big Gene's convenience store to the family-owned Ace Hardware and restaurants like King's Fast Food Chicken and Annie's Pizza, folks in the West End found a way to get the things they needed.

Except schools.

Built on the separate and unequal foundations of Jim Crow, the schools in the West End had always struggled. When the first court-ordered busing plans were rolled out in 1975 to integrate the students and remedy the problem, the backlash was swift. Riots broke out, the Klan marched, and in the years that followed white families acceler-ated their flight to the suburbs, taking their tax dollars with them and leaving the city schools, particularly those in Black neighborhoods, to fall even further behind.

My neighborhood school was Shawnee High School, which was a couple streets over from my house. Although recognized for its pro-gram in aviation, Shawnee suffered from years of inadequate funding. With all its challenges, as well as its difficulty keeping a principal, Shawnee had some of the lowest test scores and maintained one of the lowest graduation rates in the city and the state. And while there are certainly some incredible success stories out of Shawnee, it was ex-pected that many students would drop out.

Since neither of my parents had graduated from high school, they were determined that I would have the opportunities they never did. Mom started reading several children's books a night to me when I was a couple months old. I never let her miss a night, and because of her I was already reading by the time I was three. She loves to tell the story of the day she was driving and she heard me reading the street signs from my car seat in the back. "You were reading the street signs, and I never even showed them to you before. You weren't even three yet!"

From the time I started preschool, my mom framed every single award I received and hung them all up in my room. Every honor roll, every dean's list, every perfect attendance. As the years went on, they stretched nearly from the ceiling to the floor. When I opened my eyes in the morning, I immediately saw a powerful reinforcement of my abilities. I didn't fully understand the value of this as a child, but my mom was giving me the space to have confidence.

For elementary school I attended Schaffner Traditional Elementary, a high-performing integrated school not far from our apartment in South Louisville. But once we moved back to the West End, getting ahead meant getting me out of the neighborhood schools and into the better-served schools on the other side of town. Only a certain percentage of students qualified for the busing program, and I still remember my mom's joy when I got in. It was like we'd won the lottery, like there was a glimmer of hope that I would be able to get ahead. I was excited because she was excited. But I was nervous, too. It meant that I would be going to school without many of my friends. It meant a four-hour round trip every day. But there was no discussion about whether I wanted to do it or not. It was what we needed to do to get by. Which is why, starting with Barret TMS for middle school and then Male for high school, I was out at that bus stop at 5:30 A.M. every morning.

Riding the school bus from the West End to the East End of the city was always an eye-opening experience. We'd ride past the old homes and blighted lots on Market Street and through the Beecher Terrace Housing Complex on Muhammad Ali Boulevard. The legacy of segregation we rode through was etched not just in the landscape but in the people. Riding to school, we drove through many rival gang territories. Sometimes it got dangerous. One thing you learn early in the West End is the sense of ownership a lot of kids felt over their street, block, or neighborhood. It was called repping your block or claiming a set, and it was serious. Many of the kids on the bus wanted to be in a gang and acted as if they were a part of one, usually the Crips or the Bloods, though there were others. We regularly saw fights break out when kids on our bus rode through the neighborhood of a rival gang. Rocks would be thrown. One even came through the window and hit my cousin Lindsay in the face. The driver would have to pull over until the fighting stopped, making the long bus ride even longer.

The news portrayed one side of the gangs, the violence and the crime, but from the bus I could see that for a lot of kids that got involved, it wasn't actually about fighting and causing trouble. The gangs represented a sense of family and protection. Too many kids from struggling communities feel invisible, as if they have no place to belong. There's also a lot of fear and trauma in our community that kids rarely have the chance to reconcile. Gangs provided an answer to that. It was the wrong answer, but at least it was something. More than anything, gangs were an attempt to stake a claim and have a sense of identity in spaces that you don't own, almost a way of taking back some power in a place where you're powerless. In other words, the gangs didn't create the ghetto; the ghetto created the gangs. And the architects of the ghetto were not the people who lived there.

I never identified with the gangs because my family basically was my gang. I was blessed that I could look out the window and see the violence and the blighted storefronts and understand why these things were the way they were, and that was because of Grandad. My grandad was always telling stories, taking some of his deepest and most difficult life experiences and turning them into history lessons to help us understand the world beyond our block. He'd sit down at his kitchen table, get a big piece of watermelon, sprinkle some salt on it, and tell stories while the house was in constant commotion from people running back and forth. When he spoke, everything seemed to slow down. My cousins would be dancing, singing, or getting into trouble for something around the house, but I would be sitting at the table with Grandad, listening attentively. I wanted to be him. The confidence he had, the way his tank top showed his muscles as he cut the watermelon, the way he could spin a yarn even while spitting out watermelon seeds without missing a beat—I used to practice spitting out seeds like he did.

Sometimes the stories could go on for hours. He would lean back in his chair, fold his arms, and effortlessly go from one story to the next, never breaking stride. He had the uncanny ability to weave all his tales together into a seamless, hours-long odyssey through the fields of Mississippi, his tours of duty overseas, his road trips across the country, his work at the church, even the pretty women he'd ro-

manced before he settled down with Grandma. Over the course of
this incredible feat of storytelling and instruction, most of my cousins
would eventually get drowsy and go off to sleep. Before too long, it
would just be Grandad and me at the table, with him weaving together our family's history with America's history. Several times, I listened to him until the sun came up the next morning.

The geography of Louisville, Grandad told me, was governed by
race from the beginning. Its location on the Ohio River made it a
major slave-trading hub, with the trafficking of human beings taking
place in slave pens near the aptly named Market Street, the same thoroughfare my mother's house sits off of today. As the area was never a
major cotton-growing region, the enslaved people who lived here
were mainly domestic servants and laborers. And Kentucky being a
border state that did not secede, freedom wouldn't come for its enslaved people until December 18, 1865, with the passage of the Thir-
teenth Amendment (an amendment the state would not formally
recognize for over a century, finally ratifying it in 1976).

In the decades that followed emancipation, "Little Africa" sprang
up in the area west of what is now downtown. What started as nothing more than a shantytown built by formerly enslaved people quickly
grew into a thriving community run by self-sufficient Black entrepre-
neurs who built and owned their own homes, clubs, schools, night-
clubs, and parks—only to have their community seized by the city
through eminent domain to be bulldozed and paved over for the Watterson Expressway.

After Little Africa was destroyed, Black ambition rose up again,
this time in what would become the bustling corridor known as Walnut Street, Louisville's Harlem. It was the business district where
Black families could get insurance and bank loans. It was also the
nightlife district where the greatest blues and jazz performers in the
country would come to play. Walnut Street is where Dr. King marched.
It's where Muhammad Ali had his parade when he won gold at the
1960 Olympics. A place that celebrated the Black community, Walnut Street was nonetheless open to everyone.

But many in authority came to fear the growing power of a rising

Black community and its demands for equality. They also coveted the increasingly valuable real estate that Walnut Street occupied, with its proximity to downtown. Then came the "urban renewal" plans of the 1960s, which gave state and local governments the pretext to clear out what they called "slums."

"When your Mama was little," Grandad would tell me, spitting out his watermelon seeds, "we watched Walnut Street get torn down. Businesses and houses were bulldozed, Black doctors' offices and banks, restaurants and shops were destroyed. Jobs left and never returned. There was no renewal at all. The city destroyed it all."

In cities across the country, urban renewal became known as "Negro removal," and in Louisville that's exactly what it did. It pushed the Black community farther west and erected a wide, high-traffic thoroughfare along 9th Street, creating a barrier that walled off the Black community from the rest of the city, physically and in every other way. With Black families confined to the West End, the predatory real-estate practice known as blockbusting was used to drive out the remaining white homeowners, and the whole area was redlined by banks and insurance companies, starving it of the investment and mortgage capital a functioning community needs. Three decades later, thanks to the lessons my grandfather taught me, when I looked out the window on my bus ride, I didn't identify my self-worth with the crumbling, dilapidated landscape passing by me. I wasn't looking at a slum. I was looking at a history lesson written in rotting wood and busted-up concrete.

The most startling moment in the journey always came as we crossed 9th Street. On a map, 9th Street looks like any other road, but crossing over it was like entering a different world. As we rode east, the trash on the streets vanished, abandoned buildings and graffiti gave way to thriving businesses and manicured lawns. The cop cars disappeared. As we approached the wealthier neighborhoods around the school, we rode past grand houses, some with stained-glass windows that cast beautiful colors on the grass. People would be out walking their dogs, which was incredible to see. We loved dogs in my family, but nobody in the West End "walked" their dog; you just let them run around in the yard. Here, folks were strolling along with a dog leash in one hand and a cup of coffee in the other, looking relaxed and at peace, not even thinking they might have to soon run from police or duck from a gunshot. I envied that, just like I envied the other students I saw as we finally pulled up in front of school, the ones getting dropped off in BMWs and Mercedes-Benzes as we pulled up in our dusty old school bus after the interminable ride, already tired before the day had even begun.

As much as I envied the life I saw east of 9th Street, it pissed me off, too. Everyone deserves a safe place to walk a dog or go shopping. Everyone deserves sidewalks that aren't torn up and streets without potholes big enough to swallow a car. Everyone deserves to go a day without yellow tape or police sirens, no matter which side of town they live on. But the West End didn't have that. All we had was the bus, driving children over and through the problem that nobody wanted to fix, and every time I rode through the problem the anger and the sense of injustice I felt lit a fire inside me. If nobody else was going to fix it, I wanted to try.

THE DIFFICULTY OF my journey from the West End to school every morning was matched only by the slow, nerve-wracking trek through the cafeteria lunch line at noon. Founded in 1856, for over a hundred years Male High School has consistently been one of the highest-performing public schools in all of Kentucky. There was a stark divide between the students who rode the bus and those who did not. We shared the same classrooms, but it didn't always feel that way. We walked in the same halls, but it was like they were inside some sort of bubble that I was not in. The fourteen-year-old me couldn't explain it, but I could tell that these other kids weren't dealing with the stress of having their LG&E cut off at their home.

As I made my way into the loud and bustling cafeteria, walking around the bulldog mosaic in the lobby, I always tried to slip into the line between students from other classes that I didn't know, because it meant none of my friends would hear me give my free lunch number to the cafeteria lady. None of my friends would see the screen on the register that read "FREE" in big red letters when she rang me up. It was embarrassing. I didn't want anyone to know I had no money. I didn't want them to think less of me because I didn't even have the 40 cents for reduced lunch. When I managed to make it past the register without being seen, I always breathed a sigh of relief while making my way to the Black cafeteria table where my friends and I sat, always separate from most of our classmates.

That feeling of not quite belonging also followed me out of the cafeteria and into the halls. I could feel it from the clothes I had on. Wearing uniforms was supposed to be a way to help make everyone feel equal, but it didn't. At least it didn't for me. Because you could tell which students came from families with money by the Tommy Hilfiger or the Dickies logo on the back of their pants. I always wanted pants with a logo on the back, but there was no way we were going to spend fifty dollars or more for pants that I would only wear to school.

You could also tell by the brightness of the colors in the polo shirts, or by the fact that kids like me were wearing shirts that were too small because we couldn't afford new ones. One time I spilled some grease on my khakis during lunch, and no matter how many times I washed them the stain never came out, but I had to wear them anyway. I had to wear my grandad's old belts, too, using a knife to poke an extra hole in them so that they would fit me.

These details were small, but they really stood out, or at least it always felt like they did. Knowing my uniform was faded and tattered, I tried to make sure no one ever looked at my uniform at all—I made sure they were looking at my feet. Whenever I had to decide between fresh clothes and fresh shoes, I knew the shoes made a louder statement, so I saved up all my money from cutting grass and working summer jobs, and I spent it on Jordans. At $150 or more a pair, I had to cut a lot of grass to afford those shoes. But it worked. It bought me the little bit of status I felt I needed to fit in.

If it wasn't my clothes that made me stick out, there was no avoiding the color of my skin. Or my hair. There was a rule at Male that said boys couldn't have hair longer than two inches. Boys also couldn't have their hair braided. If you forgot to shave and came to school with any kind of facial hair, the principal walked around with an electric shaver, and he would stop you and make you immediately shave it off. Although this rule theoretically applied to everyone, it only seemed to be enforced with Black students. I often noticed that my white classmates who had hair longer than two inches didn't get in trouble—me, I got sent to the principal's office.

At one point I decided I wanted to grow my hair so that I could get it braided. I'd seen pictures of my grandad, dad, and uncles with afros, and I wanted to grow my hair out like them. To keep myself from getting in trouble, I'd put water in my hair to make it curl up and shrink in size. I kept my pick with me at school, and the second I left the campus at the end of the day, I would use it to comb out my afro. It always gave me a sense of relief. It struck me then that this was what folks meant when they said, "Let your hair down."

After a month of growing my hair and working to keep it matted to my head in school, it was finally long enough, and on Friday after school I went straight over to Grandma's house so that my Auntie Linda could braid my hair. "I am heavy-handed, nephew," she said as she sat me down on the floor, and she wasn't lying. The pain was nearly unbearable, and it took a couple hours to finish. It felt like my scalp was on fire. But when she was done it looked amazing. I loved my hair. It was my first time ever having braids, and my cousins all came into the front room to see my head. "You have to keep your hair braided!" they all kept saying.

I felt a little uncomfortable at first. It was a bold statement for me. But once I got over the fact that it was new, I definitely wanted to keep them in. Every few minutes I would walk by the mirror and analyze the patterns in my hair. The excitement and newfound pride I had only lasted two days though, because when I prepared to go to school on Monday, I was confronted with the reality that I had to take them right back out.

"Why should I have to take out my braids?" I said to my mom. "I like them, and it took so long to get done. It's not fair that I have to change my hairstyle when the white students don't." As my hair was taken down Sunday night, I was so angry I wanted to cry. So many people in my community wore braids, and it was never a distraction the way the administrators at Male made it out to be. The next morning, walking back into school with my afro matted down again hurt me in a way I hadn't expected.

Several other Black students I knew had been through something similar, some blow to their self-esteem or some feeling of not fitting in. But at least I had my mom. Even though she couldn't be there in the cafeteria with me, she gave me the armor to protect myself. Mom had little sayings she'd use every day for encouragement. "We are more than conquerors," she'd say. Or "You are the head and not the tail." Other times she'd look me right in the eye and say, "No matter what anyone tells you, you're intelligent, and you are strong."

These sayings became like a part of my uniform. She was getting me ready to go out into the world. She believed in me so much, and she wanted to make sure I always believed in myself. Things were hard enough for a young Black man, and she refused to let self-doubt be one more barrier I'd have to climb over. When I was little, bad grades would earn me a spanking, but fear was never what drove me in the classroom. When I got exhausted or frustrated in class, the thing that always helped me focus was my commitment to Mom. I wanted to do well, because it was the best way I knew to let her know I appreciated everything she sacrificed for me.

My mother had never spoken about race to me when I was little, and when I started busing she explained why: She didn't want me to ever feel limited by how other people might look at me. But going to Barret and Male, she laid it down plain. "You are just as good as anyone else, son," she said. "But you'll have to be twice as good to make it, and I know you will be. You do your best. You treat everyone the way you want to be treated. Don't judge people by how they look or where they're from. Don't let anyone steal your joy or make you stop being you. There will be some people who will try to do you wrong, but not everyone. You are covered by the blood, son. If you remember this, you'll find good people who will help you along the way."

Still, there was so much about my experience that she wasn't able to help me understand. I was going to a part of the city and dealing with people Mom wasn't really familiar with; many of my experiences were new for us both. I knew I deserved to be at Male, but I never fully felt like I belonged there. Taking that bus was almost like being a foreign exchange student. At Male they spoke a different language, had a different culture. Some Black students came from the West End and elsewhere and assimilated, adopting the new language and culture as their own. Others became bilingual, learning to code-switch and flip back and forth with ease. I never did—not fully. In all my years at majority white schools, I never really left the Black cafeteria table.

Part of it was self-defense. I knew I had to keep certain people at a safe enough distance, emotionally, so that they couldn't hurt me. I didn't speak to many of those folks; I kept my head down and moved from class to class. Most of the kids were decent. I was friendly with everyone, but truth be told, I was never able to cross the color line or assimilate to the point of enjoying different cultures as deeply as my own, even though I respected them.

But the Black cafeteria table wasn't only a defense mechanism. Ultimately, I stayed at that table because I was proud of the people sitting around that table. I wanted the rest of the school to know we existed—and how much the Black students at this table had to offer. I stayed at that table because I knew it was the table that needed driven, ambitious young men like me. Most of my cousins and my friends didn't have a choice about which table to sit at. Busing hadn't done anything to help them. Busing wasn't so much a solution to the problem of segregation as an acknowledgment that the city didn't want to solve the problem: Leave 9th Street where it is, leave things as they are, and help a few talented Black kids get ahead so it'll look like progress. Did life get any better in the West End as a result of busing? No. The vacant lots that were empty when I was in school are still empty today. It was a Band-Aid for a gaping wound. It was proof that we can't realize systemic change by focusing on individual success. In fact, by helping a handful of Black students find greater opportunities, busing seemed to work like a safety valve. It let off some of the pressure, making the situation seem less urgent than it actually was.

Growing up with my family I had an idea of my purpose and ministry. Sitting at my grandad's knee, hearing his stories of fighting against segregation and working to lift up the people of the West End, I knew I wanted to be a part of that fight. I knew I wanted that long before I went to Male, but my experiences there helped to reaffirm and develop my vision of the journey ahead. Seeing the stark inequality on my daily journey to school had as much impact on me as the actual education I got in the classroom. The stated goal of busing may have been "integration," but the result for me was a deep and—to be frank—traumatic understanding of the fact that the division in our city was intentional. I'm thankful for the experience, and even relieved that I had the chance to do it, but it pains me deeply that it was something I had to do.

My cousins and I were always taught that we went to school to get the education we'd need to make money for the family, and I saw my time on the bus and going to Male as my way to contribute, a feeling that Maw Maw reinforced, always giving me five dollars for every A I got on my report card. Busing, ultimately, was a means to an end. It was like a chess move toward getting me closer to a shot at having a gainful career. I'd always heard talk about people "getting out of the hood." But that was never the conversation in our house. The plan was not to leave, but to stay and make things better. I didn't see education as a way out for me but as a way up for all of us.

CHAPTER 4

A NEW REALITY

I WOKE UP with my whole body drenched in sweat, my hands shaking, my mind in a fog. It was the morning of my college scholarship interview. I'd spent the whole week preparing for it, and now I felt so horrible I was struggling even to get out of bed. By the time I sat down to do the interview itself a couple of hours later, I could barely focus on the questions I was being asked. And that was just in the first go-round. I had a whole day of interviews ahead of me. I was fighting to stay on my feet, but I knew I had to make it through no matter what. We needed the money.

My senior year of high school was supposed to be a victory lap. I was preparing to do the thing that my parents had fought so hard to make possible: walk across the stage and get my diploma. I had done well enough on my ACT to get accepted to college, but I knew we had no way of affording it. Through a co-worker, my mom knew a man named Scott Mitchell, who headed a University of Louisville program that helped low-income students get into college and graduate. He agreed to help me, went through my records, and said that my grades and test scores could qualify me for some scholarships. He told me about one scholarship that could not only cover undergrad tuition but might also help get me into law school at the University of Louisville: the McConnell Scholars Program, named after the senior U.S. senator from Kentucky. All I knew about "McConnell" was that he was someone in the government. I didn't know much about his politics or what he meant to Kentucky, and I certainly didn't have any idea about any presence he had in the West End because we'd never seen him there before. But no matter what kind of politician he was, I was going to go after any opportunity that would help me get to college. I applied and a few weeks later got a letter congratulating me for being a finalist. The last part of the application process was a full day of interviews at the University of Louisville campus.

I was so excited. It was such a huge opportunity. But in the weeks leading up to the interview I started feeling worse and worse. I was sluggish, frequently drenched with sweat, and every minute I found myself fighting the urge to drink every bit of juice in the house. We had this really thick, sugary orange drink called Tampico that we'd get from Save-a-Lot. I'd get home from school, fill a cup, and guzzle it down. But it was never enough. It wasn't just that I felt thirsty; it was that I felt I would die of thirst. Then, with each drink, I'd feel the urge to use the restroom. Soon, I was running back and forth to the restroom in the night, often several times an hour. It never crossed my mind that something was wrong, at least not to the point of telling Mom. We always tried to block out sickness as long as possible. She couldn't afford to miss work, and I didn't want to miss school, because when I missed school it threw off her whole day.

But eventually Mom noticed that something wasn't right. "Goodness, son!" she said. "You're sucking up all the juice!" Still, we had no idea what was going on. I grew increasingly lethargic. I couldn't focus in class. I was using the restroom nearly every fifteen minutes. It wasn't until my tongue got a hard coat of sugar on it that I started to get concerned. Even then, I didn't know what to do about it, so I continued to push through.

The day of the McConnell Scholarship interviews, I could barely make it out of bed. My skin looked pale with a greenish tint to it. I looked in the mirror and my eyes were sunken. I was freaking out because it looked like I was dying. Nothing was going to stop me, though. I committed to muscling through. The interviews were being conducted by U of L faculty and former McConnell scholars at one of the academic buildings on campus. As I moved from interview to interview, my feet were so heavy I could hardly walk, and it only got worse throughout the day. The questions were so basic and general. "What are your goals?" and "What do you think makes a good student leader?" I had all my answers down. I was ready to crush them. But I felt like I was flailing. It was like my mind knew exactly what it wanted to say, but my body wouldn't move my mouth to let the words come out. In one of the interviews, I got so dizzy I had to close my eyes. But quitting was not an option, so I stumbled through as best I could. I'd gone in that morning wearing a light gray sweater, but I was sweating so profusely that by the end of the day it was dark gray.

For the next few days, it only got worse. Then, one morning in Latin class, I started feeling sick in my stomach. I was sitting in the far back corner of the room next to my buddy Conrad, who looked at me and said, "You don't look good." I was still craving sugar, and even though we weren't supposed to have snacks in class I snuck a couple peppermints I'd swiped from the bowl my mom kept in the house. All I remember after that is wanting nothing but to go to sleep. I rested my head down on my desk as Mrs. Thomas was going around the class with the workbook asking everyone to conjugate verbs. All the kids were being rowdy and not listening, and then everything got blurry. My arms and legs were so heavy I couldn't move them, and then I tried to move and I fell out of my desk, collapsed on the floor, and passed out.

THE NEXT THING I remember is yellow: the bright yellow walls in the ICU where I woke up. My eyes opened slowly. They were still heavy. I could hear the beeps from the monitors in the room. I was awake but could hardly move. Mom was beside me, holding her purse in her lap with one hand and squeezing my hand with the other. I heard her whisper "Jesus" a couple times. I knew she was praying. I could sort of follow what was happening, but for the most part I was in a fog.

A doctor came in the room and poked my hand. "Charles," he said, "you're going to feel a little prick."

They were checking my glucose, and when they measured the levels, the room was in shock. A healthy glucose level should be between 80 and 120 mg/dL. Anything over 1,000 mg/dL will likely put you in a coma. Mine was over 1,300 mg/dL.

"I'm amazed he's even conscious," the doctor said.

"Will he be okay?" Mom asked, her voice trembling.

"Your son has diabetic ketoacidosis," the doctor explained. "He has a disease called type 1 diabetes. His pancreas can't produce the insulin his body needs to break down sugars in his blood, so he'll have to inject insulin into his body for the rest of his life."

At first I was confused by it all. I kept saying, "I've got homework to do. I'm missing class," and my mom kept having to reach over and put her hand on me and say, "Don't worry about that now, baby." But over the next few hours and days, the full gravity of what was happening started to sink in. I didn't know much about diabetes up to that moment, but I knew relatives and friends of the family had lost limbs from it, ended up on dialysis from it, even died from it. I slowly began to learn how diabetes affects the body. You have to take insulin because your body isn't producing it, and without it your body can't break down food properly. It all turns to sugar, which is released into your bloodstream at toxic levels. When your glucose shoots up too high, your body starts to overwork to compensate for the spikes. It's the same thing if your glucose drops too low; your body fights to get it back up. Either way, your body begins to deteriorate. That's when you get the mood swings, the blurred vision, the sweating and shaking, the arms and legs that feel like lead weights.

The news about how my diet would change was especially hard to take. No ice cream. No pizza. No sugary drinks. When you're a teenager, that's like being told your life is over. But the worst news was the shots I'd have to take. I hate needles. Hate, hate, hate them. I was terrified of them, and I had to sit there as the nurse pulled out an orange and pricked it and jabbed it with syringes, showing me how I would have to check my glucose and inject insulin several times a day. "When you prick your finger," the nurse said, pointing to different spots on my finger, "rotate around the edges of your fingertips. If you check your glucose in the same spot on your fingers, eventually your fingertips will become calloused, and you could lose feeling in your fingers."

I followed their directions and practiced on the orange. I remember crying as I did it, because I couldn't believe I would have to do this to myself for the rest of my life. When the doctors and nurses left the room after the demonstration, I laid my head back on my pillow with that orange in my hand. Mom grabbed my forearm and put her head on my shoulder. We both cried.

My family came to the hospital in waves. Sometimes I would wake up and several of my aunts and cousins would be in the room laughing about childhood stories, and I would get big hugs and join in on the stories. A few times, I would wake up to hear someone like my Uncle Will or Aunt Brenda praying for me. They would be praying so passionately you could hear them out in the hallways from my room. Grandma did not like hospitals, so when she walked in I immediately cried—if Grandma was there, it had to be serious. She leaned over to hug me, and I never wanted that hug to end.

A few times that week, my dad stopped by. I can count on one hand the number of times I've seen my dad cry, and when he saw me in that hospital bed tears were coming down his face. Each time he came he'd sit down beside me to pray. My dad was in a bit of a phase at that time. He was doing a lot of mission work in his church and had grown his beard out and started carrying two things with him everywhere he went: his Bible and a carved, wooden staff. And I'm not talking about a little cane or a walking stick. I'm talking about a staff. It was taller than him. He called it his Moses staff; he didn't care how people looked at him when he carried it.

When my dad prayed he would always open his Bible to a certain verse, like Isaiah 53:5: "By His stripes we are healed." Then he would put the open Bible on my head and pray. He would never stay long after that. I think that was the way he dealt with pain, to smile or laugh it off or not really deal with it and try to find a way for everything to be okay, even if it wasn't. So he'd say, "Everything's going to be fine, buddy, don't worry about it," and then he'd be gone again. But it meant so much to me that he came. He was still my superhero.

I was in the hospital for nearly two weeks. All along, I was doing my best to convince myself that the whole episode wasn't real. As long as I was in that hospital bed, maybe I would just get better and it would all go away. But then they told me I was fine to be discharged, and reality came crashing down. Even though they said I was stable, my symptoms hadn't fully abated, which made me realize that, in fact, I would be living with this condition for the rest of my life. I didn't want to face it. I didn't want to accept it. I didn't want to go home with this disease. I felt like I'd lost my ability to fully live. I was afraid that I wouldn't be able to take care of my mom. Even with all the family support, I began to feel like I couldn't enjoy life anymore, and if I couldn't enjoy my life, I didn't think I wanted to live my life.

Once we were formally discharged, my mom cried tears of joy that I couldn't share. The nurses helped me into a wheelchair, and Mom pushed me down the hallway. I glanced into the hospital rooms as we made our way out. In each room there was someone fighting to get better. I dreaded what awaited me outside the hospital doors.

Mom and I were quiet as we made it to the car. None of this made sense. I was a young, healthy guy who had never had a hospital stay longer than a couple hours before passing out in Latin class. How in the world was I supposed to live with a disease that would shut my body down and kill me? We got in the car, and I was upset the whole ride home, saying, "I'm not going to be able to do this" to myself, over and over. It had rained, and the roads were wet as we drove down the Watterson Expressway. Tears flowed down my face. I was angry. Heartbroken. Terrified. My faith was leaving me with every turn away from the hospital. How could there be a God if He let this sort of thing happen? My heart pounded. My window was slightly cracked, sending a stream of wind into my face that pushed the tears down my cheeks. Mom was trying to console me, but I couldn't really hear her. I could only hear the voice in my head saying I couldn't live this way. I was taught never to quit, but in that moment, I wanted to give up.

The lock on the passenger side door of the car was broken, which I knew because I was the one who'd broken it. The door would open whether it was locked or not. I was crying and punching the dashboard and telling my mom, "Ma, I'm not going to be able to do this," and she was trying to calm me down when I grabbed the door handle, swung the door open, and tried to throw myself out of the car. We must have been doing about sixty-five on the expressway, but, luckily, I was in such a daze that I'd forgotten to take off my seatbelt, so that kept me from falling out even as my head and arms were leaning out of the car. My mom was screaming, "C.J.! Get back in the car!" and she grabbed my arm and pulled me back in. I don't remember closing the door; I think the force of my mom swerving the car slammed it shut.

We were about three minutes from our exit at Muhammad Ali Boulevard. My mom pulled off the highway there, and we sat for a while. She hugged me and we were both crying, and she was praying and telling me that everything was going to be okay and that she loved me and she was sorry. I finally calmed down and remembered that God was in control, that He always had a plan. When we made it to the house, I leaned on Mom to make it up the steps. We went into the house quietly. I probably sat in the same spot for the rest of the after- noon. It was a somber day, but it felt good to be home.

Then we took our first trip to the pharmacy.

MY MOM OPENING up her purse to pay for diabetes medication shocked us into a whole new reality, a reality where we would now have to spend nearly $1,000 a month to keep me alive. I would need a dose of insulin for each meal, and then another couple doses of long-acting every day just to carry me through the day. Then, in addition to the medicine itself, we would need a near-endless supply of test strips and syringes. Mom took one look at the prices of everything and made some phone calls to different relatives, trying to see who could help us get the money. She couldn't reach anyone right then, and we ultimately had to turn around and leave without buying the medicine I needed to survive. Walking out of that store felt like a death sen- tence. I only had a few days' supply that the hospital had given me, and the frustration of having to take two types of insulin multiple times a day immediately gave way to the sheer terror of wondering when it would run out.

From that moment, Mom did everything in her power to make sure we could afford the prescription each month. Depending on my mom's work situation, there were times we had no health coverage at all. When we did, I would often go back and forth between being on her plan and my dad's plan through the Post Office, which provided better coverage; it was a part of how they juggled the shared responsibilities of custody. We only had to come up with the full $1,000 a few times before Maw Maw stepped in and told my dad to put me on his plan full-time, but even then the coverage wasn't that great. The cost went down from $1,000 to maybe $700 or so a month, still a near-impossible burden for a family that was already just getting by. When my mom's paycheck wasn't enough, she sewed clothes. She would make dresses, hem pants, fix choir robes, make curtains, tailor suits. She even cleaned up the church with Grandma to make some extra money.

Even with everything Mom did, sometimes it wasn't enough. There were months we would be short $500 dollars or more. If Grandad had it, he would give it to us. He had a good pension and was still doing odd jobs. But our family was so big, and he gave so many of us money to help with emergencies that there were times that he had to apologize for not having enough to help us. When he couldn't help, we would ask Maw Maw. My uncles and aunties would pitch in as well. It was like passing the hat at a show, collecting all the crumpled-up tens and twenties we could put together. Most months we were able to get a refill before I ran out, but often we couldn't get it in time.

I kept my insulin vials in the refrigerator drawer with the apples. I would try to keep track of how much I had, but it was always a shock to open the drawer and find an empty brown pharmacy bag. Whenever that happened, Mom would look at me with tears in her eyes, the tears of a parent who feels like she's letting her child die. To avoid seeing that empty brown bag and those tears, I would take the risk of rationing the insulin I had left. Instead of taking twelve units for lunch,

I might try to get by with six. If I was supposed to take thirty units of Levemir at night, I might try to take sixteen.

When you ration insulin, you're killing yourself in slow motion. You're setting off a domino effect where your body isn't properly breaking down the food that you're eating. Once that begins, the symptoms start to compound and, eventually, it all catches up to you. That's when you end up the way I did in Mrs. Thomas's Latin class: the sluggish body, the blurry vision, the sugar-coated tongue, the loss of balance. When it gets really bad the stomach pain and the nausea become unbearable, and you start throwing everything up, and if you go on throwing up long enough, the vomit turns dark, which is because you're throwing up bile. Throwing up bile feels unlike anything you've ever experienced. It's coming from somewhere deeper than your stomach. It feels like throwing up your whole insides.

What made the thought of running out of insulin especially terrifying was that there were no hospitals in the West End. The closest we had was a clinic in the city's historic—and predominantly white—Portland neighborhood to the north. A lot of residents from the area would use the clinic as their primary—and only—outlet for treatment. The lines were long and the wait would take hours, but if I needed an emergency supply of insulin, it was worth it. Words can't describe the wave of panic and dread I would feel seeing the last bit drip out of my insulin pen, knowing there was nothing but an empty brown bag in the apple drawer. It would send me into survival mode, and I would prepare my mind for death. I didn't want to die anymore, but the thoughts would loom over me until I managed to get my dosage and a flood of relief would hit: I could live a little bit longer.

A FEW DAYS after I got home from the hospital I had most of my strength back, but I was still a little sluggish and disoriented, and my forearm was still sore from the IVs. Eventually I was ready to head back to school.

That first ride back, I noticed *everything*. The obstacle course potholes in my neighborhood. The sun rising over the trees that blocked out the Ohio River. The cool, damp air that hit me in the face when I cracked my window. Everything mattered so much more to me now. Even riding from the West End to the East End felt different. Looking at the big houses in the nice neighborhoods, I imagined that the families living there with their beautiful cars probably didn't have to walk out of the pharmacy empty-handed. I noticed that there were hospitals downtown and in the East End, and I understood for the first time the luxury of having a hospital close to you. It's another affirmation that your life is important. The fact that we didn't meant ours weren't. But with a lot of grace and Good Samaritans, I was able to go back to school and finish out the year so I could still graduate on time, with honors.

Somewhere in the middle of all of this a letter came for me in the mail. I opened it up. Turned out I didn't get that McConnell Scholarship.

CHAPTER 5

TANESHA

THE SWAIN STUDENT Activities Center at the University of Louisville had this big ramp where everyone converged on the way into the cafeteria. One of the first things I learned when I showed up for my first semester in the fall of 2003 was how much fun it was to walk up that ramp. You were bound to run into a lot of people you knew, and if you were a people watcher, you were sure to see some pretty girls.

One afternoon I was walking up that ramp and this girl was coming down. I didn't know her, but she was with some people I had classes with. The way the sun was shining on her, I couldn't really see her at first, and then she came into view and I thought, *Who is this?!* Her auburn hair hung just below shoulder length and covered part of her face. She was tall, athletic, and really pretty. One of her friends introduced us, and I remember shaking her hand and holding on a little longer than usual. She held on a moment too long, too. As we parted ways, I thought to myself, *I'm going to find out who that is.*

Her name, I learned, was Tanesha. From that moment on, whenever I made my daily walks between classes, I always had an eye out for her. We never shared classes, but every semester we seemed to have classes in the same buildings. If I ran into her at a certain place or time, like on Tuesday morning, then I'd know she had a Tuesday/Thursday class in that part of campus, and I'd make sure to remember so I could walk that way on Tuesdays and Thursdays.

I used to light up whenever I saw her walking up the sidewalk. We always greeted each other cordially but never had much of a conversation. Still, there was an undeniable chemistry. I would briefly grab her hand or nod my head as she was walking by. She would slow up and give me a big smile. I remember she often wore a jean skirt or some shorts and a light or brightly colored T-shirt with a saying or a cartoon on it. Our exchanges were short but always meaningful. After a while, our handshakes turned into hugs.

Having been raised by my mom and Grandma and Maw Maw, I was accustomed to being around strong-willed, outspoken women. Tanesha didn't come off as outspoken at all. In fact, she was one of the most soft-spoken people I'd ever met. I'd soon learn she was almost painfully shy, but her reserved demeanor belied a quiet confidence. She had this peaceful way about her. She wasn't trying to find herself or prove herself; she just was herself. The same could not be said about me.

They say you can take a person out of the hood, but you can't take the hood out of the person. That was me in college. After all those years at Male, tamping down my afro with water and hiding my style behind the school uniforms, I was ready to celebrate who I was and where I was from. I didn't want to deny or hide anymore, I wanted to proclaim it. Even though I hadn't made it to campus as a McConnell Scholar, I did ultimately land a Woodford R. Porter Scholarship, which covered my tuition and room and board in full, plus a stipend. Between the stipend and the job I got at a Sears call center, my medical bills were covered, and for the first time in my life I even had a bit of pocket money to spare. I relished the chance to spend a little of that hard-earned cash to fully express myself. Growing up in a Pentecostal household had meant strict rules and a conservative style of dress. Mom wouldn't let me get my ear pierced while I was living under her roof, so I did that immediately, opening an account with JB Robinson Jewelers and buying a diamond earring. I also saved up for clothes I wasn't allowed to have at home, Johnston & Murphy loafers, crisp Lacoste polos, and some Ralph Lauren jeans. I still sagged those Ralph Laurens a little, too, and always kept some fresh Air Jordans or Air Force Ones nearby.

My parents had saved up to buy me a car, and I fixed it up just like my dad had with the Batmobile when I was little. I put two 12-inch kickers in the trunk so the music boomed when the bass hit. I also put on 20-inch rims. The tires were more expensive than the rims, and it took me months to save up for them. I rode around for months with those rims in the trunk. When I finally got to put them on, my friend Ronel and I rode around, blasting Lil Wayne's *Tha Carter.* My favorite song was "Go D.J." off of *Tha Carter.* (Of course, I replaced "D.J." in the song with "C.J.")

Looking back, I probably spent a lot of money I shouldn't have trying to prove something. I'd go to Von Maur every two weeks when I got paid and buy two Lacoste polos. I was determined to get one in every color. When you're young, your priorities are out of whack. You prioritize superficial things like clothes because you're overcompensating for your insecurities. When you grow up without money, it shows on you. It shows in your mannerisms. So you keep your distance from people. You don't trust them. You end up in rooms with folks, thinking, *I can't possibly relate to y'all. Y'all don't know the kind of things I've been through.*

So when I got to school and had a little money, I was thinking, *I can't look like some busted broke kid from the hood.* At the same time, with the rims and the Jordans, I was also telling everybody, "Yeah, I *am* from the hood. Just 'cause I'm from the wrong side of the tracks doesn't mean I'm not good enough to be here." It was almost an act of rebellion—a preemptive act of rebellion—against an institution that I wasn't expecting to accept me for who I was.

So there I was, walking around campus, talking to everyone, projecting all this bravado, when really I was always this poor kid who felt out of place, buying the shoes and the expensive clothes and the latest phone to fit in. Tanesha didn't do any of that. She seemed like she was above it. Over the course of my four years, we got to know each other better. She was a communications major. She had a lot of family in the West End, but she'd grown up a military brat, bouncing around during her childhood while her dad served in the Air Force, moving from Oklahoma to Ohio to Okinawa and back to Louisville. Once you knew her, the shyness would melt away and she was a light in the room, always wearing a big bubbly smile and cracking jokes. She reminded me not to take myself so seriously.

In many ways we were different, but we seemed to connect. I couldn't explain it, but I felt protective of her. I could tell that, as the oldest child, she was a nurturing person, always looking out for her friends. I noticed pain in her eyes but also a strong sense of joy that let me know she was a fighter. Her grandma passed during her time in college, which forced her to take time away from school. They were extremely close, and losing that anchor in her life seemed to make Tanesha more closed off. I picked up on that in how she interacted with me. I could tell she wasn't holding her breath for a date, but I also could tell she was genuinely interested. It was almost like she was waiting on me to stop being so busy, which I never did.

The clothes and the shoes and the rims were one way in which I was overcompensating in creating an identity for myself. The other was work. Pretty much my whole four years at U of L, I studied and I worked, and I worked and I studied. It was all I did. When I started filling out my college applications and applying for scholarships, I had no idea what I wanted to major in. I only knew that I wanted to be an advocate for communities like my own. During high school, that drive had manifested mostly in volunteering for different leadership roles at church. We had a youth group that would do community service and neighborhood cleanups and make fruit baskets and deliver them to poor families, and I did that regularly. I tutored students, from preschoolers to eighth graders. I did that four or five times a week in the afternoons.

Once I got to college, my mission to serve my community drove me to join any and every organization I could. I started off attending the Porter Scholar meetings, where they supported the scholarship recipients in leadership and professional development. I got involved in the Association of Black Students, as well as an organization called Collegiate 100, a mentorship platform for Black students under the umbrella of 100 Black Men, where I got connected to career opportunities and internships and supported initiatives like food drives.

When looking for ways to get involved, I was particularly drawn to the student leaders of the Black fraternities and sororities. They were cool, and they were popular: You saw their faces all over campus. They were doing important things in the community, and they looked good doing it. I pledged Kappa Alpha Psi Fraternity, Inc., and worked so hard I was soon elected Polemarch, the chapter president.

I did everything. Being chapter president meant I had to manage the finances, recruitment, and compliance; make sure everyone maintained good grades; and engage with administrative leaders in the university. I had to step into every role: setting up the education forums on campus, coordinating with community partners for clean-up projects, organizing can drives for food pantries and shelters, and compiling chapter reports. We put on programs to assist unhoused Louisvillians at Wayside Christian Mission. I ran seminars on campus to talk about health disparities and STDs. We led civic education events on campus, mentored middle and high school students, and did community cleanups and youth outreach at churches around the city. We performed step shows, using our performances to encourage young students to consider college in their future. We also threw a great party or two, but I never really got to enjoy them because I was always busy organizing them.

So much of the work I had to do as fraternity president involved me alone on a Saturday night, going over paperwork and catching up on some mundane task or another. One of the greatest lessons I learned from that time is that leadership is not about being the most important person in the room. Being the person who stands in front of the crowd giving the big speech is part of it, but it's only one part of it, and not even the most important part. It forced me to learn that leadership is about being humble and selfless enough to be relied upon. It's about managing great responsibility and being accountable to the trust people place in you. It is thankless and defined by sacrifice, and I didn't resent that at all. I didn't resent having to work alone and shoulder that responsibility. I saw it as what I needed to do. I was so wrapped up in having to be this crusader I believed I was supposed to be that I did it at the expense of everything else.

Before I started college, I'd made a deliberate choice: I wasn't going to look for a relationship. I had dated the same girl through most of high school, but when we broke up I decided that I wanted to focus on my studies. I wanted to dedicate my energy to my commitment to my parents and my hood. I felt like I had come to campus for a greater purpose. This wasn't a game. I was here to do whatever work God gave me, and nothing was going to stop me. Most of the time, I kept my nose down and went straight from class to the library. If I wasn't studying, I was throwing myself into some new project that I was sure was going to save the world.

At one point, I was so overextended that I actually ran out of things to do. The political student groups, the faith groups, the community service groups—I hadn't joined all of them, of course, but I'd run out of ones that looked interesting to me. I went to my advisor and said, "What else can I do? What other groups should I get involved in?"

"Charles," she said. "I know you're really anxious to do everything, but take a moment to enjoy the fact that you're here, too. Enjoy this time, because it won't last long."

I sat with what she said, and it was like something clicked in me and I realized how much freedom I had. My whole life I'd felt so much responsibility to work and get ahead. I'd had fun as a kid, but it was always fun with the pastor or my parents looking over my shoulder. Even at the parties and events we held with the Kappas, I was always working, organizing. So I said to myself, "Okay, I'm going to have my fun, and then when I go to law school I'll get back to saving the world." I started going to more parties and I started meeting more girls and I always seemed to run into one girl in particular.

Tanesha came to a lot of Kappa gatherings, where she helped promote our service events. Every week, we got together to watch the Cardinals play basketball or to host a theme night like Taco Tuesday, and Tanesha regularly came to join us. She even participated in our step show performance one year. I was always glad to see her.

Still, no matter how often we saw each other, we were just friends. I could tell that she liked me, but something was holding her back.

She never pushed me on dating or anything like that. I respected her, and I never tried to push, either. I just looked forward to seeing her in between class for those brief moments. We never dated during college. The most we ever did was innocently flirt with one another.

We had this thing. We would always talk about finally going on a date and watching *Happy Feet,* the animated movie about penguins. Tanesha loved that movie, and I promised to watch it with her. For most of my senior year in college, whenever Tanesha and I would see one another, we would ask, "So when are we watching *Happy Feet?*" We would laugh and exchange pleasantries before parting ways.

We did that for four years.

Then, the night before graduation, I spent the evening at a party with some of my fraternity brothers and friends who were also going to graduate the next day. My frat brother Chris had everyone come over to his apartment for a graduation dinner. While we were sitting around the table making toasts to honor the day, Tanesha walked in. We ended up sitting in the hallway, talking for hours, and we made plans to finally have that date. It got late, and when we left Chris's apartment, we still didn't want the evening to end. We decided to spend the night together.

The day of graduation, walking across that stage, I felt an overwhelming sense of joy. I was hyped. I was humbled. I was ready. I thought about my ancestors who had been enslaved. I thought about my grandad fighting for desegregation. I thought about my mom going without food to take care of me. I thought about all the times we nearly lost it all. This day was our time to celebrate. I put my gown on and stood outside of our house on 35th. Some of our neighbors shouted from across the street, "Congratulations, young man!" I smiled as big as I could. The sun was shining just right. This was definitely going to be a good day. I even had theme music for graduation day, the "Wipe Me Down" remix with Lil Boosie, blasting from the subwoofers in my car. Stepping up on that stage, I was so happy I could have danced. When I got the degree in my hands, the first thing I did was give it to my mom. It was hers as much as it was mine.

Tanesha and I stayed in touch over the next couple weeks, but I was gearing up for my next adventure: earning my Juris Doctor degree from the University of Louisville's Brandeis School of Law. I moved into my own apartment close to the law school's campus and was taking some courses during the summer to help me prepare for my first semester. Everything seemed to be coming together for me.

Then, one day that summer, Tanesha called me. "Hey, how are you?" I asked. I was glad to hear from her, but the call was unexpected. Her voice was shaky. She told me she was on a break from her job at Burger King and really needed to talk to me. I was over at Grandma's house, and it was loud as usual. I told Tanesha I could call her back, but she told me what she had to say was very important. I went upstairs to my cousin's room and closed the door. When I put the phone back to my ear, Tanesha said two words.

"I'm pregnant."

CHAPTER 6

KAYLIN

"**Y**OU'RE PREGNANT?" I asked nervously. Tanesha repeated the words, and I sat on my cousin's bunk bed in shock. Growing up, I'd always known that I wanted a family. I'd decided that I wanted to have two girls. I even had the names picked out. But when Tanesha told me that she was pregnant, all I could think was, *No, no, no . . . I'm not ready for this.* I wasn't even ready to be in a relationship, let alone care for a child.

In the moments that followed I felt all the emotions: excited, afraid, anxious, distraught. Having no idea how to react, I said, "Well . . . I support whatever you decide to do. Just let me know." She told me she would, and we hung up. Over the next few days I waited and waited until finally she reached out to let me know she was going to continue her pregnancy. As I prepared for the biggest challenge of my life in law school, I was now also going to be a dad.

I was afraid—afraid that I'd derailed my whole career and all of my dreams, afraid that I'd let my parents down after they had invested so much in my success, afraid that I had failed before God. Being raised in an Apostolic church, one of the clearest rules for relationships was that we were not to have children out of wedlock. More than anything, I was afraid of failing the baby. As amazing as Mom and Dad had been to me, it had always deeply hurt me that they were not together. I remembered all the times I cried when my dad took me back home to Mom only to leave me. I didn't want to pass that pain on. I wanted to be a great dad. I'd always felt like Tanesha was special, and

I could see us together, but we weren't then, and I didn't know if we ever would be.

I told my mom right away. She was nothing but supportive, offering words of comfort and wisdom like she always did. "You're going to make it through this. You're going to stay in law school. I'm going to be here to help you get through this." She never acted like it was a setback or let on that she was upset, nothing. My dad was a different story. I held off on telling him for a while, but when I did, he didn't hide the way he felt at all. He was beyond disappointed in me. I had failed. Knowing that he felt that way absolutely crushed me.

Just before Tanesha called, I'd quit the job at Sears that I'd had for all four years of undergrad. I'd secured a full scholarship to Brandeis and had originally planned to spend the whole summer getting settled in my new apartment and taking extra classes to prepare for what I expected to be a brutal first year. Instead, with no job and no roommate and nothing to do and all these negative thoughts swirling around in my head, I fell into a deep depression.

It was not a good time to be living alone. I managed to make it to my classes when I had them, but it took every ounce of strength I had. Other than those brief outings, I just sat with my thoughts all day, staring at the wall, thinking I'd have to quit law school and get a job in a factory somewhere to support the baby. The thought of not finishing school wrecked me. I stopped inviting people over. I didn't answer the phone when people called. I kept all the blinds closed, didn't turn the lights on. I didn't cut my hair, either, and after a few weeks I was looking pretty raggedy. I probably showered a couple of times, but there were days when I'd just lay on the couch the entire day. I'd go to sleep, wake up and cry, and then go back to sleep again, only getting up to maybe eat a slice of deli meat and drink some boxed wine.

That boxed wine, man. It'll get you.

Whenever I spoke to Tanesha, things were tense. Her expectation seemed to be that now we were going to be together and start a relationship, but my feeling was, "Well, we weren't in a relationship before. A baby doesn't mean that we're suddenly right for each other now." She wasn't happy with that. She kept me updated on her appointments, and I went to some of them, but it was always uncomfortable.

Mental health is not something we talked about in my hood, so I didn't seek out any kind of professional help, which I definitely should have. The only therapy I got was from my friend Forrest. Forrest was a guy I met in undergrad, a friend of a friend who lived nearby. He was one of those friends who always looked out for everybody, almost like he was everyone's parent. He knew I was in bad shape, and he'd come over to the apartment every couple days and bang on the door and say, "I know you in there! I know you on the couch! I'm not leavin'!" When I didn't answer, he'd get a stick and tap on the window and annoy me until I let him in. Some days he'd just sit and watch TV with me to keep me company. He'd make me eat something, and sometimes he'd bring food for me. But more than anything Forrest was a straight shooter, and he'd sit and talk sense to me. "Snap out of it," he'd say, punching me in the arm or even grabbing me by my collar. "You're going to be okay. I'm not going to let you sit here and wallow in self-pity. You were taught to have faith. You know that you'll be okay. You're not destined to make the decisions your dad did. You're going to law school. You're going to do great things. Your life is not over."

Forrest's words and his kindness kept me from falling apart that summer, but ultimately, the thing that pulled me out of the tailspin was the impending arrival of my daughter. As the sonograms and the ultrasounds came back and the pregnancy started to become real, life started to snap back into focus: "Okay," I said. "This is reality. This is what I'm doing. First Corinthians. Chapter 10, verse 13: God doesn't give me anything I can't bear. So let's go." I pulled myself together, I stopped hiding, got back to the business of living, shook off the depression, started going to more doctor appointments with Tanesha, and committed to the upcoming semester. Slowly, as the weeks passed I realized that this pregnancy may have been unexpected, but it was the greatest blessing in my entire life.

Eventually, I agreed to meet with Tanesha's parents. Her mom was a former cop, had competed in *American Gladiators,* served in the reserves, and had once been a professional bodybuilder. I was intimidated, to say the least. But I wanted her to know that I respected her daughter and would do all I could to be a great dad, and she believed me. I explained to her that I was raised to not have children before marriage, and that I felt like a failure for not being in a strong relationship with her daughter. I told her about my fears of not being a good father, and she told me exactly what I needed to hear to calm my fears. "C.J.," she said. "Even if you and Tanesha aren't together, you can still be a great father."

I promised her that I would be.

THAT FALL I enrolled in law school, sticking with my plan while juggling my coursework and helping Tanesha with the pregnancy, and life seemed to be back on course. Then I very nearly lost it all again.

During college, I hadn't been responsible with managing my diabetes. I had regular access to my insulin thanks to being back on my dad's insurance. But I treated the disease as an afterthought. I rarely checked my levels. I drank alcohol on weekends, didn't regulate my diet. By the time I graduated I had lost nearly fifty pounds.

More than anything, I was ashamed of my diabetes. I wanted to be normal. I didn't want anything to hold me back, and having this disease that I couldn't control made me feel weak. I wanted to feel strong and confident, and up to that point in my life, I hadn't figured out how to do that and admit I had diabetes at the same time. I scarcely acknowledged the disease to myself, and I kept it a secret from virtually everyone around me. Anytime I felt drowsy or foggy, I'd power through or play it off like it was nothing. Handling it the way I did for so long, the fact that I didn't have any major health complications is practically a miracle.

Then, that first year at Brandeis, my birthday happened to fall on homecoming weekend. My fraternity's Kentucky State University chapter was competing in a step show at the downtown convention center in Frankfort, Kentucky's capital city. For Black Greek organizations, step show competitions are for bragging rights; the winner gets a big trophy and funding for their chapter's service projects. Frankfort is about an hour from Louisville, so that afternoon I picked up some of my frat brothers from U of L and we hit the road. I hadn't eaten that day, and I hadn't checked my glucose, either. I figured I would eat after the show.

The show itself was incredible. The building was packed with students from all the different fraternities and sororities from around the region. It was a March Madness type of energy. The Kappas from K State won, and there was a huge celebration. We all got out of our chairs and ran to the stage, a couple hundred of us. It was like winning a national championship.

By the end I started getting hungry and a bit shaky, but we were so excited about the win that I ignored it. Back at the hotel, the guys passed every one of us a shot of vodka to toast in celebration. Alcohol and diabetes don't go well together, but drinking is such a big part of college life, and I was so keen to belong, that I drank my shot and sat down. The rest of the guys kept drinking, but my shaking started getting worse, and I knew I couldn't wait any longer. I told the guys I was going to drive to get something to eat and come right back.

I was already in the car and pulling out when the guys who rode down with me came running down the sidewalk yelling, "Hey, we're hungry, too!" and hopped in with me, bringing the party with them. We drove to Sonic, and the guys were out of control the whole time. In the drive-through, they were singing and yelling loudly, even yelling into the drive-through speaker. I pulled up to the window and apologized. It was all in good fun, but it was also a little embarrassing.

Once we got the food, I pulled right over in a gas station parking lot across the street so I could eat. While I sat in the driver seat eating my burger, a couple of guys decided they needed to use the bathroom, and that's when the fun started to get ugly. They were stumbling around with open containers, peeing by the dumpster in the parking lot. One of them threw up behind the dumpster, too. But I was just sitting in the car eating the bacon cheeseburger from Sonic to get my glucose up. Then, as I was taking my last few bites, there was a tap on my window. I looked up. It was a police officer.

At first I wasn't really that concerned at all. I wasn't doing anything; the keys were in the ignition and music was playing, but the car wasn't even on. I rolled the window down.

"What are you doing tonight?" he asked, his demeanor calm and business-as-usual.

"We were at the step show," I said. "We left because I needed something to eat."

"Looks like these guys have been drinkin'."

"Well, it looks like they have been, yes."

"Have you been drinkin'?"

At first I was going to say no, but I remembered I had taken that shot. "I had a little bit," I said. "Earlier."

"I need you to get out of the car."

"Why? I didn't do anything."

"You're behind the wheel, and we got a call from Sonic and I need you to get out of the car."

He reached in the window, turned the key to the ignition, and the music cut off. I looked at my brothers. They were all quiet.

As I got out of the car I was still thinking, "Well, surely I won't get in trouble. It was these guys who were actin' out." But then the cop had me do a sobriety test, walk the line and follow his finger and all that. I was still sweaty and foggy and jittery from the low glucose, and I tried my best, but I didn't do well. I couldn't walk in a straight line.

They did a breathalyzer test, and my blood alcohol was low but not low enough. "We can't let you drive," the cop said, "so we're going to have to charge you with a DUI and take you in and make sure you sober up." Then they cuffed me and put me in their car.

Now I was terrified. In that moment, I saw my whole future slipping away from me. Going to jail. Kicked out of law school. Living my life as a young Black man with a record. I knew I didn't have the luxury of having a connected family or big-money attorneys who could make this go away. Where I'm from, you don't get second chances. People like me don't normally get grace.

The officers never got aggressive or unprofessional in any way, but I'd seen enough young Black kids get roughed up that I couldn't help but be afraid they might hurt me. As we drove, I started sobbing, pouring my heart out to them to get them to see who I was as a person. With tears in my eyes, I told them my story of growing up in the West End, how I was just starting law school, that I didn't want to fail my family and my community, that I was using this opportunity to do something no one else in my family had done to make things better in my neighborhood. I told them how everyone was counting on me.

I told them my whole life story. I told them every last thing except for the one most important thing: I didn't tell them that I had diabetes. I didn't tell them that the reason I had to drive to get that burger, the reason I was shaky walking that white line, was because I had this life-threatening condition. It was so ingrained in me to be ashamed of my illness that I held back from telling these officers the one thing that might have helped them understand, and possibly excuse, what had happened back in that gas station parking lot.

I was so upset that the cops actually tried to reassure me, telling me I seemed like a decent young man and this was my first offense and everything was going to be okay, but I kept sobbing. "And now it's all over," I said, dropping my head in defeat, "because I was eating a burger."

They took me down to the precinct and sat me down on these blue plastic benches where a bunch of other folks were sleeping and detoxing. *Judge Judy* was on TV. They took my picture and charged me with a DUI and sent me home.

My close friend Ronel's stepmom ran a law firm called Legal Direction. I called her Mrs. Denise, and her firm was made up entirely of Black women attorneys. She agreed to represent me, and in my conversations with her it came up that I'd never told the cops I had diabetes. The first thing Mrs. Denise did was call the arresting officer and explain about my condition, and he said, "If we had known you were diabetic, we probably wouldn't have arrested you. We'd probably have given you a warning."

Still, the wheels of the justice system were already turning, and there was no option but to move forward. I got my court date, and Mrs. Denise explained the whole story to the judge. The judge had me go to counseling and told me that because of my clean record and the circumstances around my arrest, he would throw out my case—as long as I graduated law school. He told me he didn't want me to give up.

Once I graduated law school, I decided that I didn't want my record expunged. Getting arrested made me take my diabetes seriously, and I didn't want to wash that experience away. I also knew that this testimony might help someone else one day. I'd made a mistake, but I let that lesson help me improve.

ON THE MORNING of January 19, 2008, Tanesha called me to tell me it was time. I jumped in my car, picked up Mom, and we rushed to the hospital. By the time we got there, we walked into the waiting room, where Tanesha's family was sitting anxiously. Tanesha had just given birth, and I was able to go back to see her. When I saw my baby girl, time stopped. Tanesha had named her Kaylin. She looked like my Maw Maw. Her hair was beautiful. When Tanesha asked if I wanted to hold her, I hesitated; she was so tiny I was afraid I would break her. Everyone in the room laughed. Nervously, I got my arms ready, and the doctor handed her to me and my heart melted. I immediately fell in love. It was like my eyes were opened to some greater level of beauty that I could have never imagined.

Kaylin made my whole life make sense. When we were able to take her home from the hospital, I started staying over at Tanesha's apartment. I never wanted to be away from Kaylin. If I had a long break between classes, I would go over to the apartment, and once classes were over for the day I'd head there immediately and stay as long as I could. Tanesha would cook dinner and we'd watch a movie while the baby was laying in the little bassinet. Many evenings I'd wind up falling asleep on the couch for the night. Kaylin had us acting like a family even though we weren't one, and eventually we started to feel like one. Tanesha and I worked together well. She was very supportive of my success in law school. She made sure I stayed on schedule with my studying and even helped me at times, and I pitched in around the apartment doing the kinds of things that boyfriends and husbands would typically do. It just made sense. I started to have a thought in the back of my mind of possibly building a relationship with Tanesha that would make sure Kaylin always had both of her parents at home. I wasn't thinking about marriage yet. All I knew for certain is that I wanted to spend every second with Kaylin and that I cared deeply for this special woman who brought her into the world.

Then, that April, three months after Kaylin was born, as I was getting ready for my first year finals, I was sitting in class and my phone rang. I muted the call to get through the last few minutes of class, but it started blowing up. I slipped out into the hallway and answered. It was my cousin Lindsay. He was crying. "Grandma's dying," he said. "She's in the hospital. She's dying."

I dropped my books and started to run. I ran through a group of students and flew down the steps. I ran out of the school and across the lawn where students were sitting. I ran across the street, not looking at any cars coming. My car was at the student parking lot about a half mile away. I ran as fast as I could, tears streaming down my face with each step. I needed to get back to the West End. The drive was typically about twenty minutes. I cut that in half.

When I pulled into the parking lot of Mary and Elizabeth Hospital, I saw cousins, aunts, and uncles spread out across the sidewalk. I started to run for the hospital doors. Then I saw Maw Maw, standing in the middle of the entryway, waiting for me, and the look on her face told me I was already too late to say goodbye. Grandma wasn't gone yet, but she was on life support, unconscious and unresponsive. A blood clot had formed in her leg and made it to her heart. The doctors had given her blood thinners, but they weren't helping; her blood was seeping out of her skin.

Grandma had always been the warrior for all of us. We knew she wasn't going to stop fighting. More family made their way to the hospital, and pretty soon we completely filled several waiting rooms. Several hours later, the doctors came back out and gave us the news we'd been dreading. The room erupted. Some wailed in sorrow, some screamed and ran out of the room. I looked over at Grandad, crying quietly in his chair, and I cried for him.

About a half hour later, as we all sat in shock, still trying to process our grief, Tanesha made it to the hospital with Kaylin. The moment Mom took that little baby girl in her arms, it was as if Kaylin was pouring some peace into her, at a time she needed it most. While Mom held Kaylin, Tanesha walked over, sat by me, and hugged me. I looked around at all my cousins and aunts and uncles, and it was suddenly clear how much Tanesha and Kaylin belonged right there with us. In the days that followed, I couldn't be alone without breaking down. I even had nightmares of Grandma dying, and Tanesha would put her arms around me so I could go to sleep. I started to understand that I needed her, that we needed each other, that we needed to be a family, or at least to try.

Over the next few months, we decided to try being together. One of our moms would come in to babysit Kaylin, and we'd go out for dinner or go to the movies, just the two of us.

Maybe our relationship didn't start out the way either of us had planned, maybe our relationship wasn't exactly what I thought I was looking for, but it was the relationship that God had given me, and a couple weeks later, I was finally able to understand what God had been trying to tell me.

Looking to get some exercise one evening, Tanesha and I decided to go to Louisville's historic Cherokee Park for an evening run. Located in the center of the city, Cherokee Park is a large Frederick Law Olmsted park with several miles of trails to run. We took Kaylin over to my mom's house, got our Gatorade, and hurried to the park. The sun was going to set soon, so we were moving quickly before we lost the light. As we got started, we decided to challenge ourselves, going in the direction that would allow us to run the longest route. Our pace was good. We sang songs as we ran. Soon we found ourselves on the complete opposite end of the park. It led out into a subdivision of older, very expensive, very beautiful homes. We kept jogging because we were marveling at the houses and we lost track of the time, and before we could make it back to the park trail it was dark.

We were on the complete opposite end of the park, miles away from my car. We stood at the entrance to the park with a decision to make. Those wooded paths were beautiful while the sun was still up, but they looked like a scene out of a horror movie when it was dark. There was no other way back to the car. We looked at each other, held hands, and started running into the abyss.

I was terrified, but I fought to hide it. With each step, I thought about quitting, just sitting down on a rock in this dark, wooded park and dealing with the fact that we were stuck. That was not an option, though. Tanesha was obviously fighting the same battles in her head. She moaned and whimpered as we ran. She was breathing like she needed a rest. When I asked if she wanted to stop, she panted and said no. I admitted to her that I was a little scared. She told me that she was too. We were practically running blind. Tanesha squeezed my hand tightly, and I squeezed hers. We both wanted to stop, but it was like holding one another's hand was giving us energy. Any fear I had turned into an urge to protect her. I wasn't going to slow down or look back; I was going to make sure we got back to the car safely. I tried singing to ease the tension, but the echo was eerie. So, quietly, we kept running.

After running nonstop for several miles, we saw a shadow of light around the bend. It was the light from the parking lot where my car was sitting. That light gave us a burst of energy, and we took off in a sprint up the last big hill. The car came into view, and the relief we felt was like a mountain being lifted. It was as if we had won a championship. We both fell on the car, thanking God that we had made it out of that park. Those seats never felt so good. Sitting in the car, we recounted what happened and burst into laughter. We were fully prepared for Jason or Freddy Krueger to hop out of the trees, but we weren't going to go down without a fight.

Whenever I started worrying about being lost or tired or anxious about running in the darkness, Tanesha's hand gave me reassurance. It made me realize that I could do anything: I could dream big, I could finish law school. There was nothing I couldn't accomplish as long as Tanesha was by my side holding my hand. I held onto her through the final exams of my first year of law school, through the ups and downs of my second year, and into the third. Kaylin grew and grew and grew. She started talking, started walking, and Tanesha and I were still together, side by side, holding on. I knew I never wanted to let go of her hand from then on.

When Grandma passed, I got her Bible. Mom got several pieces of her jewelry, including Grandma's first wedding ring; because they were married so long, Grandad would buy Grandma a new ring set every ten years or so. When I told Mom that I wanted to marry Tanesha but wasn't sure what to do about a ring, she smiled, pulled out the little box of Grandma's old jewelry, put that wedding ring in my hand, and told me to use it. It was a thick gold band, with brackets for a single large stone. The stone was missing, though. I had a couple months to graduation, so I spent that time saving my money to buy a diamond to put in the ring. Then I figured out the exact right moment to propose.

The day I graduated from Brandeis was magical. I was on a cloud after a lifetime of struggle and sacrifice, tears and setbacks. My theme song for the day was a song by Jay-Z called "I Made It." I had kept my promise to my superhero, my mom, who believed in me through it all, and this day was my chance to say thank you. As I walked across that stage to get my diploma, I heard Kaylin yell out, "Daddy, Daddy, Daddy!" She gave me my higher purpose for living. Hearing her little voice fill up the auditorium was everything.

The graduation party was my time to tell everyone thank you. The Kentucky Center for African American Heritage had recently opened in the West End, and we were the first family to have a graduation celebration there. My law school mentors came, my frat brothers and college friends were there, and dozens of my cousins made it as well. Once everyone found their seats, I made my speech. It was the speech of a kid from the West End, a speech about love and relentless faith in the difficult times. It was a speech about angels like my mom, who went without food so her only son could eat. It was a speech about moving mountains and standing up for what you believe in. It was a declaration of my commitment to the West End and every community like it.

It was also a love story. I asked Tanesha to stand up. I told the whole room about our terrifying run in Cherokee Park and the peace I felt from holding her hand. Then I talked about my grandma and how much Tanesha reminded me of her. That's when I pulled out the ring. The room erupted in cheers and screams as soon as they saw it. It felt like the room was rumbling. I asked Tanesha to marry me, and the entire room shouted, "Yes!"

I grabbed her hand, looked deep into her eyes, and smiled.

PART II

CHAPTER 7

A CALLING

A T 6 A.M. on a cool March morning during my first year of law school, I pulled up and parked my car outside of what had to be one of the biggest houses in the West End. It wasn't far from my mom's, but it was on the river and had incredible views. The Ohio River wraps around most of the West End and is only minutes from our house, but because of the high trees in the parks and the fact that the beaches had long eroded away, I had never seen it this close before. Even early in the morning, the moonlight sparkled on the water. I sat and waited outside this house for about fifteen minutes. Then one of the garage doors opened, and out came a Lexus SUV. I climbed out of my car, hopped into the Lexus's passenger seat, and my journey into politics began.

My second semester had been brutal. Welcoming Kaylin into the world and losing Grandma so soon after had been an emotional roller coaster. Weeks after that, I lost my great-grandmother, too. Still, despite the difficulty, I was committed to learning all there was to know about this career, and I knew that meant seeking out mentors. I made it a goal to meet with and learn from as many different legal professionals as possible. At first I didn't know where to start. There hadn't been any lawyers around me growing up, and I had no real idea what I was getting into. So I did what Grandad taught me to do: I figured it out.

It wasn't easy to search for local attorneys online, so I went the old-school route. I grabbed the Yellow Pages for maybe the first time in years, and on my breaks and on weekends I started going down the list of every law office. I would call the office and update a template letter to mail them as well, asking them for the chance to meet. I would tell them that I was the first in my family to go to law school and I wanted to figure out how I could be successful in the field and I'd be grateful for any advice they could give me. My longer-term strategy was to build relationships so that I could then come back to folks for jobs when I graduated. I was methodical. I was determined. I was a machine. In the late hours, I would sit at my little desk facing the window looking downtown with a glass of iced tea beside me and some incense burning and knock out at least thirty or forty letters in a sitting. After sending a letter, I would wait ten days for them to respond. Then I would follow up. Most of them never got back to me.

It didn't surprise me that I was being ignored. My parents weren't attorneys. I had no connection to powerful people or elected officials in the city, so these firms had little incentive to speak with me. They were busy tending to paying clients. But I never let that discourage me. I was prepared to bug every last person in the phone book until someone answered me. Eventually, several firms responded, and I set up meetings to either stop by their office or have a conversation at a coffee shop. I gained all types of advice: everything from how to balance my schedule to which study supplements were most helpful to why I should try to get published in a law journal. But the truly life-changing moment came when I stumbled upon the name of Gerald Neal.

Gerald Neal was an attorney with a practice that handled a broad range of issue areas. He was also one of the few Black politicians elected to the Kentucky State Senate, representing the 33rd District, though I didn't know that at the time. Neal was hard to connect with due to his constant traveling, but I stuck to my process and continued to follow up. Eventually he called me back, and gave me a terse "Well, I'm busy now. Check back with me in a couple of days." So I made a note and checked back with him in a couple of days. He said he appreciated my persistence and offered to sit down with me at a restaurant near his office.

The man knew how to make an entrance. He sauntered into the restaurant, walking fast, talking loudly on his phone. He was an older man with a gray goatee and wavy gray hair dressed in a classy brown blazer with shiny brown shoes to match. He winked at the server, started looking around for me, and then, when we made eye contact, gave me a smile and joined me at a seat near the outside patio. "So," he said in jest, "we finally meet!"

That whole first meeting, it was like he was feeling me out. The man had a commanding presence, but in a reserved sort of way. He'd lean back and squint his eyes and raise an eyebrow and pepper you with questions, talking low with a gruff tone of voice: "So why do you want to meet with me for? What are you trying to do? What do you want to get out of this?" Meanwhile, I was sitting across from him, all bright and cheery like a kid at Christmas.

At one point, he came right out and said, "Are you just going to waste my time?" I would learn later that he'd stuck his neck out to mentor some other young, aspiring attorneys, taking them under his wing only to feel like they flaked out on him. I was intimidated. The meeting was a little tense, and that was quite deliberate on his part: He was probing to see if I was serious. "I'm going to give you a chance," he said, "but if you waste my time, you'll never hear from me again."

As he got up to leave, he made me an offer. "If you want to continue our conversation," he said, "it will have to be in Frankfort. The legislature is in session, and I've got too many meetings. The only time I have available is during my drive over in the morning. If you're at my house at six A.M. tomorrow morning, you can ride with me."

I'm sure he thought, *There's no way this kid is showing up at my house at six* A.M. But six A.M. came, and there I was, bright-eyed and ready to go. When I climbed in his SUV with my notepad, he was clearly a little surprised, but I noticed a smile at the corner of his mouth. "All right," he said. "Let's go."

Up to that point, my only exposure to the state capital had been driving through Frankfort one night with my father. No one in my life had ever talked about actually going inside the State Capitol building. I'd never envisioned doing anything that important. My mother had always raised me to see myself as capable of anything, but growing up in the struggle limits your ability to see how far you can really go.

I had always been driven to move forward, to move up. That drive got me on the school bus that took me across Louisville's segregated 9th Street divide to one of the top high schools in the city. That drive led me to pursue college and law school even though no one else in my family had done it before. But I still didn't have any idea what I was missing. I didn't know that my whole life I'd been dreaming too small. Now, as I was riding with a state senator to the Kentucky State Capitol, I had no idea what to expect. I only knew I would go anywhere and do anything to get to the next chapter in my journey.

THE FOG WAS heavy as we turned off Louisville Road in Frankfort. We had started driving before the sun was up, and now the new day was casting a beautiful light on the trees along the street. When we got to the bottom of the hill, I saw the most incredible scene I have ever encountered: The Capitol came into view like a beacon in the valley, its dome piercing through the fog. I was in awe. It made me proud to be a Kentuckian.

Frankfort is a small city on the Kentucky River, centrally located between our two largest cities, Louisville and Lexington. In many ways, though, it seemed as if Frankfort was in a whole different world than my hood in the West End. The whole city is no bigger than my old neighborhood, yet it is home to the political power that shapes the entire state of Kentucky. Frankfort is also the one capital city in the Union that was occupied by Confederate troops, which says a lot about the persistent struggle of political and economic power in our state.

As we drove into town, Senator Neal told me about his journey getting into law, which was still, theoretically, the reason for my ride along. But all of that began to change the minute he walked me into that building. I noticed everything: the checkerboard pattern in the evenly cut grass, the clack of my shoes on the red brick pavers around the Capitol building. I took in the beautiful columns, the marble floors, the gold-plated elevators, the remarkable dome that changed colors in the evening. There was a feeling of energy there, too. Everyone was moving quickly, as if on a mission. News cameras were posted up in the hallways. Groups of protestors lined the walls, holding signs about issues ranging from family farm programs to pre-K education. Legislators were briskly walking to committee meetings. It was electric. I could tell this was a busy place full of important people.

I also couldn't miss the fact that hardly any of them looked like me. None of the images I was seeing looked like my home or anyone in my family. There was a hall of glass cases that housed little dolls of the first ladies throughout Kentucky's history. They were all white and had on little dresses that reminded me, uncomfortably, of the outfits worn by women in the antebellum period. In the Capitol rotunda, there was a huge, looming statue of Jefferson Davis, the former president of the Confederacy. His presence struck an odd and unmistakable chord when you stopped to remember that Kentucky was not actually a part of the Confederacy. There was no WHITES ONLY sign in the Capitol building, but the statue of Davis was surely a towering monument to that shameful idea.

For the rest of the day, it felt like Neal was still testing me, putting obstacles in my path to see if I'd get discouraged and leave. He said he wouldn't have any time to talk until after his meetings, and then his meetings stretched on for the rest of the day. Constituent meetings, committee meetings, it was nonstop. The constituent meetings were private, so I spent a couple hours hanging out in the break room. Then, as soon as those were over, Neal was already on the move for his committee meetings.

"Either you can sit here," he said, "or come with me."

"I'll come with you."

I ended up shadowing him through several meetings. The biggest eye-opener was the time I spent watching the Judiciary Committee. The discussions ranged from addressing gang violence to cash bail, and as I listened, I realized the senators were talking about issues that impacted my community, that directly affected me, but many of the legislators had no clue about the consequences of their decisions. The way some of the members of the committee defined a "gang" could very well have described me and a few of my cousins walking down the street. They didn't see us as innocent children trying to survive. They saw us as a threat.

Senator Neal had a powerful voice, as did the handful of other Black legislators in the House. They definitely spoke up about challenges in the Black community, but they were all my grandparents' age. No one in the room was speaking from the point of view of a young Black man battling poverty. It was as if they were all talking about me but not exactly speaking for me.

By the time Neal was done with his meetings, we'd barely had a chance to exchange a word. On the ride home he said, "I know we didn't get that much time, but I'm going back tomorrow if you want to come." I told him I did. I told him I wanted to continue riding with him to Frankfort for the rest of the session. I told him it didn't matter how early we had to get on the road or how late we made it back in town. He told me that would be fine. I still don't think he thought I was serious, but six A.M. the next morning came, and there I was. I ended up going to Frankfort for most of the remaining days in that legislative session. At the end of each day, Senator Neal would ask, "Will I see you in the morning?" and if I didn't have class my answer was always yes.

Over time, he started to let his guard down. Our conversations about the law soon became conversations about politics. Neal gave me a history lesson that filled in and fleshed out the bigger picture behind all the stories I'd heard from my grandad. He told me how during the Civil Rights Movement, a group of young leaders had come together in the West End. Most of them were still college students. They had been activists and organizers, often slipping out of high school to lead protests to desegregate theaters and restaurants in downtown Louisville. Senator Neal would always smile when he told me stories about getting arrested for leading nonviolent protests. "I was arrested eleven times," he'd say, proudly.

Realizing that laws wouldn't change unless they took over leadership roles in the city, they set out to do just that. "We wanted to build our own power base," Neal told me. They sought not only elected office but professional and civic roles that would allow them to apply pressure from every angle, to concentrate the momentum from the Civil Rights Movement and turn it into sustained infrastructure for the Black community.

Even in 2008, most of the West End's municipal and state officials were connected to that same group of seasoned Black leaders: faith leaders, artists, attorneys, physicians, educators, and politicians. People like Rev. Dr. Geoff Ellis, Councilwoman Cheri Bryant Hamilton, Rep. Darryl Owens, Clarence Yancey, Myra Friend-Ellis, Dr. J. Blaine Hudson, Raoul Cunningham, Rev. Louis Coleman, and of course Senator Neal. They had fashioned themselves into a Black political machine, much in the same way that other activists of their generation had in urban centers across the country in the 1970s and '80s.

I was especially impressed by the stories Neal told about himself, because I could see my story in his. He'd once been a young man in a hurry, too. He'd first run for office in 1979, challenging Senator Georgia Davis Powers, a civil rights icon and the first Black person ever to serve in the Kentucky State Senate. "I had a great deal of respect for her," Neal said, "but I felt she had been in office for too long. So I went to her and told her why I wanted to run and let her know that if she didn't retire I was going to run against her." He challenged her and lost, but in doing so he made a name for himself, and he became the heir apparent for the seat when she stepped down a decade later. He won his first election to the State Senate in 1989 and had been reelected every term since, often running unopposed.

To Senator Neal, I may have started off as a young guy who was persistent in bugging him, but to me he was a mentor. Having this kind of relationship with an elected official was exciting for me. I had never personally known someone in elected office before. I looked at him like a celebrity. I started to study him: the way he talked, the way he thought through issues, his poise, the way he smiled and engaged in small talk with people in the hallways, the way he answered questions—or avoided them.

I was taking notes.

Eventually, he noticed I was soaking everything up, so he would give me instruction in real time. "You saw how we discussed funding in public schools, Charles?" he'd say. "Well, I let them talk, but then I just asked a simple question: 'Surely you want every single child to have a quality education?' Did you see how that put them on the spot?"

Neal had the spirit of a wise old owl in the legislature, often schooling his colleagues subtly and calmly even when they were making the most egregious and often racist statements. I learned a lot about how he kept his sanity as an older Black man who had seen it all. He didn't let the prejudices or blind spots of some of his white colleagues cause him to lose his cool. There was one session in which the Education Committee was debating policing in schools. The way some of the legislators were up there talking, you'd think that they believed children from my hood were violent predators. I was ready to jump out of my seat, but Neal just pushed back, softly, without losing his temper. "Well, gentlemen," he said, "we need to consider what the experiences of these children really are, what they might be dealing with at home."

Then, the moment we were in the car to drive home, he let loose. "Man, these people wear me out," he said. "Their kids cause trouble, too, but they only want the police in *our* schools." For the rest of the ride home, he let it all out. Then, six A.M. the next morning, he'd be back in his car, calm and collected and ready to head back into battle.

Day after day, week after week, for the rest of that session I shadowed Neal around the Capitol building. It transformed me. It was almost like I was coming alive, like having an out-of-body experience. It was as if my eyes had been opened to a whole new level of possibilities. My whole life, listening to Grandad's stories and seeing the injustice of segregation, I'd wanted to fight for the West End. But I'd had such a vague and simplistic notion of what that meant. It was always just, "Keep fighting. Do more. Go to college. Get to law school. Fly higher. Work harder." But I'd had no understanding of how the levers of power actually worked, or where they were, or who got to pull on them. Now, thanks to Senator Neal, I'd seen behind the curtain. I'd sat in the rooms where people were making decisions about my life and my family, and I knew I didn't want these debates happening without someone like me at the table.

I'd gone to law school thinking that becoming a lawyer was the path a person needed to take to make big changes. But the more I saw of the legal process, I realized that lawyers mostly had to work within the system as it existed. A lawyer applies the law, but what happens when the law is unjust when it's written? A lawyer can help you file for medical bankruptcy, but a lawyer can't protect you from being bankrupted by your medical bills and spiraling health costs in the first place. That happened in Frankfort, in the legislature. As I resumed my second year of law school, I decided I didn't want to be the person who navigates the rules that already exist. I wanted to be the person who rewrites the rule book.

CHAPTER 8

THE DELTA TO THE DISTRICT

O N NOVEMBER 4, 2008, in the fall of my second year of law school, I joined Grandad to stand in line outside Shawnee High School to cast our votes for the first Black president in the history of the United States. It was a special day for me, but for Grandad it was the culmination of a journey he'd started nearly eighty years before, in the Mississippi Delta, where he was born. Everyone in my family had worked and struggled their whole lives to throw off the oppressive weight of segregation and Jim Crow. But Grandad had always been the most vocal, the most political. He'd always been right there on the front lines, even as a boy helping his daddy on the farm. Those were the stories he used to regale me with when he held forth at the kitchen table for hours and hours, leaning back in his chair, sipping on a glass of lemonade.

"Charlie," he'd say, "when I was about your age, we'd take bushels of corn and soybeans to town. The white men we sold to didn't expect Black people to know math, and they always tried to shortchange us. I was always good with numbers, though, so I was responsible for keeping an eye on the weight to make sure we were paid the right amount. When the man tried to pay us, and I told him he was short, he yelled at me. He said, 'What, you think you know math, boy?'

"I hated when people called me 'boy.' They would say it to all of us, even your great-grandad. I told him that if he didn't pay us what he owed us, I'd take my wrench and hit him over the head. I grabbed that wrench and squeezed it tight—and he pulled the rest of the money out of his pocket."

Whenever Grandad told me that story, he'd clench his hands like he was that kid holding that wrench again. He was tenacious. Since his parents hadn't been allowed to read, he was determined to learn everything he could. He graduated high school as valedictorian and class president, and always sought out new challenges and committed to mastering them.

One of the most indelible stories he told me was his account of working at Reynolds Metals Company, where he fought for desegregation and equal rights. After being honorably discharged from the Army, Grandad came back to Louisville. He farmed, fixed cars, built houses, and eventually found work at Reynolds, where they made the aluminum foil that everyone has in their homes to this day. He would feed the big sheets of aluminum into the cutting machine. There was an art to doing it, because the edges of the metal were incredibly sharp, and the machine would rapidly pull the sheets into place to cut them. One false move could be deadly. Many people lost limbs or suffered major injuries from this work. Grandad was one of the best on the machine, but one day he lost control as he was loading the metal. Before he knew what had happened, three of his fingers were sliced off. It didn't slow him up one bit, though. "I sacrificed so much for that company," he'd say, lifting up his right hand. "I even lost my fingers, but that didn't stop me." Once his hand healed and he was cleared to return to work, he got right back on the machine.

The Reynolds factory was located in the West End at 28th and Hale, and it was one of the few places Black and white Louisvillians spent time together, but the Black employees were expected to do the bulk of the work and even keep the facility clean. Meanwhile, all the "management" roles were reserved for white employees. As a man rooted in the principles of respect, hard work, and fairness, Grandad demanded that Black employees receive their rightful promotions like everyone else.

"Charlie," he told me, "I demanded to be treated like the white employees. I was as qualified as anyone else, I had the most experience there, and the only reason they wouldn't promote me after years of hard work was because I'm Black. It wasn't right, and I wasn't going to tolerate it. I told them I was going to sue if I had to."

It was an uphill battle. Grandad refused to let up and encouraged other employees to stand with him. Their cries couldn't be silenced, and after his efforts attracted growing attention in the city, Grandad won. He was promoted to management, the first Black man to do so at Reynolds. He wasn't concerned about only his own opportunities. Grandad knew that his victory would open the door for more Black employees to see greater opportunities in the company. He was given a lapel pin and a tie bar, and he wore them with pride. He worked at Reynolds until his retirement.

Listening to Grandad's stories about life in Mississippi and at Reynolds, breaking this ceiling and overcoming painful discrimination, my chest would fill with pride. With every victory he won, I felt like I had won, too. Grandad had stood up for himself and for others his whole life so that I could have the opportunities that I did. Even though I could hear the anger in Grandad's voice as he told me these stories, I never saw his telling them to me as something that was meant to make my heart turn cold. I could tell he was teaching me, not so that I could be upset but so that I could know my history.

Listening to Grandad talk, I never felt anger or sadness, only pride. He taught me to take pride in being from the West End of Louisville and in being a Kentuckian. He also taught me to take pride in being an American. Not because the country is perfect, but because it's my home and because the people in it are my family. No family agrees on everything, but you always know you have a common bond that rises above all else. Because of Grandad, my faith in America is rooted in the power of that truth. We may be separated from that truth in our current politics, but that doesn't negate the fact that the truth still exists.

I felt that same sense of pride the whole time I followed Obama's insurgent campaign. Obama was taking the baton from men like my grandad and continuing that journey, showing everyone that there is no limit to what Black Americans can achieve. He had the audacity to believe something different was possible. I believed that, too, but seeing him made it real. I followed his campaign with hope, but I also had a nagging feeling that his success was too good to be true. Something that big doesn't happen to people who look like me or come from where I do. I wanted it to happen, but life prepares you for disappointment. Still, I never said that out loud. I didn't want my doubts to discourage anyone around me from supporting him. "He's going to win," I proudly said to anyone who asked my opinion.

I appreciated everything about Obama's journey, and the fact that he was doing something so big so early resonated with me. In my life and career, I had been told everything he had been told. "He's not ready." "He should wait." "He doesn't have enough experience." But I saw him handle the doubters with grace. When his wife, Michelle, stood with him, I saw Tanesha: a strong woman who doesn't like the political arena but loves people.

In the heat of that campaign, Obama's whole life was put under a microscope: his grades in school, even his pastor's sermons. The moment when Reverend Jeremiah Wright was thrust into the campaign was a critical moment for me. I saw Obama make the determination to distance himself from Wright's teachings. I didn't like the idea that he needed to do that, but I understood exactly what he was navigating. He was seeking to thread every needle that existed.

I saw Obama's slogan of "Yes we can" as a way of fighting back. It was a resounding declaration that doubt and disbelief would not win, a rally cry of courage and conviction. The type of conviction that refuses to sit in the back of the bus or be sold short on the price for a bushel of soybeans. When Grandad worked to desegregate his workplace at Reynolds Metals, it was like he was saying, "Yes we can." I saw Obama's journey as a continuation of Grandad's journey. It was a journey that could lead to the election of the first Black president—and, perhaps, whatever God had in store for me.

That night, my law school classmates were getting together for drinks, but I wanted to watch in silence. This was going to be one of the biggest moments in history, and I wanted to take it all in. At the time I lived on the eighteenth floor of Kentucky Towers, a run-down old high-rise apartment in the heart of downtown Louisville. On election night I paced back and forth, stopping occasionally to lean up against that window and pray not only for Obama's victory but for my grandad to have the opportunity to witness it. He needed to witness it. I needed to witness it. My community needed to witness it. I was taught to never doubt what's possible. I knew that through faith and hard work, I could do anything I put my mind to. However, before this night, no Black person had ever been president of the United States. There was a ceiling. An accomplishment this great seemed off-limits for us. I wanted to see that ceiling break.

As state after state confirmed their results, I started to feel like it was actually going to happen. I called my mom. She was glued to the TV, too. "He's going to win, baby!" Mom said with deep excitement.

All the lights were on in my tiny, 560-square-foot apartment. I flipped from channel to channel, trying to see who would call the race first. I was frantically refreshing the news on my laptop as well. I opened the windows in my living room to let the breeze in, and as I was waiting for the networks to make the call, I started to hear car horns. People were honking as if the Cardinals had won the championship. I knew what that meant, but I wanted to see the numbers myself. Then it happened. MSNBC and CNN had called the election. Barack Obama was going to be the next president of the United States.

I turned on the stereo and ran around my table. The station was set to B96.5, the hip-hop station that we listened to in Louisville. It was hard to hear the music, though, because the car horns were echoing into my apartment! I figured the only thing I could do was go down and join them. Our elevator took forever, so I ran down all eighteen flights, skipping steps on the way. Running to my car, I jumped in, rolled down all the windows, and pressed on my horn as hard as I could. There were cheers in the streets. Cars were driving by with people hanging out of their sunroofs. It was a celebration. I pulled out of the parking lot and headed west, pushing on my horn the whole way. I drove by a cousin's house and over to my mom's. I drove all around the West End. I wiped the tears from my eyes as I pushed on my horn. I raised my fist and smiled at people on the street. They raised their fists back, nodding in recognition of what happened. You could feel the hope in the streets.

The next day I stopped by Grandma's house, where the celebration was still going. "Well, Charlie, he actually did it," Grandad said, nodding his head. "I remember Black folks getting sprayed with hoses and hit over the head with sticks. I never thought I'd see the day when a Black man became president." I told him it meant a lot for me to stand in line with him to cast that vote. "It meant a lot to me, too, Charlie," he said. "I'm proud of you, son."

EVEN AS I watched Obama settling into the Oval Office after his inauguration, the thought that my journey might someday take me to D.C. had never crossed my mind. Then, three months later, Senator Neal walked me into the office of Robert Jenkins, one of the directors of Kentucky's Legislative Research Commission.

"Charles," Neal said as he introduced us, "if you really want to get involved in politics, you should get a job on a committee. The committees are where most of the policy work actually happens, and to get a job there, Robert is the person you need to talk to." Thus I was introduced to one of the ironclad rules of politics and power: It's all about who you know.

The LRC is the nonpartisan staff for the Kentucky State Legislature. They do everything: write legislation, perform intensive research, work as assistants for legislators, and staff legislative committees. The jobs there are very competitive. Back then, not every job got posted, and positions would be filled almost immediately after opening up. If you didn't know a legislator or already work within the Capitol, it could nearly be impossible to land a position. Of the handful of Black staffers on the LRC, none were from the West End, so it was obvious to me why no one like me was able to get a job there.

In spite of that, I was determined. I followed up with Jenkins, and he agreed to give me a mock interview, offering advice and encouragement in the weeks that followed. Neal continued to push me as well. The one thing he suggested that would really give me some hands-on experience and strengthen my résumé for the job search was an internship. "If you want to learn about policy and land a committee job with LRC," he said, "you should get experience on Capitol Hill in Washington." I decided that's exactly what I was going to do.

Up until that point in my life, I had never spent more than a handful of days outside of Kentucky. Getting some legislative experience at the federal level would not only show me a world outside of the places I was familiar with, but it would also give me an intense dive into the key issues that shape state-level policymaking. I wanted to do it. My mom thought I should as well. Tanesha was so excited for me that she started saving money in anticipation of my landing a job on the Hill. The only thing I needed to do now was figure out how in the world I was going to get an internship.

Since I didn't have many contacts in D.C., I reached out to the office of my congressperson, Representative John Yarmuth, but his internships were full. Then, when I was sitting around one afternoon with some of my college friends, I mentioned my desire to go to Capitol Hill, and one of my buddies, Kingsley, had an idea. Kingsley was one of those people who knew everybody, and he knew a young lady with Kentucky ties who was a congressional staffer. Her name was Bianca, and she was working in the office of Congressman Bob Brady of Pennsylvania. He offered to connect me with her.

After an introductory email, Bianca called me back and we talked about my goals and plans. I could hear in her voice that she was excited to help. As a Black staffer herself, Bianca seemed to feel a sense of responsibility to help me get on the Hill. At the same time, she was brutally honest about how hard it was going to be. Her advice for me was to get to D.C. as soon as possible. "You need to come up here, meet some people, and build relationships," she said. "That's the best way to help you actually get a job."

She suggested I come to town during my summer break, set up some meetings, and see where things went from there. She agreed to help me meet other staffers who could advise me, including some of my frat brothers who worked in Congress. She even told me I could crash on her couch. It was a shot in the dark, but I was willing to take it. Using most of my savings, I bought a plane ticket to D.C. I made some business cards, too, from a template I picked out in Microsoft Word. I put in my name and for my title I typed "Candidate for Juris Doctorate 2010." Then I printed them out on those flimsy perforated sheets they make for home printers. That alone was exciting. And when that August came around I was bound for Washington, D.C.—my first trip to our nation's capital.

WHEN I STEPPED off the plane in D.C., I felt Grandad walking right there with me, and I was determined not to let him down. Being in that city gave me an enormous sense of purpose. History was written on every building and spilling into every street. The monuments towered. The architecture on every block told a story. The dome of the Capitol building was remarkable from every angle. I loved it. I knew I had made the right decision to come, even if it meant sleeping on a stranger's couch.

When I made it to the House Office Building and lugged my big suitcase through security, Bianca was there waiting for me. She was petite with glasses and a short pixie haircut that said, "I'm ready to take on the world." Right from the jump she was upbeat and sunny with a big laugh, and everything about her said she was smart, professional, and official. "C'mon," she said with a big smile, "let me show you around."

The first thing we did was take a tour of the Capitol building. As Bianca walked me down the beautiful halls, I stared in amazement at the nameplates of the congressional members. We made it to Rep. Brady's office, and I got my first tour of a congressional office. Bianca brainstormed people to introduce me to and planned a full day of meetings for me the next day.

That next day on the Hill was a rapid fire of introductions and impromptu interviews. "This is my friend, Charles," Bianca would say, as if I were someone she'd known for years. The whole day she kept telling me, "I got you. We're gonna find you a job." She was so confident she made me believe it, too.

I stopped by Congressman Yarmuth's office and met Keidra King, a Black staffer there who knew a lot of the same people I knew and grew up with in the West End. Her family actually lived in my neighborhood. Like Bianca, she was so excited to help me that it shocked me. The two of them treated me like I was important. They sacrificed their time to help me out. There was no way I would have had the chance to do this without them, and I thought about all of the people who lived their whole lives without ever getting a chance like this. In my head, I said a prayer thanking God for crossing my path with theirs.

In a world where it's all who you know, all of the connections that brought me to D.C. were Black, and it's no accident that every single staffer who helped me during my time in D.C. was Black as well. What I discovered on Capitol Hill was a network of folks that really look out for one another. The Black Greek organizations were the backbone of the network. There were also listservs for Black Hill staffers as well as receptions and happy hours and certain days when the Black staff would get together for lunch. Bianca and Keidra were pulling me into that universe.

During that first trip to Capitol Hill, I rarely found myself with the opportunity to have any meaningful, substantive conversations with white staffers. They were mostly kind and welcoming, but they didn't see it as their mission to help me the way that Bianca and Keidra did. Family takes care of family, and Bianca and Keidra saw themselves as my family. One of the many tragedies of segregation is that there is power and potential in being connected, and so much of that power and potential has been squandered over the years. I wasn't even thinking about the opportunities I was missing because I wasn't connected to white legacy staffers or political operatives in a meaningful way. All I knew was that I shared common experiences with this small group of Black staffers. When you see one Black person in a room full of white people, you automatically expect to relate to how they are feeling in that moment. That feeling alone can be enough to make you want to help one another.

At the end of the day, two senior Black staffers met with me and, for precisely that reason, decided to take me under their wing. One was Mike McQuerry, who worked for Congresswoman Sheila Jackson Lee. A lot of people called him the Mayor of D.C., because he knew everyone, and the reason he knew everyone was because he threw some of the biggest and best parties in the city. The other was Brandon Webb. Brandon worked for Congressman John Barrow of Georgia. He was the only man I met during my initial time in D.C. who wasn't staffing a Congressional Black Caucus member, and he was a smart guy who managed to build relationships with white staffers and legislators. I didn't want to admit it, but I was intimidated by him. He had the look of a future congressman, and I could tell he was on his way to some sort of leadership position.

What Mike and Brandon and I all had in common, beyond our race, was that we were also frat brothers. After hearing my story and seeing my sincerity, they fully committed to helping me, pouring out a lot of wisdom for me to digest. They both suggested I come back during the winter break to try and get an internship. I thanked them for all their advice, headed back to Louisville, and started saving for my next plane ticket.

I went into my third year of law school with a lot more clarity of purpose. I became a representative for Kaplan, helping other law students get study tools and course supplements. I got more active in BLSA, the Black Law Students Association. I even started teaching in the Brandeis School of Law's Street Law Program, a partnership between the law school and Central High School, a historically Black high school in the West End.

All through that September and October, when I wasn't teaching or planning a community event with BLSA, I was contacting offices in D.C. in the hopes of getting an internship. I listed out the congressional offices by the committees the members served on, focusing on members of the Congressional Black Caucus and prioritizing the committees I was most interested in: education, judiciary, and financial services. I created a process for following up with congressional offices, using the same relentless approach I'd had for contacting attorneys during my first year of law school.

The weeks passed. The application period for internships ended, and I hadn't heard back from anyone. I went ahead and bought my plane ticket to D.C. anyway; with my limited funds, if by chance I landed an internship during the break, I'd need to have purchased the ticket before the prices went up for the holidays. I was counting on the fact that I had Mike, Brandon, Keidra, and Bianca all working on my behalf in their respective offices. Another guy who was pushing for me from the inside was a frat brother I'd met named Ben Branch, who worked for Congressman Gregory Meeks of New York. Ben had put me in touch with Rep. Meeks's office director, a woman named Kim Fuller who was responsible for managing the internship program in the office.

When I spoke to Kim on the phone, I could tell she genuinely wanted to help. She told me all the spots in Rep. Meeks's office were filled, but she encouraged me to keep checking back in case one opened up. I kept calling her every other day, and every time, she told me that they were still full. With one week left in the semester, I tried calling one last time. I worried that if I didn't get an internship before the semester ended, it wasn't going to happen. But I couldn't face that prospect. I wanted it to happen. I needed it to happen. I was pacing around the lobby of the law school, listening to the phone ring and ring, and with every ring I told myself Kim was going to pick up and offer me a spot.

She finally answered. "I'm sorry, Charles," she said. "No spots have become available."

Tears started to well up in my eyes. I told her how important this was to me, that it wasn't just about me. It was about my entire family and community that had lifted me up to get me where I needed to be. I couldn't let them down. I pleaded with her to give me a chance. When I finished, Kim hesitated. When she spoke again, there was a noticeable change in the tone of her voice. "Okay," she said. "I'll give you this one chance to convince me why I should reopen our internship application and create a spot for you."

The rest of that call was like an out-of-body experience. When she opened that window of hope, something special happened. *God,* I prayed to myself, *you have your way. You speak. Because I've gotta get this internship.* And then the words flowed out of me. "If you give me this internship," I said, "I'm not just someone coming there to get a job. This is not just you hiring somebody. This is different. I am on a mission, and this is going to help me get there. I am doing this to become the advocate that helps my community. I'm doing this to stop the killings in my neighborhood. I'm doing this to lift these people up with better opportunities. I will work harder than anyone has ever worked. If you give me this chance, God is going to take care of the rest."

I laid it all out to her. It felt like I was preaching a sermon. My life story, my journey, my plan. In the end, she was crying. I was crying, too. I'd only spoken for a couple minutes, but I was exhausted. She put me on hold. I paced back and forth in the lobby, praying out loud. I didn't care who saw me. I knew in my spirit that this was my time. I prayed so hard it made me sweat. After what felt like an eternity, Kim came back to the phone and, with tears in her voice, she told me to pack my bags. They'd decided to create a new spot for me.

I called Mom and Tanesha, sobbing with joy. I had worked myself into an internship in the United States Congress.

IN NOVEMBER OF 2009, I flew back to D.C. with all the money I could pull together, which was seventy-five dollars. I needed to make it last two weeks. The "internship" that Kim had created for me wasn't a normal internship at all. I had a badge, but it wasn't through any official program like the CBC internship. She had just convinced Rep. Meeks to let me come and work in the office for a while so I could get the experience, make connections, and build up my résumé. It was completely unpaid, but I didn't care. I had complete confidence that I was where I needed to be and that I would have everything I needed.

Mike and Brandon met me when I landed. Since I didn't have money for a hotel, Brandon let me stay at his apartment in what wasn't quite an extra room but more like a closet with a blow-up mattress that took up every inch of the floor. He also took me to Target, where I stocked up on Campbell's soup cups, which were virtually all I ate. Washington, D.C., I quickly learned, is expensive. After a few days I ran out of money and soups, and my mom had to send me another fifty dollars. Then that was gone, too. Socializing is a big part of a young staffer's life in D.C. It's how you meet the people you need to meet. Mike and Brandon went out for drinks a lot, and I didn't have money for that. A couple of times, they took me out to a club, which was rough without any money. That's the most naked feeling you'll ever have, being in a club with no money. By the end of the two weeks, Mike and Brandon were paying for pretty much all my meals. I would not have made it without them.

At the office, I responded to Rep. Meeks's constituent mail, drafted policy letters, and performed whatever office tasks they needed me to do. I was happy just to be able to run errands for people. I showed up first thing every morning and stayed until the evening. I was so eager to work that Kim had to force me to take breaks and eat lunch.

The actual work of an internship isn't very glamorous, but as a fly on the wall I got to witness intense debates over issues like financial regulatory reform, immigration reform, efforts to expand healthcare, and criminal justice reform. Rep. Meeks's district included Queens in New York City. As a kid from Kentucky, going through all the constituent mail and hearing about their experiences and concerns was eye-opening. There were letters from constituents who were fighting to keep their families together. One woman wrote the Congressman stressing that she was going to lose her home if she didn't get help. She was reaching out to the congressional office not because she knew what they could do but because she was so desperate she was willing to contact everyone. As I read her letter, I thought about my mom and all the sacrifices she made for me. I didn't know the woman who wrote the letter, but I felt like I did. Another man wrote about the high costs of his cancer treatment. The more letters and emails I read, the more I realized that people in New York are fighting many of the same fights we are battling in Kentucky.

Mostly, I would only see Rep. Meeks in passing, hustling in with his bag and disappearing into his office. You could always tell he was coming because you'd hear, "The congressman is coming," and everybody would sit up straight as he came in.

One night Rep. Meeks had the whole office working late on financial regulation reform. It was well past 11 o'clock. All the other interns had left, but I'd asked if I could stay. I was the same way I was in Frankfort; I wanted to learn everything. I was still working on constituent letters, and Rep. Meeks came in and saw me. "You still here, Charles?"

I nodded my head. "Yes, sir."

"That's a good thing. You're doing great work." He told me that he was proud of what I had been doing in law school and that he was excited that I was there, which was awe-inspiring to hear from someone of his stature.

By the time the internship ended, the office was so excited about my time there that they asked me to come back, and I made plans to come back to work during every break until I graduated. I would call Kim and say, "I've got a plane ticket. I can spend two weeks."

"All right, Charles. We'll have it set up for you."

Kim and Rep. Meeks were keeping the door open to me because they believed in me.

WITH MY EYES now set squarely on a job in D.C., my last few months of law school turned out to be the closing of one chapter in my life, and the start of my journey deeper into public service. I completed my work with the Street Law Program, published an article on bankruptcy for *The Journal of Law and Education*, and continued flying back to D.C. to work as an intern in Rep. Meeks's office every break I got. During the times I interned, Tanesha and Kaylin had to stay back in Louisville. There were several nights that I cried because I missed Kaylin, but Tanesha encouraged me the whole time. She believed in me and my mission. I would speak to them several times a day and every night before bed. Knowing that I was doing this to build a better future for Kaylin helped me keep peace while I was away.

From the time I started interning with Meeks's office, his legislative directors had been insisting that I go on a tour of the White House, and on one of my trips I finally did. I called my mom on the way over. "Mama, I'm going to go to the White House!" I said, holding back tears as I made my way up Pennsylvania Avenue, thinking about her and about Grandad and everything they'd been through to get me where I was.

I walked into the building that the first Black president called home. The security getting in was intense. I went through several checkpoints. Everyone was deadly serious. I even had to leave my phone and coat with security. The first time I walked under the Capitol Dome in Frankfort, I had been keenly aware that almost nobody there looked like me, but when I saw the picture of President Obama hanging in the White House, I saw myself. I had never considered elected office before that moment, but looking at his picture I couldn't help but feel a spark of electricity in my bones. I started to think that maybe being a legislative staffer wouldn't be where the road ended for me.

From that day on, I worked with a greater inspiration in mind.

CHAPTER 9

IN THE TRENCHES

Back in Louisville, seeing that I'd caught the political bug, Senator Neal asked me to come work for him. As a volunteer.

"I'm going to work you like I'm paying you," he told me, "although I'm not paying you." Which is exactly what he did.

For the rest of my third year of law school, if I wasn't in class, I was by his side. I was with him so much that legislators in Frankfort would ask me about him if they saw me walking in the hallway; they assumed I knew every minute of his schedule—which I did. I was his assistant, campaign coordinator, note taker, and runner. One time, I even helped him install a toilet at his mother's house. I didn't mind, though. My excitement made the time fly. Plus, I was getting an education that was worth more than money.

One of the most exciting things I got to be involved in were the regular meetings in Senator Neal's basement. The political machine that ran things in the West End was made up of several Louisville Metro Council members, local officials, and several state representatives. But there was only one state senator, which made Senator Neal's house the unofficial headquarters for much of the group's activities. He would have all of them over to his basement to talk about initiatives that he wanted to tackle, and I helped him set up the meetings. I got the coffee and donuts and parked the cars in the driveway—a job I took very seriously. Senator Neal's house was at the end of a long road that ended at the river, so I had to make sure we fit as many cars as possible in the driveway so that people didn't have to walk too far.

Some may have seen it as just parking cars, but to me it was important. Making sure everyone could attend these meetings meant that they could come together to work on educational programs and business development and campaigns for public office.

Being in that basement was the chance for me to learn and observe things that would sharpen my leadership skills. It gave me a firsthand understanding of how campaigns were run: organizing phone banks, managing canvassing events, devising field strategies. I absorbed it all. Volunteering to work on races for the school board, the Metro Council, and the state legislature, I saw the power of convening people. I saw the potential. If you could bring people together and organize them around a plan, you could create the type of pressure that would force things to change: our laws, our politics, the programs in our community, and the people serving in office. With my law background, public speaking skills, and teaching experience, I became a pretty effective organizer.

My goal was to get involved in a major campaign, and I found that opportunity in David Tandy, who was looking to become Louisville's first Black mayor. At the time, Tandy was president of the Metro Council, which is the city's legislative body, representing a district that included poor neighborhoods in the West End, parts of downtown Louisville, and some wealthier neighborhoods in the East End. Senator Neal was fired up about Tandy's race, and I was too. I started recruiting, training, and managing the volunteers. I encouraged my college friends to get involved. Even some of my cousins and childhood friends came to help. Although most of this happened in Senator Neal's basement along the river, I joined Councilman Tandy for some of his speaking events across the city. I watched him work the room, smile and laugh with the people, and then bring them to their feet with a rousing speech about his vision of Louisville as a shining city on a hill.

Ultimately, Tandy didn't win, but the fire was well lit in me. I dedicated all my energy toward finding a job in a legislative office in D.C., convinced that would be the right place for me. Every week, I applied for dozens of jobs. Every time Tanesha got paid, she put money in savings for our move to the Hill. We reserved a U-Haul and even put a deposit down on an apartment near the Brookland Metro station. Every time I was called for an interview, Tanesha and I would immediately hop in my car and drive the nine hours from Louisville to D.C. But despite my relentless commitment, I continued to get emails "regretfully informing me" that someone else had been selected. The doors just weren't opening. I'd been so convinced that God was pushing me in this direction, and I believed without a doubt that the opportunity would come. But after a few months of holding out faith, we lost the apartment and I finally had to cancel that U-Haul reservation and accept that life was telling me I needed to find my opportunities elsewhere.

Luckily, not long after, one such opportunity came along. Through an old friend from U of L, I was hired to work as a volunteer coordinator on the 2010 reelection campaign of Congressman John Yarmuth. As the representative for the 3rd Congressional District, Yarmuth was responsible for representing the entire city of Louisville. He was also the lone Democrat in Kentucky's federal delegation. Working for Yarmuth gave me a unique opportunity. Before his tenure, Louisville had been represented by a Republican legislator by the name of Anne Northup. Yarmuth ran a progressive campaign against her at a time when many didn't think that was possible. His victory sent shock waves and set the course for a new era of leadership in Louisville. Joining his campaign staff meant I would be able to see the inner workings of elected leadership and learn what it looked like to support more progressive issues in a state largely run by Republicans.

My official role was to manage all the volunteers and volunteer activities, but in my hunger to learn everything there was to know, I seized opportunities to help in every other aspect of the campaign: communications, fundraising, political strategy, data analysis, and field organizing. But the most important lesson I learned during this life-changing experience was from Yarmuth himself. The 2010 election was the year of the Tea Party wave. There was a strong backlash from Republicans against President Obama in this midterm. Though many in my community recognized that it was largely driven by racism, the proxy for this deeper, unspoken debate was the Affordable Care Act. The policy was actually popular in Kentucky, right up until the name "Obamacare" was uttered. Most politicians knew this but were unwilling to push back on the narrative and embrace the fact that the majority of Americans supported many provisions in the legislation.

Congressman Yarmuth was one of the few who didn't run away from it. He knew Kentuckians needed and deserved better health coverage and was willing to take the political heat to advocate for it. His clarity and confidence were contagious for the team. I enjoyed that Yarmuth's presence was always very direct and not calculated. During my time working with Senator Neal, I was often vexed by his calculation to hold back or restrain his answers to avoid conflict. Although I understood his approach, I often wished he didn't have to parse his answers so much. Yarmuth, on the other hand, seemed to never have such a worry. No matter what room he was in, he would say exactly what he felt. I understand there is a certain privilege to be able to do that, but I appreciated it all the same. I remember being with him one day at the Gaslight Festival in J-Town. A bunch of Republicans were grilling him about the Affordable Care Act, but Yarmuth knew healthcare backwards and forwards. He was completely dismantling people's bogus arguments about Obamacare. He was telling them straight up, "Well, you're wrong." Then he explained why they were wrong, but in a way that every conversation stayed cordial and respectful. I was so blown away by this guy who, no matter where he was or who he was talking to, always told the truth. His reputation as a straight talker gained a lot of Republican support even as the Tea Party was sweeping Democrats out of office. Even with the midterm backlash against the president, Yarmuth won the race handily. It was an important lesson for me, that being authentic is more important than trying to be agreeable.

THAT FALL, AFTER my work on the Yarmuth campaign had ended, I got an unexpected call from Councilman Tandy. I figured he was going to ask me to participate in some new program, but he had something else in mind. His legislative assistant had left to take another job, and he told me that he needed a solid legal and political professional to manage his 4th District Metro Council office.

Very few people in Louisville really knew what the Metro Council did or paid it much attention; everyone's eyes were always focused on the Mayor's Office. But what makes the Louisville Metro Council rare among similar bodies in other cities is that its individual members have discretionary budgets, money that they can allocate toward grants and projects and capital repairs. That gives them a unique power in the city. At the time, I still had my sights set on a job in Congress, but even with my experience on Yarmuth's campaign the idea remained a long shot. Plus, as I was learning, most of the positions I was qualified for wouldn't pay enough to move me, Tanesha, and Kaylin to D.C. Not only was Tandy's offer an opportunity to take on exactly the type of legislative job I'd been pursuing on the Hill; the salary was more money than my mom or I had ever seen. More than anything, it was a chance to work with a man I deeply admired.

First elected in his thirties, Tandy was brilliant, a true leader who could easily be seen as a future member of Congress. A former offensive lineman for the Vanderbilt University football team, he had a commanding presence. He stood up for the Black community, but he was also able to navigate any room and engage with business leaders across the color line. Even though he was from Owensboro, he had moved to the West End of Louisville, not far from my mother's house, which I respected; there is a difference between wanting to represent people living in the struggle and living there yourself. Tandy was maybe ten years older than me, and he and his wife Carolyn, the district director for the congressman, were young parents, like me and Tanesha.

Before taking the position at the Metro Council, I had never spent much time in Louisville's Metro City Hall. It's a beautiful, old historic place: columns, tall ceilings, marble finishes, and black and white tiles on the hallway floors. My first morning on the job, I stepped into the elevator wearing my new official badge, bursting with anticipation and excitement. I pressed the button for the second floor, which was the Republican floor of the council. Every office suite on that floor was assigned to a Republican member and their staff, except Councilman Tandy, the lone Democrat. He told me that he had chosen that office on purpose. He wanted to be close to the people he would need to persuade the most. He wanted to build relationships with the people most likely to try to block his legislation.

Tandy's 4th District office was at the center of everything: the construction of a state-of-the-art basketball arena for the University of Louisville, a new baseball stadium, downtown bridge projects, the waterfront park expansion, central district business growth, historically Black neighborhoods, public housing projects, and very active neighborhood associations. There was never a dull moment.

And yet there was also a bit of an adjustment period. When Tandy offered me the job of legislative aide, what I had in my mind was what a legislative aide on Capitol Hill does. You're right there with the representative, attending meetings, getting deep in the weeds on policy matters and position papers. I quickly learned that being a legislative aide at City Hall meant something else. You do get to use your law degree researching policy and drafting legislation, but you also learn to step into whatever role was needed: meeting with business leaders, writing grants, sitting with families grieving a loved one, staffing committees, presenting proclamations, hosting events. Even picking up trash when you had to. You find a way to do it all.

Every morning, as soon as I turned the lights on and sat at my desk, I would spin around in my chair to see the red light flashing on the phone with a mailbox full of messages from constituents. We had an office rule to respond to everyone within forty-eight hours, and I would spend several hours each day returning calls. I heard it all: trees falling on houses, rodents in a neighbor's home, semis idling on residential streets, pungent smells from meat packing plants, house fires, car accidents, shootings, you name it.

In the beginning, I can't say I was thrilled with that part of the job. I wanted to be crafting policy in Frankfort, in Washington. Taking calls about garbage wasn't what I thought I'd gone into politics to do.

Pretty soon, however, I discovered it was *exactly* what I'd gone into politics to do. Once I understood how the office helped people in the community, I was all about it. Because it was a chance to actually—often, immediately—help someone who needed it. We would get so many calls from people complaining about stuff, and I realized that I had the power to address a lot of those complaints.

Whenever I answered the phone, I always braced myself for some-one crying or yelling about something. One morning I picked up and a woman asked, "Is this David Tandy's office?"

"Yes ma'am!" I replied.

Before I could even say my name or offer assistance, she was screaming. "You all are supposed to help me, but no one cares! The yard next to me has grass that's taller than I am! Rats and possums keep getting in my yard! You all are good for nothing!"

I jumped up and grabbed my jacket, cradling the phone to my ear. "What's your address, ma'am?" I asked. "I'm on the way."

"You're on the way?" she replied, shocked. "So . . . wait . . . you're going to come right now?"

"Yes, ma'am," I replied. "You're right to be frustrated with this tall grass, and I actually do care. So I'm going to come right now to take pictures myself. We'll get this taken care of."

I put the phone down and ran to the car. I always felt like I was on a mission. A mission to not just address a concern, but to make sure this woman knew that we cared about her needs. This was my mission for my entire community. I wanted everyone to feel the security of knowing that the society they lived in wouldn't ignore them or run them over. Helping with issues like tall grass was my way of showing how government can actually benefit regular people. When I pulled up outside the woman's house, she was standing on her porch. "Are you Mr. Booker?" she asked kindly.

"I sure am," I said. "Let's get this yard fixed up."

She seemed to get a burst of energy. "You actually came!" she said with joyful surprise.

The anger in her voice from the phone call was completely gone. She showed me the side and back of the neighboring house, and I took pictures and notes. When we walked back to the front of the house, she hugged me. I promised to check on her every couple of days until the yard was cleared out. The look of shock on her face when I pulled up and the relief on her face when I left—that was as fulfilling as anything I could remember.

It meant a lot to show up for the people in my district. In their struggles, I saw the same struggles that my mom had endured to take care of me. Like her, those folks were often on their own, wrestling with hardships they should not have had to wrestle with. The work was always personal to me. As a kid, all I'd wanted was to help my mom, because that's what she always deserved. Now, I wasn't a kid anymore. I had the ability to help people, and I loved doing it. I tried to do something every day if I could. If there was a fight or a fire, I would hop in my car to see how I could help. I wanted them to know their government could actually work for them, but more than that, the chance to actually do something that helps somebody, the rush of being able to fulfill a need for someone—it's the best feeling in the world. It's like winning the Super Bowl every day.

Eventually, I grew to enjoy my time at Metro Council so much that I would go months at a time without thinking about my original plan: to work in Frankfort or D.C. I found City Hall to be a nice place to work. It was comfortable. When you come from the struggle, every day is about survival, and there were many days when I just wanted to be happy where I was. Tanesha wanted that, too. We were finally finding some financial stability, and Tanesha often told me she wished that was enough for me.

It was and it wasn't. I took pride in being able to help my neighbors. When I walked through the grocery store, people would stop me and thank me for getting their streetlights fixed or their sidewalk paved. It was humbling. The press conferences and ribbon cuttings were fulfilling, too. I had plenty of reasons to pat myself on the back and grow complacent. But at the end of the day, I couldn't do it. I couldn't forget how hurt and upset I was when I figured out that Mom was going without eating to feed me. I couldn't forget all the yellow tape I saw on the way to school because someone else I knew had been murdered. Helping constituents one at a time was fulfilling, but it was no substitute for addressing the system that left those people so vulnerable to begin with. I wanted to change that system. And that system wasn't going to change because of anything I did at Metro Council. There were too many limitations working downstream from the state legislature.

In Louisville politics, there's a steady refrain that you hear. "Oh, we can't do this because of Frankfort." I heard it so many times I lost count. "Oh, we can't address vagrant and abandoned property because state law prevents us from acquiring those properties faster." "Oh, we can't target tax dollars toward developments because the state doesn't allow us to create different streams of revenue." Most frustrating of all, in the face of the violence young Black folks endured in the West End, the state had essentially said the cities couldn't pass their own legislation to regulate guns.

As much as I wanted to be completely satisfied working at the Council, I was still chasing something. I wanted safe, thriving communities that didn't need food giveaways or resource fairs. I wanted poverty to end, and I couldn't wait to do all I could to make that happen. I knew if I was in Frankfort, I would be in a better position to advocate for accountability and, ultimately, help make sure laws were written and budgets were allocated with struggling communities like my own in mind.

But my frustrations ran deeper than policymaking. Between working on various municipal races, staffing Yarmuth's re-election campaign, and working at Metro Council, I was in the trenches of local Louisville politics for close to three years, continuing to serve as Senator Neal's right-hand man, even as I worked full-time at the other jobs. That time was a blessing beyond measure, but by the end I was feeling held back. "Be patient, Charles," was something I heard often, from Tandy and from Neal, and it was a phrase I never got used to.

I had so many deep philosophical conversations with Neal riding around in his car, about poverty, about police reform, about lack of opportunity. I was always the young idealist, saying, "All this stuff needs to change," and he'd be the wise old sage, saying, "Well, these are the steps you're going to need to take to make that happen." Because of his background as an activist, he didn't dismiss what I said, but he was always trying to educate me about how things really work, which usually involved some measure of compromise and delay. Over time I grew exhausted watching Neal moderate his plans and opinions in the legislature. I'd wonder, *Why did you do that? Why didn't you say something? Why didn't you fight harder?* But he so often kept his powder dry as a way of probing for incremental progress. It was the incremental part that left me wanting.

Much as I admired Tandy, I saw a similar tendency in him. As dynamic as he was when he spoke, he would often be quiet, observing the deliberations in the Metro Council and watching developments around the city. He wasn't passive, but I could tell he was always holding something back. It was as if he was conserving his energy. Perhaps this was the wisdom of picking battles, but I wanted to fight all of them. I could tell that he was gauging how and when to push for change. "This stuff can burn you out," Tandy used to say. I think he understood that he wanted a long career and couldn't let the stresses and challenges of public service wear him out.

I didn't want to burn out, either, but I also didn't want to wait on the changes I felt were possible now. Even if it meant I didn't have a long career. I understood Tandy's point of view, like I understood Neal's, but I had to find the balance that would give me peace. I had a fire burning in me, and I didn't want it to die out while I sat around being patient and waiting for something to happen.

Only now can I look back on that time and understand that I was going through one of the most difficult transitions a young person can go through: I was outgrowing my mentors. For three years, I'd been on a journey through state and local politics. Ultimately, it was a journey of growing and finding myself and realizing that my opinions were as valid as theirs. Neal and I would have great conversations in his car, with me making points and him agreeing with me. Then we'd go into the meeting, and if I'd start to say the same thing I'd said in the car, he would shush me. "Hold on, Charles," he'd say. "Hold on. We not there yet." Then, at the end of the conversation, it'd be, "Charles will take the notes and give you a follow-up email."

For the first couple of years, that was fine because I was there to soak up everything. I was happy to park the cars, but now it was starting to bother me that that was all I was ever allowed to do. I had my Juris Doctor degree, I was a legislative professional, and I was only being asked to "hold that thought." I held it for years, and it only intensified.

And it hurt. At times, I felt like he was using me. Eventually, I started to dread going to meetings with him. "I can't be his assistant anymore," I told my mom, almost starting to cry as I unburdened myself. "I'm more than just someone who gets the coffee. I think that's all he sees me as."

Mom tried to calm me down. "Son, you don't have to let anyone make you feel small or insignificant. If you need to pull back from working with him, you pull back."

So I did. Naturally, I started coming around less and less. I never really knew how to tell him how I felt, because I didn't know how to bring it to him without disappointing him, so I just made myself busier with my other jobs. He'd call me and ask, "Are you going to Frankfort?" and I'd come up with some excuse. It started snowballing to where I always had some kind of conflict. It was a difficult and painful thing to go through, but ultimately a good one, because it lit a fire in me to do something else.

CHAPTER 10

THE BIG DOLLARS

THE DAY SENATOR Neal first drove me to Frankfort, my mission to help the West End had taken on a focus it had lacked before. Sitting in the judiciary committee meeting where the fate of lives like mine were being debated, I knew that my journey had to take me into the rooms where the decisions got made. When I eventually left Metro Council for a new job with the Legislative Research Commission, I was one step closer; I was in the room where the money was being spent. As in billions of dollars in state appropriations. I got to see where it was going, who was getting it, who wasn't getting it, and why—and it was an eye-opening experience unlike any other.

After two years with David Tandy, all my hard work of making cold calls and meeting people and talking to anyone who might help me paid off. I'd stayed in touch with Robert Jenkins, the LRC deputy director Neal had introduced me to. The moment a job opening came up for a legislative analyst, he called me in for an interview with Director Bobby Sherman. They offered me the position, and I jumped on it.

On its face, the job description was fairly plain. Every morning, down in the basement tunnels of the Capitol Annex in Frankfort, behind a golden metal door with a big state seal and a large nameplate that read "Government Contract Review Committee," my colleagues and I would log into the computer system and find anywhere from a dozen to a few hundred contracts waiting for our review.

Our job was to assist lawmakers in reviewing all of the state's personal service contracts, memoranda of agreement, and film incentives, assessing each one to make sure it properly outlined the scope and necessity of services. Then, once we'd reviewed the contracts and made any updates in the system, we'd compile a large report for every legislator on the Government Contract Review Committee, which would later vote to approve or deny the contract.

It was a long, intensive, and frequently tedious process. As I read through contracts, I was mostly looking for errors or incomplete information. But no matter how mind-numbingly dull the actual language of the contracts might be, what excited me was seeing what the contracts revealed. It was like I was inside the machinery of the state government, seeing how it worked. These were contracts for upwards of $10 to $20 million or more in government appropriations, which was mind-blowing to me. I had never really encountered numbers that big.

America gets very caught up in the spectacle of overt racism, the young children being knocked down by firehoses, the Ku Klux Klan parades marching down Main Street, the latest outrage on Twitter. But the real roots of racial inequality are more likely to be found in the very mundane and unexciting world of contracts and law—in the dense and inscrutable legal documents that determine who gets the money and who gets the power. Seeing a ledger outlining this for the entire state of Kentucky opened my eyes to a whole new universe. So even though the work might have been boring at times, I knew it was important precisely *because* it was boring.

The job got a little more exciting when the contracts went up for review by the committee. The committee was co-chaired by a House member and a state senator. Since the House was led by a Democratic majority and the Senate by Republicans, ours was one of the few that wasn't completely driven by partisanship; critiquing the contracts at times even seemed to unify the two sides. There were regularly contentious debates, though, and they usually revolved around who deserved to benefit from tax dollars. The members would argue with one another. Sometimes they'd really grill the vendors who came before them, making them explain where and how government dollars would be spent.

In these debates, communities like mine were often not even at the table. There were no job training programs for us. Black-owned firms rarely got the big dollars for road construction or development projects. No one in my hood knew about how to procure funding for drug counseling—there was no counseling, only jail. Communities like mine weren't getting investments in small businesses or housing, either. I'd see contracts for state-of-the-art community centers being built in the wealthy districts of powerful representatives, while nothing was coming our way in the West End. If money did come to the most underserved communities, it was always a small fraction of what could have been allocated. Logging into the state's accounting system, which most people didn't know about, I saw multi-million-dollar contracts going to vendors for work that people in my neighborhood do all the time, work like carpentry and construction and painting, even cleaning and maintenance.

In my spare time I would go back to records for previous years, and I saw that a lot of the same firms got contracts over and over again, regardless of the quality of the work they'd done. They'd essentially created a portfolio where they'd gotten rich from these government contracts doing the same work as a lot of regular people who don't even know that government contracts exist for the work that they do. And missing out on those contracts has a snowball effect, because the people who got them were always in a better position to get the next one because they could build a budget, hire staff, and make investments. But if you can't get that first foot in the door, you don't have that option. I saw a lot of contracts that weren't even being put out for competitive bids. I was always suspicious of those types of contracts.

Back in the West End and even at U of L, I'd sat around with cousins and friends, frustrated at the way things were, always talking about the need to "do something." But most of what we did, whether it was the community service I performed through church or even the constituent services I performed at Metro Council, only amounted to putting Band-Aids on the problem. We were so busy running around trying to cure the symptoms of our problems that we weren't going deeper to diagnose the root causes of it all. But here, in these contracts, was one of those causes: a system that doled out opportunities to the powerful and denied resources to those who didn't have the access or the leverage to demand it. Most of the people from my neighborhood weren't seeing what I saw, because most people had no access to these documents. But I did. Every single one of those contracts told a story, and I was paying close attention.

WORKING AT THE LRC gave me the opportunity to see where Kentucky's money was going, but it came at the expense of how much money I had coming in. Taking the job required a serious pay cut. Coming out of law school, many of my peers went straight on to lucrative jobs doing corporate law with established firms, earning the big salaries that would allow them to pay down their student loans. I'd done the opposite. I'd interned for free at Rep. Meeks's office and volunteered free of charge for Senator Neal. The campaign and organizing work did compensate me, but never paid much. At the Metro Council I finally made a good salary, $51,000 a year, but we had our mortgage, car payments, groceries, and so much more. Depending on which insurance provider I had, the cost to cover my insulin and other medications ranged anywhere from $400 a month with a good plan to $1,200 a month with a bad one. On top of that, Tanesha and I were carrying tens of thousands in student loans—each. Despite my salary and hers, we were living paycheck to paycheck and barely getting by. We had practically no savings, no cushion to fall back on if anything happened.

My new salary at LRC was $45,000 a year, plus it came with the extra cost of an hour-long commute to Frankfort each way. Knowing how precarious our finances were, taking this job at all was a risk. Tanesha wasn't thrilled. "We're just now getting on top of our bills, and you want to take a pay cut?" she said. "For a job out of town?" I could hear the annoyance in her voice, and I knew she was right. I also knew, in the long run, it would be worth it, not only for our family's long-term stability but for the cause I was fighting for: Someone like me needed to be in a place like that, or nothing was ever going to change.

The basement of the Capitol Annex where our offices were was a system of gloomy tunnels lined with office suites. It had absolutely none of the grandeur of Frankfort's Capitol dome, but on my first day I marveled at it all the same, because only people with badges got to go in. Now a kid from the West End had one of those badges.

The office was so tiny that I had to set my chair at an angle to fit between my desk and the wall. It had a window, but because we were in the basement it was just this little opening way up near the ceiling that looked out into the back of a flower bed. I didn't care. I loved it. To have that space and sense of identity for myself was unlike anything I'd ever felt. The first time I walked into that office, I closed the door behind me, sat down at my desk, and prayed. I also shed a few tears. It was my own office in the Capitol Annex. I even had my own business card with the raised and embossed state seal on it.

When you move into a new office at the Capitol, they take you to this big warehouse of extra furniture, paintings, and antiques to furnish your space. When I started, I had to find a new office chair and a picture for the wall behind my desk. I wanted an image that showed the history of the grand building I was now working in, one that reflected the truth, pain, and power of seeing a young Black man like me in an office like this. I stumbled across a print of an old painting of the Capitol. I don't know who painted it or when it was from, but it showed the Capitol dome on a hazy, sunny day, with beautiful yellow flowers leading up to the building. I couldn't imagine myself in that painting, and that's the reason I chose it. I knew I belonged, and in many respects it helped to reaffirm that whenever I walked into the office. I also knew, like Grandad at the Reynolds factory decades before, that I wasn't working alone. Everything I did, I was carrying the people of the West End with me. I was always conscious of that, and I wanted to earn it and be worthy of it.

As I was often the only Black person in the hallways and meeting rooms of the Capitol, many times I felt like my presence made some of the legislators, staff, and visitors uncomfortable. It was evident in the not-so-subtle body language that you can't miss: people looking away when they see you, clutching their purses a bit tighter when you step on the elevator, loud conversations that turn into whispers as you pass by. I never let anyone dwell on it, though. As soon as I came close, I made sure to make eye contact and say a kind word. In my mind, every step I took down those halls, my block and my hood were walking with me.

Knowing there had to be other young, aspiring Black people in politics dealing with the same issues I was, I wanted to find them. It was the same mentality I had going into law school: If I didn't have peers or a support circle around me, I would seek them out. I wanted to find people who had done the types of things I was doing. I wanted to see how they found their way and take some notes for my own journey. Whenever I finished my day's work early, I would Google young Black elected officials who inspired me, people like State Representative Bakari Sellers, the youngest legislator in South Carolina, as well as the youngest Black elected official in the country; Representative Alisha Thomas Morgan, a confident Georgia legislator who knew how to command her space; and Andrew Gillum, a Tallahassee city commissioner who was running for mayor.

However, few stories inspired me like that of New Jersey's Cory Booker. As a city councilman, he'd made it a point to live in one of the toughest areas in his district. Politicians had always seemed so far away and disconnected from my experience in the West End, so knowing that someone who looked like me could speak with the poise and conviction of a statesman and still live in the hood really lit a spark in me. I studied his leadership style. He was compassionate and gave his heart to his work. He also showed a deep respect for history, regularly channeling stories from his parents or other great civil rights leaders to help make a point about a current issue in his community.

The thing that shocked me most was how he took his office out into the streets. I regularly heard stories about him shoveling snow for residents or running into a burning building to help others. It reminded me of the rush I felt when a constituent called the 4th District office with a concern, and I quickly hopped in my car to go see about them. I did it because I genuinely cared. Seeing this young legislator from Newark show that same proactive leadership let me know that not all elected officials were the same. It was a bonus that we shared the same last name.

Just being a part of it all was exhilarating. Setting foot in Frankfort was like coming alive. I wanted to do everything. I wanted to be in the middle of it all. I had a thirst for it. I read every article I could find about the state legislature. I read bills coming out of committees and the research papers behind them. At least a couple times a week, I would pop my head in at the leadership office and ask them, "Are there things I could be doing or learning before I go home for the day?" This was how I found out about legislative conferences, where you can gain knowledge on many issues. They didn't typically let staffers from my committee attend them, so I wrote a letter to the leadership explaining that I wanted to go so that I could understand more about how to interpret law and write policy, and they made an exception for me.

If I didn't have anything specific at hand to work on or study, I would simply linger around the House chamber, watching government in action just to see how it worked. Back in Louisville I had learned a great deal about political campaigning and the day-to-day functions of government, but working in Frankfort was my real introduction into the nature of power: how coalitions are built, how deals are made, how laws advance in the face of intense lobbying and division, and how leadership affects all of the above. I had never fully appreciated those things before. Watching legislators like Speaker Greg Stumbo and Leader Rocky Adkins pass a piece of legislation was like watching Peyton Manning quarterback a game-winning touchdown. Rocky's voice would roar as he brought up a bill and made a passionate plea. Then he and Speaker Stumbo would huddle near the podium, discussing strategy. Once they finished speaking, Stumbo would quietly address the Democratic caucus and the Republican leadership before going back to the Speaker's desk to bang his gavel. It was a master class on how to control a room.

The only downside to learning so much was feeling like everyone around me already knew everything and I'd never be able to catch up. I walked through those halls like I was important, my head up high, but imposter syndrome was always there like a shadow, trailing a few steps behind. It felt like everyone there was an expert—except me. There were several times where I had to call Mom for encouragement.

"Mama," I'd say, "these people are really smart."

"You're smart, too, Charles."

"Oh, I'm not smart like these people."

"Yes, you are, baby."

At that time, my mom had been struggling with some major health issues. Not long after I left law school, she'd had a seizure. The doctors didn't really know why, but from then on she started having them once a year or so. The last one had really messed her up; she was in the hospital for a couple of weeks and had to go through months of physical therapy, learning how to walk again. Seeing her fight to stay on her feet the way she did always reminded me why I was doing what I was doing. And no matter her own troubles, she was always there to support me.

"C.J.," she said, "you worked so hard for this. You never gave up, son. I am so proud of you. Everything's going to work out."

And it did.

I was excelling at my job, and the director's office noticed. Every once in a while, Robert Jenkins would pop his head in to check on me. Since I was doing so well reviewing contracts, he offered me the chance to take on some additional responsibilities for the director's office. Once I was done with my committee work for the day, he would enlist me to help draft resolutions and legislation. I learned about the process bill drafters go through to turn a legislator's idea into a bill. It required meticulous, intensive research and editing, but also speed. During the session, we were required to get working drafts back to legislators within three days of the request. I helped with several pieces of legislation, including work on a bill to cap the interest rate on payday loans. Proving myself at drafting legislation led to an even bigger opportunity: helping to draft the state's two-year budget. This was a huge deal. This wasn't just seeing where the money went in the contracts that I reviewed. The state budget was a road map for how *all* the money got spent, and Robert wanted me to join the group that would help prepare it to go to the floor and get voted on. The hard work was finally paying off.

"A BUDGET IS a moral document." That saying never meant more to me than it did when I started reviewing the billions of tax dollars allocated across Kentucky.

During my interview for the job, Director Bobby Sherman had closed out our interview by saying, "Charles, I have one last question for you. This is the question that will decide it for us. What is the most important job of someone who works for the Legislative Research Commission?"

I had the answer before he'd even finished the question. "Mr. Sherman," I replied, "the most important job of someone who works for the Legislative Research Commission is to be nonpartisan and work with high professionalism and excellence for every single legislator, no matter their political party." And that was true. The job was simply to review documents and provide factual research for legislators. As a staffer, I couldn't publicly inject my opinion, not when assisting the director on budgets and legislation or when reviewing the contracts in my office.

Still, the fact remained that I was who I was and I came from where I came from. Simply by being myself inside that department, I introduced a new perspective on the way things had always been done. I did what I could to make sure the process worked as well as possible. Whenever a contract was signed with a firm from outside the state, I asked why and made sure there was a clear explanation for the legislators. I did the same thing for every contract that wasn't bid out. And when an issue touched close to home, I found ways to give the members a fuller perspective. I would suggest to them some points to consider, questions to ask during hearings, anything I thought might pull on their conscience or appeal to their interests.

I vividly remember a contract that had to do with helping the Kentucky Department of Education provide counseling and after-school support for students battling homelessness. Tears welled up in my eyes when I read that contract. It brought back all the troubling memories of losing my home when Mr. Eugene's faulty space heater caught fire; I could still smell the smoke and feel the heat of the bright orange glow that engulfed my room. I remembered how it felt to put the little we had left in our car, with no idea of where home would be. I remembered how anxious I felt going to school, how all I could think about in class was where I would sleep that night. This contract would have provided the resources I needed back then, but I knew some legislators wouldn't understand that.

Despite my important role on a committee in the Kentucky State Legislature, I often felt invisible in the process. I would listen quietly in the committee room as people who needed employment assistance were called lazy or people battling drug addiction were chastised as immoral. Some committee members consistently asked whether we really needed to spend precious tax dollars on services that helped struggling families. Many times, I gritted my teeth to make sure I kept a calm demeanor, remembering the way Senator Neal worked so hard not to let people get under his skin.

Too often I heard statements like, "When I needed help, I didn't have a program to assist me. I figured it out myself." I even heard the word *bootstraps* a time or two. I remembered my mom working a full-time job and sewing clothes on the side so that we could get back in our home, the dread I felt walking into a store and handing the cashier food stamps to get some bread. I hated it, but we needed it. Not because we were lazy but because we were already working so hard to hang on by a thread, and that was before the fire burned it all up.

In the days leading up to the committee meeting that would decide the fate of this contract for homeless students, many of those same legislators who had unknowingly insulted my family time and again walked into the office to chat. They were respectful, looking for answers on a statute or pending contract. I would answer with a smile, mentioning a few of the big ones and making sure to suggest questions regarding the contract to support homeless students. "You should consider asking about the circumstances that the students are facing,"

I said. "You also might want to ask about the impact this service will have on the lives of Kentucky children."

I wanted them to ask so they could see the humanity behind the dollar amount. I told them I knew how hard it was for students with housing insecurity to be successful in school. I didn't expect it to change a vote necessarily, although I was certainly hopeful. Even if the answers to those questions wouldn't cause a legislator to change their mind, at least they would have to see the full picture.

Committee days were always surreal to me no matter what was being deliberated, because I actually got to watch governing in action and know that I was a part of it. In the committee room, rows of black chairs lined the large room where the audience sat. The legislators sat on elevated platforms in rows of wooden desks facing the audience area. I always felt reverent going into those meetings, even though several of the members clearly held racial prejudices. In my mind, I'd have to brace myself, thinking, *What offensive remarks will be shared in the Chamber today?* Still, at the same time, I felt great privilege just being there. My presence meant that whatever they were going to do, they weren't going to do it without me knowing about it. They were going to have to look me in the eye as they cast their votes.

I prayed before every meeting, too, that the Lord would use me. Honestly, there wasn't much I could do in the meeting once it started, but I wanted my energy present. I would think, "Maybe it will make a difference that I'm here. I can stand here with confidence and conviction. I can greet everyone with clarity in my voice. My story is here because I'm here."

The day the committee was set to vote on this contract to provide services to homeless children, there was a feeling in the air like something important was about to happen, like church when it's about to get started. As a kid from the hood, I never expected that my own struggles would influence major business in the halls of government. Then, the moment came.

"The next item on the agenda is a contract to provide support for students facing homelessness," the chair asked. "Is there anyone here to speak to the contract?"

I watched as Department of Education members came forward. I had given the agency reps data to share and suggested questions to the members. Now all I could do was sit in my chair, back straight, and hope. And it worked. From the mouths of the legislators came the questions I'd suggested, and the agency representatives were ready with answers that I knew would reflect my own experience. They told harrowing stories that showed what homeless children go through before they get in the classroom and how it stops them from learning.

Several of the legislators acted as if they had no clue that being hungry or not having a bed to sleep in might affect you in the classroom, but the testimony they heard was undeniable. I remember one of the agency representatives getting emotional talking about what some children go through, and I was getting emotional too, trying to keep it together. Tears came down my face, and I wiped them quickly away, hoping not to be too much of a distraction.

In the end, the conversation moved the needle. After a few minutes of discussion, the contracts were approved. I closed my eyes briefly, thinking about the nine-year-old version of myself. From now on, children would get the help I didn't have back then, and that felt better than anything.

I knew that I was making a small difference, but at the same time I realized that if I truly wanted to change things, I needed to be the decision-maker, the one who actually votes for the contracts and the budgets. The experience of being one of the only people like me in these rooms showed me why things weren't changing. I explained this to some of my friends back in the hood, various activists and organizers. "We want things to change," I said, "but how do we ever make that happen? We protest in the streets, but that's not the only way to wield power. We've got to have a multi-pronged approach. We need people in the streets agitating and disrupting the status quo. But we also need people in the spaces where decisions are made, making sure to be accountable to us. To change the system, we have to do it from the outside in and the inside out. Until we find a way to be leaders ourselves, nothing is going to change."

CHAPTER 11

WHERE I NEED TO BE

AFTER MY FIRST three months at LRC, it felt like life couldn't get any better. I was learning something new every day, I was passionate about the work I was doing, and that work was being recognized. I was offered a raise, which I gladly accepted, and day by day Tanesha was getting more involved in community leadership as well. Although she was naturally shy, her love for Kaylin pushed her to take on roles with the PTA and other community organizations in our neighborhood.

Like me, she was new to the political arena, and one thing she struggled with was going to the big events and galas. The pomp and circumstance of politics annoyed her. I wasn't really a fan of it either, but I could tolerate it. I always wanted to be back at the office, in the trenches, doing the work. After several years, I lost my patience for the ribbon cuttings and the theater of it all. Still, as much as I felt like none of this stuff should matter, I knew that it did matter. This was a big part of getting into these decision-making spaces, and I had to learn how to hold my own.

I naturally light up in rooms of people, so I had the knack for it. Tanesha was the opposite; she preferred to disappear. One night, we were invited to the Wendell Ford Dinner, an annual event of political hobnobbing hosted by the Jefferson County Democratic Party and the Kentucky Democratic Party. All the elected officials and candidates attend this grand ball at the Crowne Plaza Hotel in Louisville. Everyone was dressed in their best, the men in tuxedos and the women in formal gowns, and the line for the bar stretched all the way across the room.

"Charles," Tanesha whispered in my ear as we arrived. "I don't feel comfortable here. I'm sorry, but you should have just come by yourself." I could see the tears in her eyes as she said it. She didn't want to let me down, but the bright lights and wonky conversations made her uncomfortable. "You're a natural, Charles," she said. "You stay, and I'll go."

But I didn't want to be there without her. "I'm as nervous as you are," I whispered back. "I don't come from this world, either. I don't always feel like I'm smart enough or good enough, either. But I know I deserve to be in any room I walk into, and I believe in my spirit that I'm supposed to be here. I'm not going to do it unless you're with me, though. So if you want to leave, we'll leave together." She nodded, grabbed my hand, gave me a few minutes to say hello to some county leaders in the room, and then we quietly slipped out before the night was over.

Not every event went like that, though. Sometimes she forced me to stay and watched alone from her table as I worked the room. Senator Neal and Councilman Tandy were born retail politicians. They had mastered the art of laughing that big laugh as if whatever's being discussed is the most hilarious thing they had ever heard. I'd watched them in action and learned, always making sure to greet everyone in the ballroom before the dinner was served and the keynote began. As I would mingle, every few minutes I would glance across the room and try to make eye contact with Tanesha. I could tell she was miserable, but she was doing her best.

It took me some time, but I eventually learned that the best way to make sure Tanesha was at ease at these types of events was to let her be herself and accept whatever energy she wanted to put out. If she didn't want to smile at everyone that night, I respected that. Once she realized I was accepting her for who she was, things got easier. She started to loosen up, and we even began to have fun. Sometimes we would sit alone at our table, laughing about how serious we were trying to be in this strange new world. I soon realized that no matter what room I was in, the most important person there was Tanesha. This whole thing was an uncharted journey for me. I chose to hold Tanesha's hand and let the rest of the details handle themselves, just like that night in Cherokee Park.

IN THE SUMMER of 2012, all the Democrats could talk about were the plans for the upcoming Democratic National Convention in Charlotte, North Carolina, where the platform would be set and the Democratic nominee for president confirmed. President Obama was running for a second term as the country's first Black president, and we all knew how important it was for him to win. For many of us in the Black community, his victory was not just about his policies of expanding healthcare or restoring the country following the Great Recession. The unspoken truth was that it was about making sure he won so that the nation would know that a Black person could win the presidency twice, that it wasn't a fluke.

The convention wasn't even on my radar as something I should or even could be involved in. It felt far above my pay grade. Then one day while I was cutting the grass, an old blue pickup truck pulled up, and I heard, "Hey, baby!" in a loud, cheerful voice. It was Mr. Yancey, who lived a couple houses down from me and always stopped by. That day he had on his favorite blue jean overalls and a bright smile. Clarence Yancey was like a godfather, a longtime political operative in the West End. Anyone who was in elected office or hoping to be in elected office knew him. As he would tell you, they didn't win without him.

"You got the yard looking nice, baby," he said to me.

"I'm trying, Mr. Yancey," I responded, laughing.

I expected him to pull away like he normally did, but this time, he paused. "You know what, baby? You should run to be a delegate for the DNC. You could be a delegate for President Obama. If you want to do it, I'll help you."

I had never considered the idea before, but as soon as I did I thought, *Yeah! I absolutely want to do that.* I told Mr. Yancey I loved the idea, and as his truck pulled off, I called Tanesha to let her know about the conversation, and much as she preferred to avoid engaging in political events, she was on board with it right away. She didn't really know what being a delegate meant—honestly, I didn't either—but I told her, "If I get selected, we'll get to go to Charlotte, and we'll get to see the president and the First Lady." That was enough for her.

After winning the election to become the youth representative for District 43, on Mr. Yancey's advice I launched a phone and email campaign to reach out to every legislative district chair in Kentucky, letting them know all the reasons why they should vote for me at the upcoming Democratic state convention, which was being held at the Kentucky Exposition Center in Louisville.

The day of the state convention, the Expo was bustling with Democrats from all over the state who'd come to vote for party leadership and determine which Kentucky delegates would cast the formal votes for the Democratic nominee for the president of the United States. Tanesha and I filed into the meeting room where the vote was being held. After all the names of the candidates were read, it was time for the representatives from every district to cast their ballots. As the youth representative from the 43rd District, I got one, too. So I was able to vote for myself.

Once the vote counting was done, the executives called the meeting back to order and slowly began reading the people selected to be delegates from the 3rd Congressional District. After what seemed like forever, I heard it. They said my name. It was one of those things where it was so dramatic that it wasn't. On the outside I kept my cool, but on the inside I was jumping up and down, thinking, *Man, this is the greatest thing in the world! I'm headed to the DNC!*

As a delegate, I was able to attend both the convention and many of the special receptions happening around the city. With this privilege came the chance to bring one guest, which I knew would be Tanesha. As nervous as I was, knowing that we would step into this big moment together meant a lot to me. There was only one snag in our plans: I didn't quite know how we were going to find $1,000 to pay for a week in a hotel. And so, as they had many times, Mom, Dad, Grandad, Maw Maw, and my mother-in-law chipped in to help us.

The drive to Charlotte was long and monotonous, but when the city's skyline came into view, I knew this trip would be one to remember. The streets of downtown were packed with people, big signs and balloons everywhere, people on every corner selling Obama T-shirts. All the different TV stations were set up outside with the bright camera lights and their logo—MSNBC, CNN, all of them. The skyscrapers shone bright in red, white, and blue. Tanesha and I bought matching shirts and held hands as we explored downtown. It was like a movie. Then Tanesha spotted a familiar tuft of white hair moving along the sidewalk across the street. "C.J.," she said, squinting her eyes. "Look over there. I think that's Bill Clinton." We saw the entourage, the crowd of people—it was him. A former president of the United States was walking on the same street we were on. I squeezed Tanesha's hand. I couldn't believe that before the end of the week, we would see President Obama and First Lady Michelle Obama too.

Each evening, when it was time for the convention program to start, everyone filed into the Time Warner Cable Arena, as it was called at that time. Since I was a delegate for Kentucky, I had a special pass to sit in the lower level in the area designated for our state, but it was always so packed that it was hard to find seats. Tanesha was allowed to sit with me as a guest, but only if we got there on time. Each day, we fought through the crowds to get a good seat. One of the speakers who came out to fire up the crowd was Mayor Cory Booker. "Tanesha, that's Cory!" I screamed over the roar of the thousands in the arena. I rushed to take out my phone to get pictures of him as he spoke fiercely about the future of our country. I couldn't believe I was seeing him in person. I could hardly believe I was in this place to begin with. I was looking into a world that seemed so disconnected from everything I knew growing up on 35th and Market. I was seeing political leaders up close, people I had only read about or watched on TV. I was able to see them as regular people—and if they were just regular people, it was a little less impossible to imagine I might be one of them someday.

In the evenings, we got dressed up and went to receptions with all the important people. Tanesha had on her "Michelle Obama" dress: a beautiful sleeveless number with an elegant, midnight-black top that fit close to her body and a flowing champagne-colored skirt that tiered out. She glowed with it on. We felt out of place as kids from Kentucky amid important people from all over the country, but we had fun anyway. Enjoying one another made the evenings fly by. Every once in a while, we would come across one of the legislators from Kentucky with their spouses and felt a little more at home. After a reception at the NASCAR Hall of Fame, we found Councilman Tandy and his wife, Carolyn, and walked to a large outdoor area where a concert was about to start. Since all the big names come out for the DNC, we knew the headliner was going to be someone good. When the lights hit the stage, John Legend walked out onstage and grabbed the microphone, and everyone went nuts.

For the president's speech on the final day of the convention, the plan had been to move to the Bank of America Stadium, where the Carolina Panthers play, to accommodate the larger crowd. However, because of rain, we learned we would remain at the basketball arena. This meant nearly half of the attendees would not be able to come— including delegates' guests. The whole week I had been telling Tanesha how special it was going to be for us to see the first Black president together, so when I got the news about the venue change, I was crushed.

From the moment I'd been selected as a delegate, the main reason I wanted to do it was so that Tanesha and I could experience it together. This wasn't about the speech. It was about our lives, the journey we were on as a family. I didn't want to travel this road without her. Seeing the president wouldn't mean anything if she wasn't there with me.

"Tanesha," I said, "if I can't go with you, I'm not going."

"Go without me!" she said. "I'm always holding you back. You want to see the president. I'm not going to let you miss it just because I can't go."

I shook my head in disagreement. "No," I said. "We'll figure something out. We're going together."

Tanesha's guest badge could get her into the outer perimeter of the arena but not the main area where the Kentucky delegates were seated. We made it into the concourse about an hour before President Obama was set to take the stage. I showed my badge to security and walked into the lower level, and Tanesha stayed at the entrance, waiting to see if I could find her an extra spot.

Once I made it into the arena, I looked everywhere. I walked up and down every row, asking if there were two seats available. No luck. I ran back out to report to Tanesha that I couldn't find anything. "Charles," she said. "I'll go sit up at the top of the arena. You go down there so you can see the First Family."

So that's what we did. I walked her up to the top of the arena where the overflow crowd was gathering. From that high up our state delegation was a tiny square. You could see the people onstage but couldn't make out who they were. Even the massive screens felt as small as a TV at home. "Don't worry about me," Tanesha said. "Get back down there before Barack comes out." I promised her that I would try again to find a seat for her and ran down to the lower level.

When I made it back to the Kentucky section, several of the delegates were waving and shouting at me to grab my seat. The arena went dark as a video started to play. Several speakers were still scheduled before Obama would come out to accept the nomination. I took that time to walk around the arena again, looking for two adjoining seats. It was absolutely packed. President Clinton was on the stage, and the crowd was preparing for President Obama. I sat down, torn.

Then it hit me. I couldn't let President Obama walk on that stage without being by Tanesha's side. I told everyone around me that I had to go and wasn't coming back. I got up and ran as fast as I could to get up to the top of the arena. I had to climb several flights of stairs, skipping steps on the way up. I was still running to Tanesha's section when the lights dimmed and the crowd started to roar. I knew he was coming. I made it to the upper deck and started sweating as I looked for Tanesha. The thought of her being alone made me want to cry.

Then, just as President Obama appeared on the big screen, I saw the top of Tanesha's head. I walked up quietly, sat down beside her, and grabbed her hand. She looked over at me in shock. "What are you doing up here?" she whispered urgently. "You won't be able to see President Obama!" I squeezed her hand and told her I didn't care. The whole time I set my sights on being a delegate, my focus was on reaching this historic accomplishment on behalf of my community and my family. However, when the moment came, all I wanted to do was share it with Tanesha. A huge concrete column blocked my view, but it didn't matter. I understood what was important. The president came out. I couldn't see him, but all I could do was smile. I was exactly where I needed to be.

MY RETURN TO work after that DNC trip was a blur, but everything was moving in the right direction. Then, one day in early January, I got a call from David Tandy's wife, Carolyn.

One of the big elections in Kentucky that year was the matchup for U.S. Senate, with Secretary of State Alison Lundergan Grimes taking on Mitch McConnell. Carolyn wasn't working for or affiliated with the Lundergan Grimes campaign, but they'd reached out to her in an effort to connect with people in the West End.

"Charles," Carolyn said, "the Grimes campaign is trying to find a young mother living in the West End who would speak about her life experiences in a major political ad. Can you think of anyone who might help?"

The call excited me. The producers were in a time crunch and needed someone right away. I wanted to find a young mother who could shine a light for people like my own family—a real person, not a politician, someone who would say exactly what she felt. At the time, I knew a lot of young Black mothers in the West End, but I didn't know many who would be up for this kind of endeavor.

The truth of the matter is that a lot of Black people don't trust politicians and completely avoid politics. They stay away from it because they're afraid of being hurt by it. In the hood, anything that makes you stand out can only bring problems. So imagine going around the hood and asking a young, struggling mother to be featured in a video that the whole country might see. Most people in the hood don't move like that. You typically stay quiet and avoid trouble, and calling out Mitch McConnell was nothing but trouble. Very few people in Kentucky actually like Mitch McConnell, but that doesn't mean they're eager to pick a fight with him. He's too powerful.

I knew it would be a challenge to find a young woman living in the West End who would jump to do a video like this, especially at the last minute. I thought about some of my cousins, but I knew they would be uncomfortable with it. Given the time crunch, I knew the campaign and the crew would move on to another area if I couldn't find anyone, and I didn't want to let that happen. And then it hit me: I knew just who to ask.

That night, I was sitting at our dining room table while Tanesha was going back and forth through the room, folding laundry and straightening things up. I carefully pitched her the idea, knowing it might take some coaxing to get her to say yes. "Tanesha," I said, "I know you don't like speaking in front of people, and this might make you uncomfortable. But your voice is so powerful. You're the perfect example of hard work, selflessness, and determination. You're an incredible mom and an inspiration to more people than you realize, especially Black women. If you do this ad, it won't just be for you, it will be for our grandmothers, our mothers, our aunts and cousins, and most of all our daughter." I couldn't hide my excitement as I shared the opportunity with her. I knew she was a shy person, but I also believed in my heart that she was perfect to speak truth on this big stage. I knew how much she loved to help others. I knew that she could be a leader. I knew she would honor the women in our community well, and I figured this would be a catapult to push her to embrace her voice.

"I don't know if I can do it, Charles," she replied with a little sadness in her voice, not wanting to disappoint me. "That stuff is not for me."

I told her I understood and asked her to sleep on it. After that conversation, I backed off it completely. I didn't want to come off as pressuring her. But I could tell she was mulling it over through the

night, and the next day she came to me, looking and sounding resolved, and said, "I'll do it."

On the day of the taping, the camera crew showed up at our house,
and I took Kaylin and went upstairs so that Tanesha could shoot the
video. She was nervous, but I knew she would step into the moment
and tell her story. I paced back and forth upstairs. Part of me wanted
to be down there to cheer her on, but I also wanted to be invisible so
that the film would be entirely her own.

As the shoot progressed, the film crew told Tanesha that they
didn't think the footage was telling her story the right way. They
shouted for me to come downstairs, and I went down to see what they
needed. "We love what Tanesha's saying," the director said, "but right
now it seems like she's a single mother, which she isn't. We'd like to
show you and Kaylin in the video with her."

I looked at Tanesha, who was sitting quietly on the couch, to see if
it was okay with her. "I want you to be in this with me," she said.

I hadn't planned on being in the video at all. In my mind, this stage
was going to be Tanesha's all by herself. Up to this point in our relationship, I was the one that got all the attention. It made her feel
small, and I hated that, because I never could have been as bold as I
was without her support. I wanted her to show everyone the strong,
confident person I knew she was.

So I hesitated at first. I didn't want this to be another thing that
centered around me. But when I looked at Tanesha, I understood why
she was asking me to be there. It reminded me of how I felt at the
Democratic Convention. That was a big moment for me, but all I
could think of was being with her. This was the same situation in reverse. We were meant to go through these moments together. I wanted
to be with her and hold her hand in this important moment, just like
we did in Cherokee Park. So I stopped protesting and changed my
mind. "Okay," I said. "I'd be happy to be in the video with my wife." I
put my hand on her shoulder and sat down next to her on the couch.

From that moment, I resolved I would do whatever I was asked to
do if it helped Tanesha tell her story. After we sat on the couch for

some B-roll, I drove the crew around the West End so that they could film Tanesha talking about the neighborhood. The whole time we were filming, I didn't stop to worry about what being in the video would mean for my job in the state legislature. I had asked my fellow staffers about the rules for getting involved in a political ad for a federal race and had looked up the department policy on it. There was a strict prohibition against getting involved in state-level races, but there was no formal language that addressed federal races. I shared with my committee supervisor that my wife was doing a video called "Tanesha's Story" and that it was going to be for the U.S. Senate race. I explained the message in the video, and I also let her know I was in a couple scenes. She and I talked about the aim of the video and went back and forth on the question of what type of political activity staff can be involved in, and after we spoke I felt confident this didn't violate the prohibition on state legislative politics, so I didn't bother asking the department director.

That said, I knew that bringing political attention to myself, even if not expressly prohibited, could potentially blow back on me. However, this was such an important opportunity to tell a story about our community; no one ever came to the West End or asked what we thought. So I felt the risk was worth it. It felt like one of those "ask for forgiveness instead of permission" moments, so I didn't even mention it to Director Sherman or to Deputy Director Jenkins. To me, the worst-case scenario was that the leadership staff would slap me on the wrist for bringing attention to myself.

When I saw the final cut of the ad, I knew it was special. I was so proud of Tanesha and grateful to her for using her voice. When the spot landed the following week, everyone at work was excited to see it. All our family members called. They were so proud! The video started with a shot of the Louisville skyline. As the city rose up on the screen, I swelled with emotion. Kaylin held her head up the entire time. She was little, but not nervous at all. I could tell she was proud, too. The message Tanesha shared in the video was true: We are fighters in the West End. Even in the tough times, we keep getting up. We keep loving. We keep working hard. We keep fighting to make it.

The pride I felt was quickly deflated by a story about it that broke in *The Courier-Journal* soon after. It was written by a local writer, Phillip Bailey. It wasn't a news item. It felt like a hit piece. It highlighted my experience with Yarmuth and Tandy in a way that made it seem like I was some kind of campaign operative concocting a story for this ad that wasn't actually true—that Tanesha wasn't really a typical West End mom with a genuine story but rather the wife of some super-connected Democratic Party insider, which I was not. It was not a secret that I had worked for Yarmuth and Tandy in the past, but this article made it seem like hot news. It framed my being in the video as a bombshell revelation, when really I was just some staffer behind the scenes.

The story cast a shadow over my head the next day when I walked into the Capitol. Up to that moment, the staffers who'd seen the video were excited for my wife and proud of me for supporting her. Now, the whispers had started. We started to hear about a push to get me fired. Since it was the end of the week, I hoped that things would blow over by Monday morning. I didn't want to lose my job; I felt so alive working in that big, beautiful building, giving my all to honor my family and community. Lastly, and most importantly for me, was the support my work gave Tanesha and Kaylin. My salary was covering the bills. We couldn't afford for me to lose this job.

On Monday, when I walked through the basement tunnel to head to my office, I had a feeling things were about to change. "Good morning, Kim! Good morning, Becky!" I said to my colleagues in my normal cheerful tone. But Kim had a concerned look.

"Charles," she said, "the director's office wants you to go over to the Capitol office before you get started today."

I put down my bag and coat and headed over to the Capitol through the Annex tunnel like I always did. The same hall that gave me so much joy as I nodded at legislators and said hello to students on field trips was empty that morning. The only noise was the clack of my footsteps on the marble floor. The elevator was old and seemed to take forever to get up to the third floor. When it finally stopped, I stepped out and looked up at the rotunda. I could hear the hum of a vacuum or the rumble of a cart with cleaning supplies being pushed by one of the janitors. Other than that, the place was quiet.

When I opened the door to the LRC suite, the entire office looked solemn. Robert Jenkins was sitting in his office with Roy Collins, the HR director. They waved me in. I sat on the same couch that I had sat on when I interviewed to get the job. Roy asked me about the video.

"Charles, *why*?" he said. "Why did you do it?"

I wasn't going to give him the satisfaction of assuming what he was talking about. "What do you mean?"

"You didn't have to be in the video," he said, his tone exasperated. Robert, meanwhile, was quiet, with his head down and his hands in his pockets. "We love you," Roy said, "but we gotta let you go."

"Well, what did I do wrong?"

"You know what you did wrong."

"No, I don't. You're going to have to explain to me what I did wrong."

"You know that staff can't be involved in politics. You have to be nonpartisan."

"Well, my understanding is that the distinction was for state-level politics, not federal."

My palms were sweating. I knew my job was at-will, meaning they didn't need a reason to fire me. I also knew that I'd bent the rules. When you're a staffer, you want to be invisible and do the work. But to say that I'd broken the rules to the point where I'd committed some fireable offense? I didn't see it that way.

"You're going to have to show me that's the rule," I said, "because that isn't what the language says."

We all had our legal hats on, and we were going back and forth, and eventually they conceded that I had a point. Roy said, "Okay, Charles. The language doesn't say that you did anything wrong, but you still shouldn't have done it, and we still have to let you go. You brought too much attention to yourself. It's created a distraction. I'm sorry.

"But Charles," he added, "don't think that we want to get rid of you. I wish you hadn't done this. Everyone here loves you, but we're getting a lot of pressure. We need to let this die down. If you resign, we'll keep everything quiet and after the election, we can bring you back."

They gave me the rest of the day to think about it. They also said I could collect unemployment even if I resigned. I hugged Roy and Robert, wiping tears from my eyes. They were wiping their eyes as well. I walked out of there shell-shocked and crushed.

Initially, resigning felt like the right thing to do. I could protect my family from more media attention and then come back to work after the election. But then I called Tanesha and told her what had happened. She was devastated. "So you have to quit your job because of me?" she asked. I felt terrible. My wife had shown incredible courage. The idea that her speaking out had cost me my job was like a slap in her face. She blamed herself, and I couldn't let her do that. If I quit, it would be like throwing her under the bus, so I decided I would rather throw myself under the bus. I would rather have them fire me and bear the responsibility of what I did myself rather than make it seem like she did something wrong.

That night and the next day it was all I could think about. As I sat at my desk, preparing to let the director's office know my final decision, I thought about how and why I'd come to this crossroads. The whole reason I'd wanted to work in government was to be a voice for my community. Now, the moment my wife used her voice, I was being forced to resign and quietly go away or stand with her and face the consequences.

But before I let myself get absorbed in that fact, I let my thoughts float back to my family history. I thought about Grandad facing threats and gross insults for taking a stand to demand that Black workers receive the same treatment and opportunity as their white co-workers. I thought about the many documentaries and articles I had studied while sitting in that office. I remembered Dr. King's letter from that Birmingham jail cell and Mandela keeping his faith while serving time in prison for dedicating his life to ending apartheid. What I was going through was nothing compared to what those two men endured, but if they could go to jail and put their lives on the line for simply believing that everyone should be treated justly, surely I could withstand losing my job to honor my wife's courage.

I had no excuse. Quietly resigning from this defining moment was not an option. I chose to straighten my back and stand up for what I believed was right. I withdrew my decision to resign, and they fired me. I felt in my spirit that this was a special moment for my partner, and that her shining was a part of this larger journey for the both of us. I didn't know where it would lead, but I knew that the work God had in store involved us as a team. Once I got over the initial shock, I felt entirely at peace about it.

I was proud that I lost that job. There was only one problem. Now I had to find another one.

Me at five years old, in one of many outfits my mom made for me growing up.
Courtesy of Earletta Hearn

My childhood home at 35th and Market, after years of updates and repairs.
Courtesy of the author

Me at three years old (in the foreground), with a couple of my cousins, Latarius (left) and Terisha (center), and my big cousin C.J. (seated), at one of our regular family dinners.
Courtesy of Earletta Hearn

My maternal grandparents, Lindsay E. Hearn, Sr., and JoAnn Hearn. *Courtesy of Earletta Hearn*

My Grandad, Lindsay Hearn, in his seventies, standing in front of his black Durango in the driveway of their home on 38th and Parker. *Courtesy of Earletta Hearn*

My mom on Mother's Day, wearing one of the suits she made for herself; I had surprised her after church with some flowers. *Courtesy of the author*

A family portrait with my dad, Charles Booker, Sr.; he was still rocking his curl at the time. *Courtesy of Earletta Hearn*

My paternal grandmother, Flora Bauer, and her husband, George; I proudly call them Maw Maw and Paw Paw. *Courtesy of Earletta Hearn*

Graduating with honors from Louisville Male High School in 2003.
Courtesy of the author

Holding Kaylin when she was nearly two months old. I was still in law school, and this was one of the many times I stayed over at Tanesha's apartment after class.
Courtesy of the author

At a birthday party with Tanesha, a year after our marriage and my graduation from Brandeis School of Law.
Courtesy of the author

With Senator Gerald Neal on the House floor in the Kentucky State Capitol in 2019.
Photo: The Kentucky Legislative Research Commission

With Tanesha at the United States Capitol for the inauguration of President Obama following his reelection in 2012. It was freezing. *Courtesy of the author*

With Tanesha by my side at the 2012 Democratic National Convention, as I cast my vote for President Obama in my role as a Kentucky delegate.
Courtesy of the author

My first hunting trip with the Conservation Leaders for Tomorrow class at Max McGraw Wildlife Foundation in Illinois. *Courtesy of the author*

Meeting President Obama while serving as a driver in his motorcade during a presidential visit to Louisville in 2015.
Courtesy of the author

With a pregnant Tanesha on the site of the proposed FoodPort project, standing in front of an old billboard that I'd had redone, hiring a young local artist to replace an old cigarette advertisement with a positive message for our community.
Courtesy of the author

On the steps of the Kentucky State Capitol after filing my candidate papers for my run against Senator Neal. Around me are Tanesha (left, holding Prestyn), my cousin Kim (center), and Grandad (right). In the next row are my cousin Cory (left), Tanesha's aunt Pretty and her husband, Ronnie (center), and my cousin Geno (right). Behind them are Tanesha's brother-in-law, Marcus (left), her sister, Jennifer (center), and my mom (right).
Courtesy of the author

With my uncle Tyrone Booker (my cousin T.J.'s father) during my run for State Senate against Senator Gerald Neal in 2016. I had just put up this yard sign on the fence at his house.
Courtesy of the author

Doing the Wakanda salute during my swearing-in on the floor of the Kentucky State House chambers in 2019, standing between Representative Lisa Wilner (on my left) and Representative Danny Bentley. *Courtesy of Beth Thorpe*

With Rep. Danny Bentley as we testified together before the Health and Family Services Committee about HB 64, "Kevin's Law," a bill we were co-sponsoring to provide emergency access to diabetes medication.
Photo: The Kentucky Legislative Research Commission

Joining the women and men of UFCW Local 10D in Lawrenceburg, Kentucky, during their strike against Four Roses Bourbon; their benefits were being cut, and I stood with them in protest. *Courtesy of the author*

In Harlan County with Scott Shoupe (left), a miner from Eastern Kentucky who is advocating for sustainable opportunities like solar, and his father. *Courtesy of Scott Shoupe*

Canvassing in a holler in eastern Kentucky during my run for U.S. Senate in 2020. *Courtesy of the author*

With Senator Bernie Sanders at "Breeway"—the site of the year-long protests following Breonna Taylor's murder, formally named Jefferson Square Park—as we spoke with organizers about the work to ensure justice for Breonna Taylor and every Kentuckian.
Photo: Booker for Kentucky Campaign

Standing on West Broadway with my campaign staffer Joshua (to my right) and hundreds of residents, raising our fists and standing in silence as the body of David McAtee was viewed by his family. McAtee was killed when the Louisville police department and the National Guard came into our neighborhood and shot at his restaurant in what they called a response to protests.
Courtesy of the author

My mom wearing the campaign shirt my great-aunt made to help me in my run against Senator Neal—my very first campaign shirt.
Courtesy of the author

Onstage with Kaylin (left), Tanesha, and Prestyn at my State House general election kickoff event following my historic primary win in a seven-way race.
Courtesy of the author

CHAPTER 12

FISH AND WILDLIFE

"**H**AVE YOU EVER shot a gun, Charles?"

Tim Farmer had stopped by my new office to feel me out. I was less than three months into my new job as director of administrative services for the Kentucky Department of Fish and Wildlife Resources, and Tim, like everybody else in the department, was curious about the new guy from the West End of Louisville.

The stated mission of Fish and Wildlife is "to conserve, protect and enhance Kentucky's fish and wildlife resources and provide outstanding opportunities for hunting, fishing, trapping, boating, shooting sports, wildlife viewing, and related activities," which it does from its main office in Frankfort as well as in camps, wildlife management areas, and satellite offices across the state. For a kid from the hood, it was like visiting the other side of the moon.

Unlike me, Tim Farmer was a rock star at the department. At the time, he was the host of *Kentucky Afield,* the department's Emmy Award–winning outdoors show that highlighted the state's beautiful wildlife and rich natural resources. Whenever he came into the building, people would call out, "Tim's here!" and everybody would get excited and line up to talk to him. He was not a standard employee in any sense. He also looked like Jesse from *Full House,* with the jeans and the leather jacket and the motorcycle glasses and the hair swooped back.

Tim was also a military veteran, a musician, and a skilled archer. The man was cool. If his talent, accolades, and good looks weren't re-

markable enough, there was also the fact that he accomplished everything that he did with one arm. Back in the 1980s, he'd been badly
injured in a motorcycle accident. But that hadn't stopped him; he'd
learned how to be an archer by pulling the bow back with his teeth,
and he could hit a bulls-eye pretty much every time.

I knew nothing about Tim or about *Kentucky Afield* before coming to the department. I'd never seen a single episode. The answer to
his question was that, no, I had never shot a gun. Although several of
my relatives loved to fish, I didn't fish much or bow hunt, and I had
never even gone camping other than with the Boy Scouts when I was
little. On top of that, I was also the only Black executive, and one of
few Black employees total, in the entire department.

Like everyone else, I was instantly a fan of Tim Farmer. You
couldn't help but like him, and I could tell that he hadn't just stopped
by my office to "check out the new Black guy." He was reaching out
because he genuinely wanted to connect. He wanted to help.

One thing I knew, going into such a foreign environment, was that
people would never trust me or accept me if I pretended to be something I wasn't, so I told Tim the truth. "I come from a family of people
that loved to fish," I said, "but I never had the privilege to do it much.
And in my neighborhood, when somebody's got a gun, it's not to
hunt deer. So, no. I've never shot one."

"Well," he said, "let's change that. Because to earn the trust of the
people who work in Fish and Wildlife, it's important to know how to
handle a gun. I like you, Charles, and I can tell you're a good man. So
if you want, I'll bring you out to my ranch and teach you how to
shoot."

Tim was right. I still had a lot of work to do to make the new job
feel like home. Indeed, the whole aftermath of getting fired from the
Legislative Research Commission had been incredibly difficult to
navigate. The morning after I was terminated, I woke up to find myself
in the national news for losing my job. "LRC Staffer Fired for Appear-
ing in Lundergan Grimes Video," read the headlines on my laptop
screen as I sat on the couch, my head in my hands, sitting motionless

for what felt like hours. As proud as I was of myself for standing up for Tanesha, I hadn't expected to be in the national news. The only consolation was that at least people across the country were taking a moment to learn about the West End.

Worse than the public embarrassment was the pain of not being able to provide for my family. No matter how hard we worked, with me in the public sector and Tanesha at her job processing medical claims, we were always living paycheck to paycheck. Now my paycheck was gone, unemployment only covered about a third of what I'd been making, and our little bit of savings was gone in a heartbeat. Meanwhile, we had the mortgage, car payments, groceries, my medical bills. I managed to sell some furniture and an old stereo I had. Tanesha started selling plasma; I think she got $60 or $90 each time. The worst was when we had to start getting payday loans, which I did not want to do because I knew once you start taking them, the interest will eat you alive. But we didn't have any choice.

As we scraped by week to week, I was back at square one with my career, cold calling everyone I knew, scrolling through job postings, emailing my résumé everywhere under the sun, filling out dozens of applications every single day. I looked at jobs all over the country, anything in the realm of what I might be qualified for. I had a couple of responses, but nothing ever panned out. Then, after four months of searching and searching, I finally got a text from Delquan Dorsey, who oversaw the Office of Minority Empowerment under Governor Steve Beshear's administration. He had a very unlikely job interview for me, something so far off my radar I never in a million years would have thought to apply for it: Director of Administrative Services for the Department of Fish and Wildlife Resources.

The job description terrified me, to be honest. All the department's administrative functions would be my responsibility: human resources, payroll, overseeing a budget of close to $17 million to run a statewide department of over four hundred employees. They didn't have a policy handbook; I would have to create one. They hadn't done ethics and harassment training; I would have to implement it. Never mind the hunting and fishing piece of it; I had never taken on anything close to a managerial role of this scale. "But whatever," I said. "I'll do anything."

I put on a suit, drove to Frankfort, and interviewed for the job. When they called back to extend me the offer, I accepted on the spot. At that point, it didn't matter how far the job deviated from my original career path, I just needed to work to support my family. But the Lord, as they say, works in mysterious ways, and this job I grabbed onto as a life raft in a desperate moment turned out to be one of the greatest blessings of my life.

I RODE OUT to Tim Farmer's ranch with Michael Gray. Michael was the other Black guy at Fish and Wildlife. He was also from Louisville and was in my fraternity as well. Michael was a middle-aged guy, a fast talker with dark skin and a short goatee who loved to smoke cigars and drink bourbon and always had on some cologne that reminded me of church. He worked in marketing.

Before I even started work, people were telling me, "You're going to Fish and Wildlife? You gotta connect with Michael." Like everybody else at the office who was curious about me, Michael popped his head in my office on the first day. "There's some things you need to know to work here," he said. "Let's get together off-site so we can talk for real." Michael understood what I was up against. Since news of my hiring had gone out, people had been talking about me on Kentucky sportsmen blogs. In some of the comments, hunters and anglers were questioning whether I could do the job. "He needs to go back to the ghetto where he's from," one commenter said. Another referred to me as a nigger. It hurt to read that people who cared so deeply about Fish and Wildlife didn't want me. I prayed and shook it off.

Inside the department, people weren't hostile like what I was facing on the blogs. Arriving at the Frankfort office my first day, the reception I got was cordial and professional, but I wouldn't characterize it as a warm embrace. All the people who stopped by my office, I could tell that behind their big smiles they were sizing me up, waiting for me to prove myself. They would say, "You know, I love this place," intimating that they cared about it more than I did and that I'd better not screw it up. I'd walk into a conference room, and folks would be in the middle of a big, loud conversation, then see me and suddenly fall silent and nod in my direction.

People regarded me as an outsider, not just because of my race but because I wasn't one of them. Fish and Wildlife was its own distinct and insular world. For the people who worked there, it was more of a way of life than a job. They lived and breathed Kentucky wildlife, day in and day out. They even made their own furniture. They had woodworkers on staff who made custom desks and chairs for everyone to go with all the stuffed and mounted deer and elk heads on the wall. That's how unique a place it was.

As a workplace culture, Fish and Wildlife was the definition of an old boy network. Part of the reason I'd been hired was because it had become too much of an old boy network, even for the people who worked there. It was too insular, too stuck in its ways. For years they almost always promoted from within, and the lack of new blood and outside perspectives had fostered an unhealthy environment. Several people, including my predecessor, had departed under a cloud of allegations involving harassment within the department. There was an ongoing scandal over the mismanagement of certain funds, as well as a great deal of mistrust between the leadership and the staff. Knowing all of this to be an issue, the state sent me in to try and shake things up. So the fact that I didn't fit in was a large part of the reason I got the job in the first place, which was why both Michael and Tim Farmer knew I was going to have a difficult time adjusting and why both of them wanted to help me out.

When Tim first invited me to go shooting, my only interest in guns was in making sure I didn't end up on the wrong end of one. A gun had taken my uncle's life. Living in the West End, I heard gunshots every day; it was so commonplace that me and my cousins could name the type of gun by the sound of the shot. But there's one thing I've learned as my life has taken me into worlds that are different from my own, and that is to set aside my own preconceptions and take the opportunity to learn something new. So I overcame my reluctance, and one evening after work, Michael and I followed Tim out to his home, which was on a large piece of land, hidden behind some rolling hills.

Naturally, he had his own shooting range.

Tim went up ahead of us to his house, and we waited outside. I changed my shoes and took off my tie. When I looked up, Tim was walking out holding this big wooden tray with various handguns on it, plus a couple of shotguns slung over his shoulder. He looked like an action figure.

In my mind the whole time I was thinking, *I'm not actually going to shoot those guns.* It was like somebody daring you to eat octopus. You say, "Yeah! I'm gonna do it!" But you're not really going to do it.

Tim handed me a shotgun, and I felt uncomfortable. I still remember the weight of it. But the way he described it made me feel safe. He told me the history of the gun and how it shot and what the bullet would do on impact. His voice was calm. He was patient. I could tell he was trying to quell any anxiety that I had, and I decided I was ready to face my fear. We lined up and took aim at these targets he had out in the field. He shot first and showed me how to hold the gun. "Don't close your eye," he said. "Rookies close one eye." I took aim and fired.

Very much to my surprise, I was a good shot.

"Do you play basketball?" Tim asked.

"Yeah, man. I love basketball."

"You got a good jumper?"

"Yeah, I do."

"I can tell. You've got good hand-eye coordination."

All told, we fired something like twelve different guns, different gauges of shotguns, a 9mm. Then he brought out an AR-15. If the other guns caused me a bit of discomfort, that one triggered some real PTSD, because I only knew that gun in the context of people being murdered.

"Charles," Tim said, "if you're uncomfortable, you don't have to shoot this one."

I shot it, though. The bullets fired off so fast into the dirt that I immediately handed it back. Tim understood completely. "Honestly," he said, "I never use this gun because it's pointless for hunting. You're going to damage the meat. But I wanted you to see it." I'd seen it and seen enough of it. But the experience as a whole was exhilarating, and it made me understand why people like guns.

When the shooting was done, we went into Tim's house and tasted different barbecues. I sat at the bar and tried different types of burgers and sausage while Michael and Tim traded stories about how they loved to cook. Because Tim also has his own cooking show that he does with one arm. The dude is unstoppable. I was glad that I'd come. I knew the day would come with this job when I would be asked to go on a hunting trip, and Tim had made sure I wouldn't embarrass myself. Plus, I knew that if Tim Farmer was taking a liking to me, I was on the right track.

IN AN EFFORT to improve morale and fix the broken culture of the department, one of my first tasks was to conduct the annual ethics and harassment training in every single office, department-wide. Since most of the employees worked in offices and wildlife management areas outside of Frankfort, conducting those trainings gave me a joy and a privilege I might never have enjoyed otherwise. I got to visit every corner of the Commonwealth, and my travels showed me that, without question, Kentucky is the most beautiful place in the world.

Prior to taking the job, I had never seen much of the state beyond Louisville and the hour-long drive back and forth to Frankfort along I-64. Now, driving down the Wendell H. Ford Western Kentucky Parkway, the fall leaves outside my window looked like an oil painting. Walking along the Ohio River in Paducah, I got to see the famous murals depicting the city's charm as well as its rich yet painful history, including the important part that the area once played in the Underground Railroad.

Kentucky has incredible waterways all across it, and working at Fish and Wildlife gave me the chance to see many of them. The department had a conservation camp called Camp Currie on the Kentucky Lake in Western Kentucky. The lake was man-made but sprawling and beautiful. I used to sit down by the water and watch the boats cruise by, the sunset sparkling on the peaceful water as evening approached. The serenity was like medicine.

Traveling east on the Martha Layne Collins Bluegrass Parkway, I finally saw the bluegrass I had heard so much about growing up. It blew in waves, and when the sun hit it just right, you could see the blue. The first time I paused to look at the Appalachian Mountains, I felt the pride that folks in Pikeville and Prestonsburg have known their whole lives. I was just as proud of the West End of Louisville, but the scenery here was unmatched. The hills surround you, towering along the roads and creating the bends that reveal large valleys surrounded by tree-covered mountains. One of the things I loved most about Eastern Kentucky was the way the mountains are a part of everything. It always amazed me to see huge high schools, hospitals, and universities nestled up against the slopes.

From skipping rocks at Camp Webb on Lake Cumberland to watching boating lessons at Grayson Lake, I savored the chance to finally see Kentucky. The rolling hills in the Daniel Boone National Forest and the cliffs and waterfalls at Red River Gorge all made me even more proud of my home state. The greatest gift of doing training sessions for Fish and Wildlife is that we always had the best natural backdrops. The grand beauty made our work easy . . . especially since that beauty was our work.

The department had two primary responsibilities. The first was to serve as custodians of the state's natural resources, to nurture and protect them. The second was to provide the people of the Commonwealth access to those resources. But the way I always saw it, the people of Kentucky are also a part of the state's incredible bounty, as much as the rivers and the trees and the rolling bluegrass, and those people need nurturing and protection too. Our government was failing to provide that to people all across Kentucky, and Fish and Wildlife was failing to provide it to its own employees.

In the wake of the department's harassment and corruption scandals and all the staff turnover that followed, morale was way down. "Charles," Michael told me on my first day, "you're going to have to show the department that you won't up and leave. You're going to have to show them that you are here to help them. You're going to have to show them that they can trust you."

When I started and folks were coming by and poking their head into my office to see what my story was, it was funny to see how they interacted. Everyone who came in would nod at the person who'd just left and say, "You can't trust that guy." That happened over and over. There was so much backbiting and mistrust.

It reminded me of life in the West End, to be honest. In that neighborhood, we had so much love on a personal level, but our morale as a community was severely damaged. We were isolated from the rest of the city, all but ignored, creating an insular culture that couldn't respond well to change. When politicians came into our neighborhoods, we got mostly empty promises and exploitation. Whenever people came into our hood presenting themselves as leaders, most residents looked at them with great skepticism, which then stood in the way of residents working together to mobilize to fight for what they needed.

Keeping that in mind, I committed to being the type of leader I'd always wanted to see in the West End. That meant showing up, facing the mistrust that people have, being accountable to their concerns, and showing through my actions that I was actually there to work for their best interests.

To gain trust in my division, I set up meeting after meeting after meeting: one-on-one meetings, team leader meetings, and division-wide meetings. I gave everyone a chance to vent their frustrations. I wanted to create a space where everyone knew they could be heard, and the stories I heard were exactly what I expected to hear.

In any culture that's run on the old boy system, there are no rules and procedures to follow. It all becomes about personalities and politics: who to curry favor with to get anything done, who to avoid because they'll screw you over, and so on. And all that comes at the expense of doing the work that you're passionate about. That dynamic can be particularly hard for anyone who's an outsider, who doesn't know how, or can't, navigate the rules and rituals of the old boy culture.

That hadn't really been a problem for Black people at Fish and Wildlife because there weren't any Black people at Fish and Wildlife, just Michael and a few other folks at other offices around the state. It had definitely been a problem for women. One of them, I'll call her Susan, sat in my office and told me her story. Several of the staff used to go out for drinks after work. Some of the men would get sloppy, and they'd gotten physical with her, harassing her and touching her, which terrified her because she already knew the stories of the women who'd rebuffed the advances of their bosses, only to be ostracized at work. When she told me what had happened, she was physically shaking. She'd never been able to tell anyone before because of the overall lack of trust in the department.

Then there was the department's financial issues, which had long been covered up and papered over as well. The department had issued what they called procurement cards, or "pro cards," which worked like department credit cards. But they were doing a very poor job tracking and reconciling who was spending what each month, and certain individuals were taking advantage of it, spending thousands of dollars on things that had nothing to do with the department. One of the directors was even believed to be having an affair and using Fish and Wildlife resources to cover expenses. Everybody knew it, but no one could report it for fear of retaliation.

Once you establish a culture of dishonesty, it infects everything else. I reversed that by opening up. I shared my story of growing up and explained who I was and where I came from. By being transparent and honest with them, I was encouraging them to do the same with me, and I worked hard to listen to everyone else, especially the employees who were not in leadership but did the bulk of the work. I met with all of them and just listened. Once I established that they could trust me even though I was an outsider, they slowly realized that they could trust me precisely because I was an outsider. I wasn't a part of the old boy network. I was able to be an independent sounding board and authority. You could talk to me without worrying about it getting repeated somewhere else. It helped that, as the director of administrative services, I was the one who signed off on everyone's paychecks—even the other directors—so in a lot of ways, they all had to report to me, and I had the leverage to implement new policies and guidelines. But it was also that they liked and respected me.

About six months after I showed up, three of the other managers—the grants manager, the accounting manager, and the purchasing manager—came in my office, closed the door, and said, "Charles, we all want to thank you. None of us knew what to expect when you got here. We thought you might leave as soon as you saw how bad things were. But we can tell you really care. We never had a manager that treated us like we actually mattered and went to bat for us." I get choked up thinking about it now because they were so grateful, and they hadn't expected me to do what I did. They didn't want the department to be sloppy because they really cared about this stuff. For them to feel like I was there to do my part for them because I knew how much they cared, that meant the world to me.

There was this narrow back hallway that I walked every morning to get to the kitchen area where I would put my snacks and my lunch. Initially, when I would walk through, everybody was always a bit quiet, like my presence had put them on edge. "The boss is here! Shape up!" It was that kind of vibe. But as I went through, I made a point of stopping and speaking to everybody, getting to know them and asking about their families. Slowly, they started to lighten up, and some of them even started making snacks for me. I could tell they lit up when I came in, like they were relieved that I was there because they knew I was going to have their back.

As a Black man who'd lived his whole life feeling ostracized from people who didn't look like me, I was heartened to see so many at Fish and Wildlife open their arms to me. It even forced me to reckon with some uncomfortable truths about myself. Before I went to work at Fish and Wildlife, I never would have admitted being prejudiced in any way. I felt that I didn't look down on other people or other cultures. Stereotyping was something other people did to me, not something I did to other people. But that wasn't always true. There was a certain type of guy who used to always set off alarms for me. He always had a particular look: middle-aged or older, overalls and boots, and he probably spoke with a deep Kentucky twang. I'd take one look at that guy and think, *Man, that person's not going to like me. I'll bet he looks down on me.* But why would I assume that a man has hate in his heart just by the way he dresses or looks? That's a negative stereotype, too.

Fish and Wildlife had a deal with a bunch of Kentucky grocery stores through which they'd give us all their misshapen and expired food to feed to the animals. The expiration date is only for commercial purposes; usually the food's fine. But one day I started getting complaints about an employee stealing the food. I called him into my office, and when he came in, he had that typical rural Kentucky look, and all those alarms started going off. He sat down across from me, and the mood was a bit uncomfortable, and everything about his look led me to think, *This guy's not going to respect me. I'm going to have problems with him.* But that didn't happen. Instead, the man humbled himself. He opened his heart and said, "Charles, I just . . . I just needed something to eat. My family . . . we ain't got any food."

It was a powerful moment. I looked at this man who I was sure I was going to have problems with, and in his story I saw my own. Although the work at Fish and Wildlife required high-level expertise, many of the jobs were lower-level jobs that didn't require extensive formal education. Too many people who worked for us were just getting by. I remembered all too well what it was like to not have any food, what it was like for my mom to go without dinner so that I could have enough. Only a few months earlier, I'd been selling my furniture to pay my mortgage. I arranged with the department to set aside food for him so that he wouldn't have to sneak it out. More importantly, I started applying whatever pressure I could to get workers like him a long-overdue raise.

Fish and Wildlife was also where I first learned about the opioid epidemic. One day this old guy with no teeth came in, and he was going on about "I need my license." As one of the employees showed him over to the IT division, which was where they issue the hunting and fishing licenses, one of my staffers said to me, "Man, that guy's been coming here so long I remember when he still had his teeth."

"What happened?" I asked.

"Drugs."

There were stories like that one all the time. You'd see the people struggling with opioids because they all came in to get disability hunting licenses, which come at a discount, even though they weren't permanently disabled. They were suffering from opioid addiction as a result of a painful injury or other health problems. It was so pervasive that you'd see whole families addicted to opioids. Grandparents, parents, and grandkids. All of them.

Tim Slone, the department's education director, told me, "Charles, many of these folks that don't work are perfectly able to work, but they're on drugs." Their stories reminded me of my uncle Lamont. He was a great guy whom I loved deeply, but after some health issues, he consistently battled drug use. He struggled to keep a job or a home. These rural Kentuckians weren't labeled as criminals in the same way that people in my hood were, but they were definitely suffering from the same problems.

Working at Metro Hall and at the LRC in Frankfort, my drive had always been to get the perspective of people like me into places where it wasn't being heard. What I learned at Fish and Wildlife was that I needed exposure to other people, too, in order to broaden my own perspective. Before that job, I hadn't fully grasped the ways that all Kentuckians—and all people, really—are as physically and emotionally interdependent and connected as we are. Because of my faith, I always knew we were spiritually connected; I've always understood that when I see a person, I'm looking at a human being first. But my new job showed me in real terms that I have more in common with white Kentuckians in rural areas than I ever expected. It was a powerful lesson for me about the ways we so often fail to connect and communicate and understand one another. The distance between me and the department when I showed up, my preconceptions about the man caught sneaking the food—both of those stories could have gone a different way. Both of those stories could have ended up with everyone being more divided and more suspicious of each other than we were at the start. It was only through a conscious, deliberate effort to open up and understand each other that we were able to make progress.

IN MARCH OF 2015, about a year into my tenure at Fish and Wildlife, I found myself fitting in and getting along in ways I never would have imagined when I started. I even got to go on that hunting trip that Tim Farmer had so kindly prepared me for. During one of our executive team meetings, Gregory Johnson, the department commissioner, announced to the group that he was encouraging me to attend a national conservation camp. "We all love Charles," he said, "and since he's in leadership here, this would be a great experience for him." The program was called Conservation Leaders for Tomorrow, and it was a weeklong retreat at the Max McGraw Wildlife Foundation in Illinois. We would learn about the history and challenges of wildlife and habitat conservation, and at the end of the trip we would go hunting. It was the dead of winter, so it was going to be cold, too. The other directors were all smiling and patting me on the back, saying, "So, ready for your first hunting trip?! You excited? You scared?"

If the same thing had happened my first week on the job, I probably would have thought they were trying to haze me and alienate me, to make sure I remembered that I was an outsider. But now, having been around awhile and forged such strong connections with everyone, I could take it for what it was, just lighthearted joking around.

Still, the fact that I'd never hunted before felt like a chip on my shoulder. I knew, deep down, they would never fully accept me as part of the team until I had been hunting. The thing is, I had no interest in hunting. With so much gun violence in my community, I didn't want to shoot a gun at anything other than a clay pigeon. Everyone was so excited to see me shoot that I was walking around acting cool with everything, but inside the idea of actually killing a living thing filled me with dread.

Of course, I do eat meat. I buy it every week at the grocery store, which is no better than pulling the trigger yourself. In some ways it's worse, because you're not taking the same kind of responsibility for your choices. So when they told me, "Whatever you kill, you're gonna eat," that helped me make peace with it. I could tell myself that I was doing it to provide food for my family.

Hunting proved to be a revelation in more ways than one. I expected to be bored on the trip, but the experience was far from dull. I learned how to break down and put together a rifle. I learned more about the science behind conservation and how important it is to manage diseases and the destruction of habitats. I also learned more about the history of hunting and gained a better appreciation for how hunting wasn't just for sport, that there are ways to hunt that made sure the animals didn't suffer.

More than anything, I got a glimpse of the peace that hunters feel sitting quietly in the woods, waiting to get their shot. Hunting means accepting that you're not in control of what's happening. Nature is in control. Once you accept that fact, you can let go of the stress of daily life and become attuned to the world around you, the feel of the wind on your face, the beat of your heart slowing down as you gather yourself to shoot. It's calming, almost meditative, which I never would have imagined. Being outdoors in nature felt spiritual, to be honest, and it gave me a lot of respect for people who hunt.

On the day of the hunt, we headed out to shoot pheasant in these pickup trucks with wagons hitched up behind them, kind of like a hayride. My dad had been so excited for me to work at Fish and Wildlife, and he bought me boots, a big Carhartt jacket, and thick white socks with blue stripes on them. "You're going to need this to keep your feet warm," he said, and he was right. There was over a foot of snow on the ground, and the wind was whipping by. We had these little beagles and hunting dogs with big, floppy ears, and we let them out and they were rushing through the snow, puffs of white powder shooting up in the air as they were zigging and zagging this way and that. As they flushed out the game, we took turns going out in pairs to take our chance at shooting a bird to take home.

My first trip out, I didn't hit anything. My dog had a tough time finding any pheasant to chase out of hiding. The few times it did, the birds were too far away, and I shot and missed. I think I missed because I was okay with missing. I was still averse to shooting an animal. But when I got back in the truck, I realized I was the only one who didn't get something. My competitive streak took over, and I turned to my instructor. "There's no way I can go home and tell these folks I didn't get anything," I said.

"You want to go back out?" he asked.

Everyone looked at me, encouraging me to do it. I was so cold already from standing in the foot of snow, but I decided to give it another shot. I drove back out, got a different bird dog, and this time the pheasants flew low and close. *Bang!* I hit one on my first shot! My instructor and the other group that was still out there all cheered.

To be honest, it was exhilarating. Not the idea of killing the bird, but the fact that I aimed for a target and hit it, and the fact that I was going to get to keep the bird for dinner, put me at ease about it. My adrenaline was pumping now.

"You want to keep going?" my instructor asked.

"Yes!" I said.

We moved deeper into the field, and the dog rustled up two more birds. I quickly hit them both. I shouted to the group, "I got three!" The feeling of redemption was awesome. With each shot, the dog would grab the bird, and the instructor would put them in a bag that was wrapped around my waist. Seeing the bag of birds felt weird, but I blocked it out. I pushed myself to do something I had never done before, and I didn't give up.

After we all were done hunting, they showed us how to remove the innards and cut the pieces of meat that we were going to freeze and take home with us, and once again I blocked out the queasy feeling I had and cleaned my birds. When I made it back to town, I showed Tanesha the meat.

"Where did you get that?" she asked.

"I shot it," I replied. "This is going to be our dinner."

She looked slightly disgusted, but she helped me cook the meat. It didn't taste as good as chicken, but with some hot sauce on it, it wasn't too bad.

MY TIME AT Fish and Wildlife was going as well as I could have imagined. I'd helped the department create policies around purchases and compliance, crafted a $12-million-plus annual budget, implemented reorgs, and made sure the agency met EEO standards. Every day that I left home and took that drive from the West End to my beautiful office on the lake, I reflected on how blessed I was. Tanesha helped me manage my diabetes because I had to be out of town all day for work. She bought me a big lunch box, and every morning she filled it with meals for breakfast, lunch, and dinner, plus fruit for snacks in between. We stopped worrying about our lights being cut off. Everything felt right with the world.

Still, I never wanted to forget the mission that led me to law school: using my experience and my position to help improve lives in the West End. Now that I was a director in a statewide agency, I felt even more responsibility to help break down barriers for folks living in underserved communities like my own. One of the biggest frustrations I had about living in the West End was the fact that we were practically on the river, but because of divestment in our neighborhoods and infrastructure, it seemed like we were walled off from the main waterway that drives our city. There had been a time when both Shawnee Park and Chickasaw Park had sand beaches. The parks were segregated, but Black residents were able to go to Chickasaw Park and feel the waves of the Ohio River lap against their feet. When the lock system was put in to allow larger boats to travel the portion of the river that wraps around the West End of Louisville, the higher boat traffic and changes in the water patterns eroded the beaches away. Louisville had invested in restoring the downtown waterfront but hadn't done the same for the West End. As a result, a large wall of trees lined the river, and the eroded banks became a steep twenty-foot drop-off. It was like the river no longer existed for us.

Working at Fish and Wildlife helped me understand the health benefits of being connected to outdoor spaces. When anglers talked about their time on the water or hunters talked about the quiet time spent waiting for a deer or turkey, I heard the deep reverence in their voices. It was a sacred experience, and it was something that we were completely deprived of in the hood. I talked about my concerns with Councilwoman Cheri Bryant Hamilton, the councilperson for our neighborhood in the West End. She shared the same frustration and told me about her aim of getting a boat ramp put in at Shawnee Park so that people could finally get access to the river again.

"I think I know what to do," I told her.

The engineering division of Fish and Wildlife builds boat ramps all over Kentucky. As a director, I was able to join the executive team in proposing new projects for the agency. I worked with Councilwoman Hamilton to get the details for the plan together and then presented the idea of having Fish and Wildlife build a boat ramp at Shawnee Park at our annual meeting to discuss priorities for the upcoming year. The proposal was unanimously adopted on the spot. I don't recall a single objection. In fact, the engineering director came over to me and said, "This is a great idea. I've been wanting to do something like this, but we didn't know who to talk to or where to start." And as the meeting wrapped up, the commissioner took me aside and said, "Charles, I want to help make sure that you get this done." And he did.

The West End boat ramp project would take years to reach completion, only opening to the public in the spring of 2021, long after I'd left my office at Fish and Wildlife. We also successfully got a second boat ramp installed in the West End in the Portland neighborhood, just minutes from my house. Once the Portland ramp opened, I would stop by some evenings to see if anyone was using it. Every time I did, I would see some old man fishing on one side, a Black kid skipping rocks, or some people preparing to launch a canoe, and it filled my heart with so much pride. We deserved resources like this. We deserved experiences like this.

My time at the Department of Fish and Wildlife gave me a new family. To know that I could go into a space where practically no one else looked like me or came from where I came from and still build bonds and accomplish big goals was the greatest affirmation. I met hunters and found people who cared about their families, loved sports, and took pride in Kentucky like I did. I came into it seeking to get my bearings in a new environment and left knowing the people behind the work. Our political differences were irrelevant. We all wanted to take care of Kentucky's natural environment. That's what brought us together.

Working in the department gave me a deeper respect for the hood, too. Before taking that job, I had never thought about the people in my community who wanted to go fishing but had no access to the river. I never thought about the students who might love archery, if only there was a program in our part of town. I never thought about the ponds in our parks that were contaminated by neighboring chemical plants. I never thought about the reasons people would want to own guns beyond killing my cousins. I never once thought about having a boat ramp in our part of town, let alone imagined that I would help get one built and that people would actually want to use it. This was a common bond that existed for folks in my hood, and one that fell in my own blind spot.

When the boat ramp was complete, Tanesha's uncles called me their hero. They loved to fish but had never had a way to do it close to home. Their genuine excitement brought a tear to my eye. I was so proud I had done this for them. The leadership at Fish and Wildlife was so excited to help me get this project done, too. They wanted more people to enjoy the outdoors and didn't know how to start forming connections with places like the West End. It wasn't that they didn't care; they just didn't know where to begin. There was so much goodness right around me that I was not even aware existed. We were blocked from opportunities, but that didn't mean we didn't want them.

CHAPTER 13

DREAMING BIG

IT WAS MAY 2015. I was sitting on the couch, getting ready to leave the house and grab something to eat, when Tanesha came down the steps and sat beside me. I looked over, ready to ask what she wanted, and before I got the words out she handed me a pregnancy test and whispered, "I'm pregnant, Charles."

I heard her, but the words didn't register. Our eyes met, and she smiled and said it again. "I'm *pregnant*, Charles."

"Really?" I said with a big grin.

I was shocked but strangely at peace. This time, I felt ready. I looked down and stared at the test, thinking about how far we'd come as a family. When Kaylin was born, Tanesha and I hadn't really known each other, but over the last eight years we'd grown together and found love. This new baby was a testament to that, and although we hadn't been planning for it, I knew it was a blessing. We sat for a while, and she rested her head on my shoulder. I told her, "We'll be okay."

The pregnancy changed everything. The prospect of having a bigger family forced me to evaluate my long-term career plans. Working at Fish and Wildlife was more than a job. It was a whole universe and a way of life unto itself, and to be an effective leader there required me to make a full-time commitment. I didn't want to leave, but staying would mean more and more time away from my growing family. At the same time, as much as I loved working on the issues facing the agency, after my work on the West End boat ramp I found myself looking homeward. If I was going to continue to make Fish and Wildlife my world, I wouldn't have time to do the deeper work in and for the West End. I wouldn't have the time to go to neighborhood meetings and stay up-to-date on things that were happening, to be an advocate for all the issues I was most passionate about. Part of me was feeling more and more like God was calling me back to the West End.

On the other hand, Fish and Wildlife represented stability, and in some ways it was an escape. It felt good to be accepted at the department. It felt great having a stable income for my family. The exposure to Kentucky's beauty was amazing, too. Tanesha and I even considered moving out of the hood and closer to Frankfort so that I could give more time to my work and less to my commute. I found myself enjoying the fact that I worried less about the shootings in my hood. From time to time, I even caught myself thinking, "Maybe the challenges of the West End aren't my burden to carry right now. Maybe it's my turn to unplug and be comfortable with my family."

I kept going back and forth. I told my mom that I was considering a change. We both started to pray about it, and then, out of the blue, I got a call from Congressman Yarmuth's office that helped make the decision for me. The congressman's office was assembling a team to join President Obama on an upcoming visit to Louisville that was a part of his push to highlight advancements in science and technology across the country. It would be his first trip back to Louisville since the 2008 presidential primary. Because of the work I'd done in the city, they wanted me on the team. Naturally, I accepted immediately.

The day the president arrived, I walked through the security clearance at Standiford Field at Louisville International Airport, and the Secret Service and the White House advance team handed me the keys to the car I was assigned to drive, along with a lapel pin that would identify me as a member of the motorcade. All of the vehicles were white. Mine was a brand-new Dodge Charger. Initially, I was assigned to drive one of the visiting ambassadors, but as everyone was scrambling to get into vehicles, the ambassador ended up in a different truck, and I ended up driving around Valerie Jarrett's luggage for the day. I didn't mind one bit.

We drove in a line out onto the tarmac and waited for Air Force One to land. The sky was gloomy. A few drops of rain sprinkled on the windshield of the car as I stared at the low sky. We had been hearing that the visit might be postponed at the last minute due to some national security issue that was breaking that morning, so as we waited on the tarmac, I kept my fingers crossed that he would actually be able to make it. Then, suddenly, the clouds parted, and that big, big Boeing 747 nose came through. For me, it was like time froze. As the plane landed and circled around, I read the words UNITED STATES OF AMERICA emblazoned on the side as I fumbled with my phone trying to hurry up and grab a picture.

We were asked to turn our vehicles on and be ready to drive, but all I could do was watch the steps of the plane, waiting with anticipation. One by one, staffers and dignitaries came down the steps, each of them getting my hopes up. Then, finally, I saw the silhouette of a tall, slender man trotting down the steps. I was alone in the car, but that didn't stop me from shouting "That's him!" and clapping my hands in excitement. The president moved with ease, his hand in his pocket, then glided into the presidential limousine, just as smooth in person as he was on TV. We weren't allowed to call anyone while in the motorcade, but I wanted so bad to call Tanesha and my mom. I could hardly believe I would get the chance to meet him.

We drove the same route I used to travel from high school back to the West End, along the same roads that had helped to segregate our city. When we made it downtown, we filed onto East Main Street, right in the heart of the neighborhood, to visit a business called Indatus, a tech company that created cloud-based applications for business and also provided coding training. It was a chance for President Obama to showcase that innovation was happening in places that got overlooked—places like my own hometown.

Outside the venue, I waited with the vehicle to be ready to help the president get to his next location. After about thirty minutes, a Secret Service member knocked on my window. I was told to come around to a back entrance. Once I walked in, I saw him. He was standing in front of a row of flags, shaking hands with VIP guests. I was put in a line with the other drivers to get the chance to speak with him. Watching as the line got shorter and shorter, I knew I would only have a few moments to talk to him. My mind had gone completely blank, so I scrambled through my thoughts to figure out what I wanted to say. I was so nervous to see him up close, my hands were sweating. But I finally worked up the courage and walked up to him.

"Mr. President," I said, looking him in the eyes. "My name is Charles Booker."

He tilted his head up, a big smile on his face. Then he squinted his eyes a little, extended his hand, and said, "It is a pleasure to meet you, Charles."

"Sir, I just wanted to say welcome to my city. I was a delegate for you in 2012. Now I'm working in state government to be a voice for my community, and I want to thank you for showing me what is possible."

He squeezed my hand. "Well, Charles. I'm proud of you, young man. Let's take a picture together."

He was a little taller than me, and his hand was slender but strong. I lifted my chin, fixed my tie, and smiled as big as I could for the picture. It was like I had completed a journey, one that started the day I stood in line with Grandad to vote for him, continued with my trip to the DNC, and had come to its conclusion here. Shaking his hand felt like, *Wow, he's real. And if he's real, then these ideas I have could be real someday, too.*

When our day was finished, I returned to the airport with the motorcade and sat in amazement as the president trotted back up the steps and turned to wave at us before the door closed behind him. Once the plane was out of view, I called Mom to tell her everything.

Shaking the president's hand reminded me of the inspiration I felt in 2008 when he was elected. My decision about Fish and Wildlife was made for me. I knew where I belonged. I knew it wasn't my time to unplug and be comfortable. I was in the spaces I found myself in for a reason, and I needed to do all I could to lead for change. It wasn't time to leave the West End. It wasn't time to look away. It was time to dig in.

THE MAYOR'S GALLERY sits in the center of Louisville's Metro Hall. It's a grand space filled with paintings and figurines made by local artists, including some high school students, as well as a rare copy of the Declaration of Independence. The floor is made from pieces of glass that reflect hues of red and orange up into the large rotunda overhead. Every office in the mayor's suite connects off of the gallery, and it's where I found my office the first morning I showed up for my new job as a project manager for the mayor's Innovation Delivery Team.

Once I made the decision to leave Fish and Wildlife, one of the first guys I reached out to was Ted Smith, a chief officer for Mayor Greg Fischer and a brilliant guy I'd met while working for the Metro Council. It was Ted who told me about a fellowship in the Mayor's Office with the Bloomberg Innovation Delivery team. The task of the team was to assess challenges in the city and utilize a multimillion-dollar grant from Bloomberg Philanthropies to research and implement creative ways to solve those challenges. It sounded exactly like what I was looking for.

Even though I knew I was making the right decision, leaving Fish and Wildlife wasn't easy. I wasn't leaving a job; I was leaving my new family. Getting to know these folks was transformative for me. I had always figured that they thought they were in an exclusive club and didn't want someone like me in it. But over time I learned that they were regular people who loved, cared, cussed, and cooked. They danced and sang. They believed in prayer. Just like I did. I was going back home to be with my family, but I was going to cherish those bonds I'd made. The responsibility I felt for the West End I now felt for the state as a whole. I knew that somehow, someday, I would find a way to step up for all of Kentucky again, but at the moment God was calling me back home.

On my first day at my new job, my heart was bursting with excitement. I'd walked through the Mayor's Gallery before, but stepping foot in it now, empowered by my new position to actually make change, I appreciated it so much more. I took the elevator up to the top floor and made my way into a makeshift workspace in what appeared to be an unused area of Metro Hall. The office suite was a big open room. It was dusty and dim, but it was where ideas that could help our city would first see the light of day.

When I arrived, the team was about to start a meeting. Ted briskly walked in behind me and rolled up to the big table in the conference room. "All right, everyone," he said. "We've been focusing on issues of neighborhood blight, overcrowding in our jails, neighborhood Wi-Fi, and vacant lots. What ideas do you have? Dream big!"

We started going around the room and somebody said, "The internet is terrible in the West End."

"All right," Ted said. "How do we fix it?"

A few ideas bounced around until somebody said, "We've got trash cans on every corner. What if we put solar-powered Wi-Fi hotspots on trash cans to create a mesh network?"

"Awesome! See who can make it happen."

And that's what we did, all morning. We brainstormed on everything from pollution to overcrowded jails to broken sidewalks. Anything that somebody could be pissed off about, we tried to figure out a way to create an innovative solution. Then, because we were a special division in the Mayor's Office, once we had an idea, we had the latitude to study it and work with various city departments to implement it.

One problem I was keen to tackle were the abandoned houses all over the West End. On most blocks, you could find a home with a rotting roof and boarded-up windows. In places where the old houses had caught fire, you'd even find vacant lots overgrown with weeds and overrun by rodents. My mom's house on 35th had a longtime rental home beside it. One family after another moved in, never staying long. Eventually, the house sat empty for a long time, attracting roaches and mice that kept migrating to our place. I hated it.

Recounting all of this at the table with the team, I made the case for us taking on the issue of vacant and abandoned properties. They agreed, and during that summer, we got a lot done. In an effort to take out the tall grass and replace it with something more manageable, we researched species of plants that don't grow beyond a few inches in height. We put together tool shares, where residents could rent lawn mowers. For the vacant lots, we organized weeks of outreach in the West End to see what residents wanted done with them. We turned one vacant lot into a public art space with a community orchard.

Taken together, those initiatives amounted to a series of solid base hits, but I knew we needed a home run, and one project in particular looked like a walk-off grand slam. One of the largest vacant lots was a twenty-six-acre parcel blocks from my mom's house. It was an old to-bacco company site at 30th and Market that had shut down during the industry's decline. It had been designated as a brownfield, mean-ing the land was so contaminated that a special clean-up would be required to rehabilitate it for development. Some developers wanted to transform it into a regional hub for healthy, Kentucky-grown pro-duce; they'd named the project FoodPort. Since access to fresh food was high on the wish list for the West End, I was particularly inter-ested in it.

The site itself was a complete mess. It had been abandoned and run-down for most of my life; I'd ridden my bike by it all the time when I was a kid. Overgrown weeds had turned into trees. The grass was taller than me, making it impossible to see the other end of the street. There were mounds of broken concrete, syringes, shattered glass, moldy couches, tires. The plants spilled over the sidewalk and into the street, making a walk on that sidewalk more like a trek through a jungle. Whenever I passed by, I often crossed the street so the bugs and rodents wouldn't jump on me.

Walking on the site for the first time was actually breathtaking. I was blown away by how huge it was. Once I got past the grass and the trees that blocked the view from the sidewalk, I could see large paved areas where cars used to park, an old shed, and a small building that looked like it had been the security booth. I walked around that lot all afternoon the same way my mom walked through our old, dilapidated house for the first time when I was seven years old. All around me was blight and decay, but I saw only potential. The site was perfectly located, adjacent to two bus lines, and its sheer size alone conjured up hundreds of possibilities.

As I learned more about the FoodPort project, I was deeply intrigued by the idea of helping our corner stores and groceries get more fresh produce on their shelves while simultaneously helping small family farms and local business owners scale up by investing in the West End. I felt that if it were done right, it had the potential to be the most transformative project for the West End in my lifetime. I didn't know much about the developers or the politics behind the project, but I knew I wanted to see more fresh, healthy groceries in our community. I decided to start going to the neighborhood planning meetings to learn more. It wasn't technically part of my job. Mostly I was going as myself: a resident of the West End. But the fact that I held a position with the Mayor's Office meant that my presence counted for more than the average citizen.

The first meeting was held on a Thursday evening at the Shawnee Clubhouse, which sits on the Shawnee Golf Course, one of the few public courses in the city and the only one in the West End. I did see some Black golfers there from time to time, but I personally never felt like this place was for us. We never went onto the course itself. The clubhouse, however, was a different story. It was where we met for community meetings and events. My high school graduation party was held there, and every month, Metro Councilwoman Cheri Bryant Hamilton held the 5th District community meeting there to update residents on what was happening in the city.

After I parked outside, I got out of my car and ran up to hold the door open for some elderly residents who were making their way in. The crowd for this FoodPort meeting was largely the same people that always came to the neighborhood meetings. People like Ms. Bonnie Cole, who was president of the Shawnee Neighborhood Association. There were maybe a couple of people there my age, but for the most part, everyone who attended was over sixty.

The meeting was being held by Seed Capital Kentucky, the developers of the FoodPort project, and the residents were as curious about this project as I was. The room was filled with chairs lined up in rows facing a projector screen and large white tables where the FoodPort team was seated. There were a few seats open in the back, so I quietly made my way to one of them. "Hey, young man!" whispered a few of the elders, smiling.

Caroline Heine, the co-founder of Seed Capital, was leading the discussion. Right from the jump, I could tell she was in trouble. She was talking like she was in a boardroom giving a grant presentation for investors. "You see, it's going to create this much energy for the grid" and "We'll be able to connect additional farmers to the commercial industry so that their produce can get into grocery stores." It was all very technical. Meanwhile, the questions people were throwing at her were all personal. "What does this mean for me?" and "How are we gonna get some food?"

For decades, developer after developer had come through offering folks in the West End some great new deal. Time after time, it almost always fell through. So a lot of people were justifiably skeptical of Seed Capital's motives and legitimacy. It reminded me of my own effort to introduce myself to the employees at Fish and Wildlife, with the onus on Caroline as the outsider to earn the trust and respect of this community. As I sat there listening, I could feel the conversation growing tense. Caroline said that her organization sincerely wanted to hear our concerns and ideas, but several of the residents simply didn't believe her.

The main point of contention arose over news articles that had recently been published outlining plans for the FoodPort to install anaerobic digesters, a new technology that would break down food waste and convert it into methane gas that would be fed back into the city's energy grid as renewable energy, which would in turn lower utility costs for surrounding residents. It sounded like a win-win on paper, but these digesters were a foreign technology for the residents. The notion of methane gas collecting onsite immediately raised fears of an explosion, and considering the West End's history with toxic plants and deadly emissions, it was understandable why some residents were against the idea.

I was used to loud neighborhood meetings, but in that room it was getting hard to hear anyone speak. Spirits were running high. At one point I heard Caroline saying they would be willing to consider removing the digesters from the project, but her attempts at compromise were being drowned out by the raised voices in the room. "What is this project?!" "Where did you all come from?!" "How is this going to help me get food?!" "Why would you bring methane gas to our neighborhood?!" "Do you want this project in your own neighborhood?!" "We've had enough chemical explosions!" "This ain't even about us. They just tryin' to get rich off us!"

Caroline stood before the room like a deer in headlights. Realizing that nothing she said would help, she stood quietly while the questions and comments piled up. Against a sea of upset Black residents, this poor white woman stood defenseless. There were plenty of valid questions about the aim of this shiny new project, but a lot of the anger and frustration directed at Caroline was due to forces beyond her control. It had built up over generations from people who were sick and tired of being ignored and taken advantage of by big-money developers who got rich while we stayed broke. Pretty soon folks were getting up and preparing to leave. The meeting was falling apart, and it looked like the whole project was about to go belly-up.

As I sat there, all I could think was, *Well, here we go again. This is what always happens.* Because it was true that many of the West End's development problems stemmed from people exploiting us or straight-up ripping us off. But it was also true that so many positive things never came to fruition simply because the people of the neighborhood and the leaders of the political and business class regularly missed the opportunities to communicate and cooperate. I believed the FoodPort was a good opportunity. I didn't want to see us lose it just because we were so used to being hurt. We had to figure out a way to do something different.

Something compelled me to stand up and speak. It wasn't something I normally did at public meetings like these, but the urgency in that moment drove me to my feet. I saw the development walking out the door, and I saw the disappointment that was sure to follow. The two sides weren't that far apart, but they were shouting past each other. The room needed to hear from someone. It had to be me. So I stood up. I waved my arms to grab everyone's attention, and then I took the floor.

"Hey!" I hollered. "Listen up, everybody!"

Everyone stopped and looked at me in anticipation. The room got quiet. People sat back down. "Go ahead and speak, Charles!" one of the residents shouted out. Several of the others looked at me with a smile. I was one of their neighborhood children. They knew my experience in local and state government, and many of them had been there to lift me up with every step in my career. They trusted my perspective.

"I hear you," I said. "I hear your concerns. But we need fresh, healthy food in our community. This is something we all know. These developers are looking to come into our community, redevelop this contaminated land, and turn it into a place that will allow all of us to get more access to healthy produce. I agree with everyone here that they have to earn our trust, but it looks to me like they want to work with us. You say you don't want the digesters, and I'm hearing the presenter here saying they would be willing to remove the digesters. If we all think that is a good idea and still would like to see a project that helps us all get more healthy food, then I encourage you all to take them up on their offer. Let them hear your concerns and let them earn your trust by responding. If there is a way to remove these digesters and work together, we should explore if that is actually possible."

Once I was done, many of the elders in the room seemed to calm down. Some of the residents started to applaud. The rest of the meeting went much smoother. People shared their concerns, and Caroline listened attentively. Once the meeting was over, she made her way to me and gave me her card, thanking me for speaking up that day. Then Councilwoman Hamilton walked over and shook my hand. "Charles," she said, "you did a good thing today. We needed you to do what you did."

AFTER THAT CONTENTIOUS community meeting with Seed
Capital Kentucky, I had the chance to sit down with Caroline Heine
and the Seed Capital board chair, Stephen Reily. I pressed them on
the project and voiced the concerns I had heard from residents about
this being another broken promise in the making. They told me they
were creating a community council where residents could learn about
every aspect of the project and help make decisions about it. They
would also remove the digesters from the plan. I said I thought they
were moving in the right direction.

I walked away from that meeting hopeful about what the development could do for the West End. My fellowship with the Innovation
Delivery Team was scheduled to end shortly thereafter, but I enjoyed
the work I was doing trying to get the FoodPort off the ground. So I
had an idea: I would pitch Seed Capital on the idea of hiring me to
help build the FoodPort. I reached out to Caroline to make my proposal, and ironically, she suggested the exact same thing. So when my
fellowship ended, I transitioned seamlessly from one to the other.

My title with Seed Capital Kentucky was Director of Strategic
Partnerships. My responsibility was to help the organization build relationships across the Commonwealth, starting with my own community in the West End. I headed up the FoodPort Community
Council, a collective of residents from each of the nine neighborhoods that make up the West End. The council, which convened at
least once a month, was tasked with giving input on every aspect of
the development as well as helping to define the sustainable benefits
FoodPort should provide to the community. We were going to create
one of the city's first community benefit agreements: a contract with
the residents to codify the promises the organization was making. If
we were successful, we would create a template for other developments in the city.

To get the project moving, I traveled across Kentucky talking to
local growers about the opportunity to work together to compete in
the commercial market. As I spoke with farmers around the state, my
message was simple: Your farms grow the produce Kentuckians need
to live healthy lives, and in communities like my own, we don't have as

many open acres to farm, but we eat what you grow. By working together, we can help family farms increase their production and profits and also increase access to fresh, healthy food in the places often referred to as food deserts. We had a common bond, I explained, and if we joined together we could create new economic opportunities for everyone. The chance to tie the hood to the rural parts of Kentucky I'd grown to love at Fish and Wildlife meant so much to me. It was fulfilling to sit down with older white men and share this idea and then to see them nod their heads in excitement. We had the potential to do something big.

The same thing was happening in the West End, too. The community was embracing the fact that the developers pulled out the plans for anaerobic digesters, and there was some rare momentum in the neighborhoods around the site. That autumn we threw a huge community festival called the Harvest Festival, where the block alongside the proposed FoodPort was blocked off for a day of music, games, vendors, and hayrides. There was even a pumpkin patch for kids—the first time I had ever seen a pumpkin patch in the hood. Excitement for the project was riding high. People were starting to believe that something good was going to happen.

Change was coming to the West End, but the neighborhood wasn't the only thing changing. A thought had been planted in my head the night of that first FoodPort meeting at the Shawnee Clubhouse. I hadn't been looking for a chance to be a community leader that night. I was simply trying to do my part. But that moment when I stood up and felt everyone's eyes on me, it reminded me of the anticipation I had always felt waiting for my mom to sing or preach at church. It reminded me of the audiences I stood before in school as I made presentations before assemblies at the University of Louisville. It reminded me of those nervous moments standing before the Appropriations Committee at Metro Council to advocate for grants to neighborhood projects. It reminded me of the way residents looked at Cory Booker in that documentary when he was running for mayor—or the way I looked at President Obama when I shook his hand. It reminded me of all those times I was the only person in the room that knew what it was like to be a young Black man from the hood. When I stood up that day, I started to realize that everything I had accomplished and seen in my young career was pointing me in a new direction. I felt like I wasn't merely being called to serve my community; I was being called to inspire, speak for, and lead my community.

CHAPTER 14

READY TO RUN

W HEN I FIRST went into public service, the thought of running for office myself never occurred to me. I don't think I ever even considered it until I started working for David Tandy's office at Metro Council. I was all of twenty-seven years old at the time, still volunteering for Senator Neal, running errands and parking cars, and one evening Neal said to me, "You ever think about running for office, Charles?"

"No," I said. "I don't think I ever have."

"Well, I won't be in office forever," he said, "and I want you to know I've been thinking about you."

When he said that, I didn't show a big response, but on the inside I was blown away. An actual legislator had told me that he thought I could do something as big as run for office. I was stunned that someone of his stature would think of me that way, and of course once the seed was planted, I found myself thinking more and more, *Well, maybe . . . yeah. Maybe I could run for office someday.*

I didn't see elected office as the only route for change, but I knew it was critical. I also understood that it aligned with my strengths as a leader: being able to craft policy, build unlikely coalitions, speak through the noise, navigate complex challenges, and see solutions to systemic problems. I was taught that God would have messengers in every venue, including politics, and I gradually grew to believe that, someday, public office was the arena in which I would minister.

Working for Tandy, the things that I loved most about that job—

responding to complaints and creating a legislative vision—were the very things that made it clear to me I didn't want to be a staffer all my life. I had my own vision for leadership, and I knew I wanted to find a way to bring that vision to pass. I even started planning my policy platform and my brand, including my campaign colors. I landed on crimson and Tiffany blue. Crimson because, in addition to being my fraternity's color, it was a color that represented soul and depth and maturity. The Tiffany blue was an idea given to me by a fellow legislative aide. It was a color that was bright and lively but not threatening. It seemed to complement my combination of boldness and deep conviction with a sense of quality and inclusion. I found a necktie with those colors, cut up little squares from the material, and had my mom sew them into lapel bars. I wore them on my suit jackets every day. In my own mind, I was laying a foundation. As I did good work in the community, I wanted people to see those colors. By the time I ran and used them for my campaign, people would naturally associate them with my leadership. When I shared all of this with Tandy, he smiled and said, "Wow, man. You're getting yourself ready."

I was doing just that. And as the years went by, I saw running not merely as possible but necessary. When I first met Senator Neal and the elder Black leaders of the West End, I was in awe of them, their accomplishments, and their status in the community. But as I spent more time away in Frankfort, I was able to gain a deeper perspective. Since the push for transformational change in the 1960s and 1970s, it seemed to me that our leaders had assumed more of a gatekeeping role to protect what limited power the Black community had, more or less accepting the de facto segregation of the West End as a permanent fixture.

I also felt like the old guard had little trust or hope that the greater community could mobilize to change things, which resulted in a small group of Black leaders who held a degree of power not shared with others. The broader community in the West End was kept in the dark while that handful of Black leaders worked with white leaders on development and policy decisions. I'd received a powerful lesson in this when I started helping Senator Neal launch an organization he named the African American Initiative, or AAI.

"Charles," he told me, "I want to create an organization to bring information to the public focusing on all of the issues that impact our community. As a senator, I can bring experts to dig into these issues."

I lit up when I heard that. This was a program that would finally break down the silos of information and equip our community with knowledge about what was really going on so that we could create an agenda for real change.

"And once we bring this information to the community, we can help them shape an agenda!" I said, enthusiastically.

He shook his head no. "This isn't about determining what happens after they get the information," he said. "It's just about giving it to them."

Honestly, I was disappointed. Simply giving people information wasn't enough. Our community had been crippled for so long, it needed people on the inside of the power structure, like Senator Neal, to help them understand what to do with the information.

Everything Neal did, it seemed, was about making the best life we could inside the status quo, but it was never really about changing the status quo. There was no expectation of things ever changing. Kentucky was majority-white and increasingly Republican, and they had the power. It was what it was, and you did your best with it.

The AAI felt like an incredible opportunity to mobilize that I didn't want us to miss. But as the years went by, I noticed more and more missed opportunities like that one. Senator Neal often talked about his age and regularly mentioned that new leaders like me would eventually have to take over. I do believe he meant it, but I don't think he expected that time to come anytime soon. Whenever we did talk about my running, it was always for the House.

Kentucky's 43rd State House District had been held by State Representative Darryl Owens for many years. Owens was a good man, one of the few people that I looked forward to hearing speak on the House floor. He didn't always talk, but when he did, people listened. Although he was an elder in the West End, over the years I began to see him as a friend. The fact that we were frat brothers didn't hurt.

For years, Owens had been making noises about stepping down, but then, like Neal, he never would. In both of the election cycles that followed, first in 2012 and again in 2014, Owens decided to stay in office. But by December of 2015, as we were heading into the 2016 election, Owens was growing increasingly adamant about this being his last term, and Senator Neal made me feel like I had the inside track to be his replacement. "Charles," he said. "I'm telling you this because we trust you. Rep. Owens is telling me he plans to retire. I think you should get yourself ready to run and ask him to support you. I can't speak for him, but you should see if he'd support you. At least, that's what I would do."

The timing couldn't have been better. For the moment, I was stuck in a holding pattern at Seed Capital. Our good-faith efforts on the FoodPort hit a snag when the residents learned that the city was discussing another anaerobic digester at a distillery in the area. It was a different site that had nothing to do with ours, but the mayor and his economic development team were facing intense pressure from residents to keep anaerobic digesters outside of the city limits and the city put an indefinite hold on executing any development agreements. We had already spent a few million dollars in site assessments and mitigation work, but the construction couldn't start until the city transferred ownership of the site. Due to circumstances entirely beyond our control, everything had momentarily stalled out. I continued to lobby with different partners and constituencies around the state, but there wasn't a whole lot for me to do, and with Tanesha getting closer to giving birth to our second little girl, I felt it was time to make the bold move I had started contemplating after that first FoodPort meeting.

I started quietly laying the groundwork of a campaign so I'd be ready the moment Rep. Owens announced his retirement. Then, right before the holidays, I stopped by his law office in Old Louisville to touch base and take his temperature on what his plans were; in my mind, this was the meeting where we would talk out the timeline of how he would retire and then endorse me to succeed him.

I rang the buzzer outside and waited as he walked down the hallway toward me. He welcomed me inside, offered me a drink, and motioned for me to have a seat. We spent a few minutes talking about college basketball, as always. Then he got down to business. "Well, Charles," he said, "I know you're here to talk about running for my seat. And I was planning on retiring. I really was. But the Speaker is pushing all of us incumbents to stay in so we can keep as many seats as we can. So I won't be leaving—not this term."

It was not what I was expecting to hear. I was hurt, confused, and deeply frustrated. I felt that both men, Neal and Owens, had been nudging me toward this exact moment, and now the rug was being pulled out from under me. With Owens, I didn't take it as personally; I think he was genuinely ambivalent about whether or not to retire. With Neal, I saw it differently. I felt like he knew I was getting restless, and maybe he'd been suggesting Owens's seat for me as an incentive to sit still and "be patient" and "wait my turn."

Beyond my personal disappointment, it didn't seem like this decision was in the best interest of the community. Owens and Neal both knew the 43rd District was one of the few majority-Black districts in the state and was nearly 90 percent Democrat, which meant it was more or less impossible for this seat to succumb to the Republican wave without some unprecedented organizing effort, which we knew the Republicans were not going to do. The disappointment hit me in my stomach, nearly knocking the smile off my face, but I managed to keep my composure. It was his decision to make, and I could only respect that. I had so much reverence for the man that I wasn't prepared to express anything but graciousness that he was even talking to me.

Still, as much as I appreciated Owens's voice and his lifetime of service, I also felt it was time for new leadership. I was impatient about the change I believed our community needed. It was hard to balance the respect I had for him with the growing feeling that it was time he handed off the baton. I pushed back, explaining that all the trends suggested Republicans would take the House, which meant that it would be better to succeed him while Democrats still had the leadership. Otherwise, he would be leaving an open seat after Republicans took the majority. He acknowledged my point but repeated that his plan was to seek re-election one more time. Discouraged, I thanked him for letting me know and walked out.

I didn't know what to do. With all my years working in different levels of government, I knew that a different type of politics was possible, and I believed that a new generation of leadership could make a difference. Most of all, I thought about Kaylin and the baby Tanesha was carrying. My mom had faced hard times raising me. What was I going to do to make sure that I wouldn't be passing down the same hard times to them? I felt an urgent need to lead for change. Waiting my turn was a luxury I did not have. I called my mom and told her about Rep. Owens's change of heart. Then I got a call from Senator Neal, who knew about the meeting with Rep. Owens. I told him how the conversation had gone and told him that I felt an urgency to do something. I told him that I still felt the imperative to run.

"Charles," he said, cutting me off. "If you decide to run against Owens, I will take it personally. And if you do it, I'll have to crush you."

I couldn't believe it. He had never spoken to me that way before. It caught me completely off guard. I didn't understand it, either. To me, these offices belonged to the community, so the idea of running—even against someone I liked—didn't seem like a personal attack. In hindsight, it was a naive opinion to have. My intentions were pure, but intention and reality can be different things. There is a big difference between wanting to influence power and building your own power. By looking to run for office, I was seeking to build power, even if I didn't see it that way. The way the older generation saw it, I was trying to take power away from them that they weren't ready to relinquish. I didn't yet appreciate how personal politics is; I didn't fully grasp how people in public service vested their identity and sense of self in the offices they held. I was coming from a place of genuinely wanting things to change and knowing that more could be done. I had deep respect for both Rep. Owens and Senator Neal, but I felt something pulling on my spirit that I couldn't ignore. It was the same pull that told me I was going to law school, the same pull that gave me the words when I convinced Rep. Meeks's office to give me a congressional internship. I knew I had to run, and I couldn't wait.

I called a close friend of mine, Jacie Rowe, to ask his opinion. Jacie was a young man around my age. He wasn't from the West End, but he cared deeply about it. He was involved in city politics and had the same vision that I did about changing the system. Considering the fact that there weren't that many young Black men out there trying to be political operatives, he and I had become fast friends.

Jacie had always been a bit of a revolutionary, both in his temperament and in his politics. Anytime there was a choice between a safe option and a risky one, he'd tell you to take the risky option, and that's exactly what he did when I called. "You aren't just running to be in office," he said. "You want to be a leader. So you should run for the position that will give you the greatest platform to lead. That isn't the State House. It's the State Senate. You should run against Senator Neal."

I almost laughed in his face. The idea was absurd. But he wouldn't let up on me. For the next hour, he kept going. "Charles, this needs to happen," he said. "The community is so complacent. The leadership never changes, and then nothing ever happens, and then we don't expect anything to ever be different."

As he went on making his argument, I did my best to dismiss it. "I can't do it," I said, over and over. "There's no way I can do it."

But in the back of my mind I kept thinking, *Or . . . can I?*

Jacie stayed on me, questioning my faith and asking me if I was backing down because I didn't believe. I assured him my faith wasn't lacking. When I got off the call, I ran upstairs and talked it through with Tanesha. She thought I was crazy, but she understood why I might feel it was something I had to do. I called Mom and told her the same thing. "Baby," she said, "if you feel in your spirit that you need to run, I will support you."

In the end, Senator Neal made the decision for me, in a way. Not long after that phone call with my friend, he asked a group of young Black professionals to his house to talk about working together on different projects for the West End. The group was full of my peers.

They all walked in, bright-eyed and optimistic about the meeting; they reminded me of how excited I was the first time I attended a meeting in that basement. They asked about investing in Black businesses, stopping gun violence, and improving public education, among other issues.

"What can we do to change things right now?" one person asked.

"Nothing is changing," someone else blurted out.

But when Senator Neal responded to their questions, he didn't really answer them. He acknowledged their frustrations but essentially told the room there wasn't much he could do about the problems they were raising. Every answer was, "Well, that's going to take a long time," or "Here's why you shouldn't get your hopes up," or "There's nothing we can do about gun laws at the local level." Every answer boiled down to the fact that the Republicans held the leadership in the state senate, and the issues we cared about in the West End were pretty much on hold.

I was beyond frustrated. Here was a group asking to be inspired, asking to be mobilized as citizen lobbyists applying pressure in Frankfort. Instead of seizing that energy and harnessing it, Senator Neal gently tamped it down, explaining on issue after issue that little could be done. I dropped my head, crushed that these people had come out to his house with hope and would be leaving with disappointment. In that moment, I felt like nothing was ever going to be different until the leaders that had been holding power since before we were born passed the torch down to us.

When I first met Senator Neal almost a decade earlier, I would have laughed hysterically at the notion that I would ever challenge him directly for his seat. When I first got in his truck that morning, he took me on a trip to a place that changed my life. Pulling onto the Capitol grounds and seeing that towering rotunda had felt like traveling to outer space. Walking in next to him, I admired his poise and the smoothness of his walk, so much so that I even tried to emulate it. I walked into the Capitol with big eyes and a huge smile, unaware of the battles that were fought there. Senator Neal opened the door and gave me the chance to see on the inside. I was able to peer behind the curtain of power in Kentucky and learn the ins and outs of how to maneuver there. I appreciated every second and was relentlessly eager to learn more.

Senator Neal took a chance on me and allowed me to imagine a path bigger than I could fathom. He'd set my sights on D.C. and pushed me to explore opportunities in local government. I owed so much to him that the idea of running against him made me sick in my stomach. I loved him dearly and found myself wanting him to be proud of me in the same way I longed for my own dad to be. I didn't want to hurt him or disappoint him.

But this wasn't about any of that. I had to follow what God was putting on my heart. Life has taught me that this is the only thing that matters. With the little bit of time I have, I want to do exactly what God is calling me to do. My constant prayer in the midst of that conviction is that I hear God correctly . . . that I don't mistake my ambition for the Lord's voice. I sought within myself to make sure I was not being misled by my own will. I almost hoped I would feel that way and back out. But I didn't feel that. I knew this was real, and it was bigger than me.

Ironically, if I challenged Senator Neal, I would be following in his footsteps, challenging him the way he first took on Senator Georgia Powers when he was the young upstart refusing to be patient and wait his turn. I was now in the same position Neal had been in then. I was ready to take risks. I believed we needed to inspire people, not urge them to accept the way things were. I believed we could mobilize a movement to redefine the way politics was being done. As uncomfortable as it made me, the longer I sat with it, I couldn't resist the feeling that this was something I had to do. I made my decision.

I was not going to run for the House seat. I was going to take on my mentor. I was going to run against Senator Neal.

PART III

CHAPTER 15

T.J.'S STORY

"MY NAME IS Charles Booker. I am a husband, father, son, and dedicated servant," I said to the camera as my cousin Jarvaun shot my first campaign video. We were standing at the TARC stop in front of St. Columba church near my mom's house at 35th and Market, right where Mom and I always used to catch the bus when we didn't have a car. Jarvaun's small camera was hardly what you'd call professional grade, but the quality of the recording device didn't matter. What was important was that I had a message I needed to get out. I wanted to show how we could bring the community together. I wanted to lift up a message of how the people can come together to demand more from our elected officials. I wanted to show how an office like state senator could have a direct impact on the problems that plagued our neighborhoods.

When we first shot the video, my announcement was still pending, and Tanesha was still pregnant. "Do you really think I can do this while we bring a new life into the world?" I asked her. I knew what I was being led to do, but I also knew how much time and energy it would take to run a campaign on top of my job at Seed Capital. I was worried about making sure I could be by Tanesha's side every step of the way as she prepared to give birth to our second daughter.

"You know you're going do it anyway," Tanesha replied, understanding me all too well. I wouldn't say she was excited about the idea of my running, but she'd long since accepted the fact that this drive was simply a part of who I was. "We'll figure it out," she said. "All I know is that if you don't follow your heart and run now, you'll be miserable."

She was right. I wanted to be the best dad for my girls. At the same time, things were only getting harder in our community, and using my experience and passion to lead for a brighter future in Kentucky was part of my responsibility as a parent.

About a month after we recorded the video, Tanesha's water broke. The baby was coming a month early. We grabbed the suitcase we'd packed, dropped Kaylin off at my mom's house, and as we raced to the hospital I thought about how ready we were this time compared to when Kaylin was born. We were rushing, but we were calm. With Kaylin, I wasn't even able to be at the hospital the moment she was born. Since then, Tanesha and I had made our way through the journey of building a relationship, and now that our second daughter was coming, I was going to be there right when she opened her eyes.

Holding Prestyn for the first time was magic. When I heard her cry, I knew I'd do anything to take care of her. Despite the premature birth, the delivery was smooth, and we were able to leave the hospital after a couple of days. Kaylin wanted to carry her sister out of the hospital. "Can I do it, Mommy?" she asked, excited. We compromised on letting her carry the car seat while Tanesha was rolled out with Prestyn in her wheelchair. Kaylin carried that empty car seat with so much pride. I walked behind them, thinking about my responsibility to all three. I was going to run this race, and I was going to do it for them.

Once we were settled at home, I called Jarvaun. "We need to edit the video," I said. "Prestyn needs to be a part of this." Jarvaun agreed and came over and shot and edited some new scenes of the nursery and us holding the baby. The video was complete. Now we just had to tell Kentucky the news: The 33rd Senatorial District was actually going to have a primary this year.

I ANNOUNCED MY candidacy on Tuesday, January 26, 2016. It was the last day to file, and I walked into the Secretary of State's office in

Frankfort minutes before it closed, timing my launch video to go out simultaneously. Several of my relatives carpooled to Frankfort with me. Grandad and Mom were there. My in-laws and a few of my cousins came. Tanesha was by my side, holding Prestyn. I wanted Kaylin to be there, too, but she was at school. (As much as Tanesha supported me, she drew the line at Kaylin missing school.)

My filing sent shock waves through the Capitol, because everyone in the building knew about my relationship with Senator Neal. The news cameras followed me as I walked to file my paperwork.

"How does it feel to run against your mentor?" one reporter asked.

"This isn't about me running against Neal," I said with a smile, holding Mom's hand on one side and Tanesha's on the other. "This is about me running for the community." Which was true, but that didn't mean Senator Neal saw it the same way.

When Neal told me about his decision to challenge Senator Powers for her seat in 1979, it reminded me of what Allen Iverson used to say about getting his chance to finally play against Michael Jordan. He had so much respect for Jordan, but his love for the game was greater than his reverence for the GOAT. So when he stepped on the court, he took the ball, went at M.J., and crossed him over. On the basketball court, challenging another player is a sign of how much you respect their abilities and experience in the game.

As I prepared to challenge Neal, I felt like Allen Iverson at the top of the key. I was showing the courage to stand up and run on what I believed in. Even though it meant challenging my mentor, it felt like the deepest sign of respect. It was the student becoming the teacher. In my mind, if anyone could understand what I was preparing to do, it would be Neal.

I was mistaken. Politics, it turns out, is nothing like basketball.

In the car on the road back to Louisville, I called Neal to formally acknowledge what he surely already had heard. I wouldn't say he was angry. He was confused. He legitimately did not understand why I had decided to run against him. I explained all my reasons about needing to push harder for change, but he still couldn't fully wrap his head around it. Finally, he said, "Okay, young man. Looks like we've got a race. I'll see you on the field." It was an awkward conversation for sure.

The primary election was slated to take place on May 18, 2016, which gave me a little over sixteen weeks to bring my message to the people of the district—sixteen weeks that turned out to be a crash course in the realities of politics and power. The first speed bump I hit was the abrupt appearance of a third candidate in the race. My initial plan had been to take control of the race by drawing a clear one-to-one contrast between Neal and myself. Then Judge Toni Stringer announced her candidacy. She was from the same generation as Senator Neal but was backed by a group that was similarly frustrated with the state of things in the West End. Having her in the race complicated the simple narrative I had hoped for, but I believed my message needed to be heard and, more important, it was a message that only I could carry. I was ready to go.

The second speed bump came once I started dialing for donations and endorsements. Part of what had inspired me to run was the fact that I'd always had so many people telling me they thought I should. "Whenever you decide to run," they'd say, "I'll help you." It was a regular refrain that often came with a hug and a big smile. Then, once I announced, I quickly learned that running against a twenty-five-year incumbent meant that hardly anyone would help me. Night after night I'd sit at my kitchen table, calling and calling, but I got nothing. I called people like Ron Jones, the director of University of Louisville's Black Diamond Choir. He knew my family, and I knew he supported me, but when I called him, none of that seemed to matter. "Charles, I'm so sorry," he said. "I really am proud of you, but I can't support you against Neal."

That's how it went, call after call after call, my confidence about running a successful race battered over and over by cold, hard reality. My willingness to take a huge risk didn't mean others would take the same risk just because they liked me or worked with me. All the relationships I had built, with labor unions and community leaders, with other elected officials and wealthy families in the city, were strained by my decision to go against the grain. My running put them in an uncomfortable spot, because it forced them to make a choice about sticking with Neal and the status quo, even as I was forcing them to reckon with the shortcomings of the status quo. A lot of West End elders were even upset with me. One lady for whom I had a lot of respect told me never to call her again. A former congressional staffer called me up to say, "I'm so disappointed in you. How could you stab him in the back?" I tried to explain that I wasn't trying to stab anyone in the back; I just believed the community needed a different type of leadership that couldn't wait. She wasn't hearing it, though. To her, I broke a rule you never break.

I only crossed paths with Neal a handful of times during the campaign, and I quickly understood what was going on. He was avoiding me, treating me as if I didn't exist. It was a smart strategy, too, and it made it hard to run against him. We both knew that the contrast in our vision for the State Senate would offer a compelling choice to voters, and that mine might look favorable by comparison. He showed up at two or three candidate debates and events, but several he skipped outright, and with him never showing up it was hard to show people what that contrast was.

I'd been warned about the dirtiness of politics, the relationships that are built and destroyed, the posturing and the dirty tricks. A candidate debate was scheduled at St. Stephen Church, but I never got a formal invite. I only heard about it when several people called me to let me know that the debate had been announced on the local AM radio station. We knew that much of the leadership at St. Stephen was supporting Judge Stringer, so it wasn't a big surprise. I had to reach out to the church myself to let them know I was coming.

When it came to staffing my campaign, I knew or had met virtually every seasoned campaign operative in local Democratic politics. Almost none of them would go against Neal. I did have two close friends from college I was counting on to help me. One was Jacie Rowe, who'd pushed me to run against Neal in the first place. The other was Perry Green, a brilliant organizer who thrived on politics. Both of them worked as assistants in Councilwoman Cheri Bryant

Hamilton's office. Where Jacie was the revolutionary, Perry was bold but pragmatic. Anytime I talked to them Jacie would tell me why I should take a risk, and Perry would tell me the consequences to consider. They balanced each other, and between the two of them I usually found enough helpful clarity to make a plan.

The three of us had agreed years before that whenever I ran, we would all come together to win the race. When I announced, however, Jacie had to be out in California and couldn't come back to town, so Perry and I made do. We found a couple other young people unafraid to challenge the status quo, and together we mapped out our strategy.

In terms of fundraising, for a state-level campaign like mine, the rule of thumb is that you want to be able to spend at least a dollar for each resident of the district. The average population of a State Senate district in Kentucky at the time was a little over one hundred thousand people. We raised $16,000, which is only slightly better than raising nothing. I made most of my campaign literature at home, designing quarter-page flyers on Microsoft Word, tailored for every church service and event I attended. I had mounds of white cardstock at my house, and I printed everything on that. I couldn't afford campaign stickers, so I bought sheets of labels from Kinko's and printed my logo on them. The adhesive on the back of the labels wasn't the best to use on clothes, so they regularly fell off while I was walking and shaking hands, and I would never notice in time to grab it before it hit the ground.

There's a rule in politics that says you need to touch people at least seven times for them to remember you. That includes literature, phone calls, yard signs, canvassing, TV, radio, events, and any other way you can find to get your name, platform, and vision in front of them. To make the kind of personal connections you need, there is no substitute for getting out there and making them yourself: talking to people, hearing their concerns, and showing them you're the best person to address those concerns. Since we didn't have many volunteers to help out and go door to door, in the end the field team was me. But we made it work. Perry and I both knew how to cut turfs to canvass using Votebuilder, and because of my work with Neal over the years, I knew well the areas where people had never had a campaign knock on their door. I made it a priority to go to those places.

Perry went with me occasionally, but many times I was alone, walking up every street, knocking on every door. When you're by yourself, it's tough trying to keep up with the streets and addresses all while holding a stack of literature. I was pretty good at it after years of canvassing, but it was still a challenge.

Some days it went well, like the day I met Ms. Nannie Bibbs. I was canvassing in the Russell neighborhood, walking through a small cluster of older homes that were divided by a sidewalk instead of a street. No one answered until I got to the last house, where a little old lady with pretty gray curls and thin-framed glasses resting on her nose appeared at the door. "Good afternoon! Are you Ms. Nannie Bibbs?" I asked as I glanced at my sheet to make sure I had the name correct.

"Why yes, that's me," she replied. I started to introduce myself, and she immediately cut me off. "I know who you are, baby! I heard you on a radio interview. Son, I had never heard of you before, but when I heard that interview, I knew you were something special. You remind me of Obama. Not only do you have my vote, but for the first time in years, I am going to get out and volunteer for you!"

She was absolutely fired up. Seeing this elder have genuine excitement for new leadership gave me hope. From that day on, Ms. Nannie would regularly send me words of encouragement. She came to my events. She would call into WLOU to talk about me. She became an outspoken advocate on Facebook, which was funny because she didn't know how to use it that well and she would type in all caps, so her posts were always like, "PLEASE SUPPORT CHARLES BOOKER. HE'S A MAN OF GOD." Or, if I posted a picture of my family, she'd say, "OH LOOK AT THE BABIES! I'M SO PROUD OF THIS YOUNG MAN." As much as Ms. Nannie said I inspired her, her fire truly inspired me.

Other days it didn't go so well. In fact, some days were downright brutal. The 33rd Senatorial District covered more than just the entirety of the West End. It went down into South Louisville and spanned east into the downtown business district and some surrounding neighborhoods. I'll never forget the day I had to canvas the subdivisions off Dixie Highway, which was clear on the opposite end of the 33rd Senatorial District from where I started.

This street in the South End was full of hills, so my legs were burning from the cardio. I had on my standard white dress shirt with the sleeves rolled up twice. It was a hot, humid day, and the heat was making my sticker fall off my shirt. Having some kind of sticker or identifier was important to me, especially since I was alone. I wanted people to get a chance to know who I was before they opened the door, so they'd be less inclined to open the door with a gun pointed at me.

Since I was walking alone, I was struggling to keep track of all the addresses. I had a clipboard with the walk lists in one hand and a stack of my literature in the other. After dropping a leaflet at a door, I would have to put the stack under my arm, put the clipboard against my knee, and do my best at writing notes on the walk lists. More than once I dropped my stack of literature. One time a car drove by and the driver looked on as I chased down a campaign flyer that was escaping in the wind.

I knocked on the door of one lady who had a huge dog. I couldn't see it, but the barking was loud and angry and deep. In my mind, it had to be big enough to easily knock me down. The woman didn't open the door all the way; she seemed wary. "Who are you?" she asked, struggling to keep the dog back. I quickly told her who I was and handed her a piece of literature and turned and walked off as quick as I could before she lost control of that dog. I wasn't sure if she heard anything I said. I was relieved to get away from there in one piece.

Door after door, street after street, I kept getting the same responses: "No, thanks." "Not interested." "Come back later." "Booker who?" "You're running for what?" "State senator, what's that?" Some days are like that, and it can be terribly demoralizing. Eventually you find yourself praying that nobody's home as you ring the doorbell.

By the time I got to the last house on my list, climbing up what felt like twenty steps to the front door, looking around to make sure there wasn't a dog loose, I was cooked. I'd knocked on maybe seventy doors in the last two hours. I wanted to slide my literature inside the screen door and walk away. My glucose was starting to drop, and sweat was beading up on my face. "I am going to knock on this last door," I told myself as I double-checked the list, "and then I'm getting something to eat." I pressed the doorbell and was prepared to drop my literature and leave when the door opened and a middle-aged man appeared.

"Hello. How can I help you?" He had a Spanish accent and looked like he was busy.

"Good afternoon!" I said, digging deep to get my energy back up. "My name is Charles Booker, and I am running to represent you in the Kentucky State Senate." As I was talking to him, a little child walked up to the door and stood beside him. I handed the man my literature and gave him my little speech about how I was running because I knew our district deserved better, how I was doing this for my children, and his, too.

Unexpectedly, his face lit up. "Charles," he said. "I've never had someone knock on my door to ask for my vote. No one comes to talk to us. It means so much that you actually came to our house. You have my entire family's support."

We shook hands, and I waved goodbye to the little boy. Walking back down those twenty steps, I smiled to myself. That excitement the man felt just from knowing I cared about him, that sense of hope and reassurance, was why I was running. I wanted everyone to feel the way that man felt. I wanted everyone to know that they mattered, and that we could do big things if we stood together. The breeze picked up as I walked back to my car. It was a perfect ending to a very difficult day, and on that campaign I had more difficult days than not.

I knew the odds were overwhelmingly stacked against me, but I never felt like I made a mistake joining the race. It seemed like every time I got down and needed a shot of hope, I would catch a little glimpse of something that confirmed the importance of my making this run. What I found, more often than not, was that the lack of a real competitive primary or general election in the district had bred a certain level of complacency and disinterest among voters. People knew that there was a guy in office who had been there nearly thirty years, but they couldn't really tell you what he did. Nothing people did was going to change anything, so why should they care? Just by running, I was changing that. I was taking the time to explain the legislative process, to talk to people about how the state legislature shapes the laws that govern our city, to tell them about the billion-dollar state budget, and how there were millions of dollars that get allocated to economic development and community revitalization that never make it to the West End. I got to tell people how we could work together to lobby for more investment in our community, how we should be getting more rural communities to organize with us since they have so many of the same struggles. With many of my conversations, I saw the light-bulb come on. People were beginning to see the possibility of doing something different. It felt electric.

In spite of getting minimal support, we were building momentum. People across the city started to acknowledge that there was a real primary. I never attacked Neal, but instead talked about my own vision and called out the realities of my lived experience. Eventually, even a few of the people who were upset with me for running against Neal recognized that I was doing a good job. When I showed up for events now, there were cheers and applause.

One of the debates with Senator Neal and Judge Stringer and myself was held at King Solomon Missionary Baptist Church. Rev. Charles Elliott, another local civil rights icon, was the head pastor. He'd marched with Dr. King and was a vocal leader in the West End. I wasn't sure how he felt about me running, and I expected him to voice disapproval like many of the other leaders who were involved in politics. Instead, once the debate was over, he applauded me. "I'm proud of this young man," he said, addressing a group that had stayed after the event. "We need new leadership, and young people like Booker have to step up to carry the mantle. I respect Neal, but it's time for Booker."

THE LAST SUNDAY in March was Easter. With about seven weeks left to go until the election, Tanesha and Kaylin were sitting in service watching our church's annual Easter play, which, at our church, was a major undertaking, like a Broadway production. There were life-sized crosses in the pulpit, and the actors playing Jesus and the two criminals were actually hoisted up on them, towering above the congregation. Every year, this powerful reenactment of the Crucifixion and the Resurrection kept us all glued to the stage, wiping the tears away as the story unfolded, right up to the moment when the stone was rolled back, revealing that Jesus had risen.

Sitting in service, I was inspired for the road ahead. We were celebrating new life, and that is how I saw this moment in our community. That is, until my phone vibrated. To keep up with news in the city, I'd set up my phone to alert me when our local news outlets were reporting a breaking story. I slid Prestyn over slightly so I could reach for the phone in the pocket of my blazer. It was another shooting. A young man had been shot and killed outside of a convenience store, just minutes from our church. I shook my head in disappointment. Another act of senseless violence. Another young man dead. I didn't click on the alert. These shootings happened so often, I didn't really stop to think about this one. I put the phone back in my pocket and continued watching the play.

Walking into the house after service, I noticed a few missed calls from my dad. It was unusual for him to call me, so I suspected something was wrong. I dialed him back.

"Buddy," he said solemnly. "I was calling about your cousin, T.J."

T.J. was one of my younger cousins on my dad's side, and whenever I heard his name, I thought about how the city had nearly destroyed him. A couple years earlier, a series of fights had broken out on the waterfront. The news called it a riot. A large group of teenagers were caught in the fights, and it spilled over into some adjoining streets downtown. The news cameras captured some of it. Kids were running through the streets, knocking trash cans over. A few stores were damaged with broken glass, and several people sustained injuries. All the news stories focused on what this meant for downtown Louisville and the need to address violent crime. It was a major blow to downtown development.

The mayor announced that cameras would be installed at the waterfront and made a forceful declaration that the people who instigated the events of that night would face the consequences. This led to the arrests of four young Black men, one of whom was my cousin T.J. But T.J. and the other three had never even been at the waterfront. Nonetheless, they were identified by a witness, and my cousin was arrested and put in jail for something he didn't do. Unable to afford the bail, he and the other three men stayed in jail for months. T.J. missed his high school graduation, lost his job, and nearly lost parental rights to his son.

T.J. and I had always been cool, but given our age difference we were never terribly close as kids. Our relationship really started to grow in the wake of what happened after his arrest. I couldn't call T.J. in jail, but I regularly talked to Uncle Tyrone to check on him, and T.J. would call me when he was allotted phone calls. I tried to encourage him, and he was naturally such a bright and high-spirited guy, but depression was taking hold of him and his spirit was breaking.

After a public battle and lawsuit against the city, T.J. was released. The "Misidentified Four," as they were called, in a nod to the Central Park Five, received a multi-million-dollar settlement from the city. The settlement changed T.J.'s life. Once it was split up and the attorney's fees came out, it was something like a half a million for T.J. alone. He was able to help out his family financially. He bought a brand-new red Dodge Charger, jewelry, a new wardrobe. It was like he'd made it to the NBA. But all that money put a huge target on his back. When my dad told me he was calling about T.J., I dreaded what he was going to say next.

"Buddy," he said, "T.J. was murdered today. He was shot and killed in his car, right outside of a convenience store on Oak Street."

Time slowed to a stop as I heard the words. The alert I'd seen on my phone had been about my own cousin. I slumped to the floor and sobbed. I was devastated. My soul was crushed. It was like a part of me died at that moment. Tanesha walked over and tried to ask what was wrong, but I couldn't even put the words together to tell her what happened. I closed my eyes as the tears fell on my suit jacket.

At first, I questioned if I could continue running my campaign. I told Perry and the team what had happened, and we agreed to take a few days off. It was clear to everyone that I was taking this loss very hard. I wasn't getting sleep, and bags seemed to stay under my eyes. There were several campaign meetings where I had to take a break to walk outside. I would hurry out of the room before the staff saw the tears come down my face.

For at least a day or two, I was convinced that I'd have to drop out. But as I sat and cried and reflected and prayed, I suddenly saw what I needed to do. I couldn't quit. What happened to T.J. was the exact reason I was running for office to begin with. I needed my campaign to keep going to help tell his story.

For months, gun violence had been one of my main issues on the campaign trail. As a young man, I was in a position to speak about it from current experience, unlike my opponents. Senator Neal and Judge Stringer saw gun violence through the lens of elders who were no longer in the streets. They spoke about violence from the standpoint of getting problem people off the streets, which is necessary, but only part of the solution. It doesn't speak to systemic challenges like poverty that create the environments where violence is the likely outcome. When I spoke of gun violence, I talked about not only the tragic seconds when the trigger is pulled and a life is taken but about all the events and environmental conditions that make that horrific moment possible. To me, gun violence is a symptom of so many deep inequities and generations of trauma. It's the product of hopelessness and abandonment. It's the result of a society that has left so many young people with no other options. I saw it clearly. I knew so many young men who were victims of the environment that caused murder to be seen as acceptable. Gun violence isn't just a personal tragedy; it's a public health crisis. When a shooting takes place, the person harmed isn't only the person who's shot. It's the family of the person, the neighbors, the first responders, the city as a whole. Even the person who pulled the trigger. Addressing gun violence is a bigger conversation about how we realize healing in our communities.

That had been my message for months. I just never expected to be personally thrust in the middle of the issue as I was running for State Senate. My cousin could no longer speak for himself, but as a candidate I could be a voice for him. After the shooting, everywhere I went, I told people about T.J. Every church, every picnic, on every panel. I told people about how smart and talented he was, about how the system took everything from him, about how he was murdered in the car he bought with the settlement check from being wrongly accused by the city. I wrote an opinion piece in *The Courier-Journal,* too. I wanted to shine a light on the painful realization that we had all become too comfortable with murder.

T.J.'s murder changed everything about the race. At a panel event on gun violence for candidates, a woman named Kristal Smith came up to me with tears in her eyes and told me that reading my *Courier-Journal* piece on T.J. made her want to do something. She became a member of the gun-reform group Moms Demand Action and started telling her own story as a survivor. We stayed in contact from that day on, and she even volunteered for my campaign. The media started paying more attention to what I was saying. Even Senator Neal reached out to express his condolences. I wasn't expecting his call, so when I heard his voice, it stopped me in my tracks. I was grateful that he still cared about me enough to tell me he was praying for my family.

T.J.'s death further illuminated why I was running. It gave my words greater meaning and caused more people to better appreciate my sense of urgency. My resolve grew even stronger, and my perspective came into focus. I saw my campaign as a tribute to T.J. I saw my voice and my work as a debt I owed him. I wanted to honor his life, and I didn't want to let him down. In addition to my daughters' future, I was now running for my cousin's legacy.

BY EARLY MAY, it was obvious I wouldn't be able to catch up to Senator Neal. I had raised a good amount of money for a first-time candidate but was still severely outspent. I couldn't pay for mailers or TV ads, and I knew I couldn't knock on enough doors all by myself. The odds were clearly against me.

I had all my hopes pinned on the last debate before the election. A lot of people who'd learned about me were planning to attend and make a final decision on who to vote for. If I was going to make up ground, it was going to be on that stage. I was going to acknowledge my love and respect for the senator and tell everyone exactly why we needed to applaud him for the work he had done, then step up to chart a new path forward. Perry and I walked into the church where the debate was being held. Mom, Tanesha, and the girls were with me as well. I was exhausted but ready. "God, have your way," I said to myself as I prepared to walk up to the podium. I looked over my right shoulder as I waited to be called to the stage. In the crowd, I saw my dad and my Uncle Tyrone, T.J.'s father. The crowd clapped loudly as I was introduced. Judge Stringer was on the stage as well, along with another gentleman no one had heard of before the debate. Only one person was missing: Senator Neal. He didn't even bother to show up.

I was absolutely deflated. I'd lost my one chance to tell the whole story as a contrast to the incumbent. I immediately knew it would be all but impossible to win. It saddened me, but I found my voice nonetheless. There was a message I needed to deliver on that stage. I spoke about the importance of this race, but also about the greater work before us. I poured my heart out and told everyone in the room that I loved them. The future may not have entailed a victory in this election, but that night I felt victorious. No matter how the election ended up, I made it clear we were just getting started in the work to transform Kentucky.

Election Day was rainy and gloomy. I'd worn myself out getting to the finish line. After making stops at all the polling stations, I went home, prayed over the day, and closed my eyes. That evening, the family gathered with me in the basement of the office building where I worked. Tanesha got a cake, although I was too wound up to eat it. As each precinct reported, it became more and more clear: I was going to lose. I went in my office and put my head down on the table.

I ended up coming in third, with just under 20 percent of the vote. I called Senator Neal to congratulate him. It was a deeply embarrassing thing to have to do, but I knew it was the right thing to do. As the phone rang, I felt my nerves. I didn't know if he would be angry with me or insult me. When he answered, his voice was calm. I told him that I wanted to do everything I could to make sure he won the general and stressed how much he still meant to me. His response was cold, but he at least managed a "Thank you." Then he said, "Charles, I still don't understand why you did this. Maybe to set yourself up for a future run? Maybe it just isn't for me to understand."

I told him I was following what I believed God was pushing me to do, that I had never intended to disrespect him in any way.

"You ran hard, Charles. Thank you for calling me."

After I hung up the phone, I put my head down on the table again. I didn't want to face my family as a loser, but Tanesha came in the room and grabbed my hand, and then we made our way out to where my family was waiting to hear from me. I apologized to them for not winning and thanked them for believing in me. As sad as I was, I told them all that this was clearly the beginning of great things God had in store. I hugged everyone in the room, then went home for the night.

THREE MONTHS LATER, the plans for the FoodPort fell apart, which was crushing on so many levels, both professionally and personally. I'd worked so hard and we'd come so close, but in the end all I could do was sigh and say, "Well, no surprises here. This is what always happens to us. Nothing nice ever happens for the West End." The final blow came in August when the anchor tenant, a massive indoor vertical farming company that had planned to invest over $20 million into a 60,000-square-foot facility, pulled out of the development. Their departure made the whole enterprise unsustainable for the smaller tenants and farmers who'd intended to join. Two months later the entire team was let go. Not only had I lost the race, but I was out of a job, too.

After Senator Neal won the general election, I reached out to him in hopes of making sure we were in a good place. But it was clear that my running had deeply upset him. It had turned into a personal in- dictment of the man, even if that was never my intent. He avoided me for a while, but then grudgingly agreed to sit down and have a cup of coffee at Heine Brothers on Eastern Parkway. He came in with his windbreaker on, and we sat down at a small table.

"So," he said, very abrupt. "What do you want?"

His demeanor put me on my heels, and I fell right back into that earnest and humble tone I always used whenever I was around him. "Well," I said, "I just wanted to meet with you to let you know that now that the race is over that I appreciate everything that I've learned from you and that I want to support you and be helpful."

"I'm fine," he snapped. "I don't need your help." Then he softened a bit. "If you want to work together, we can do that, but I still don't understand why you did it." I started to give him my same answer about needing to push for change, and he cut me off. "No, no, no, after all I've done for you, I don't understand."

"I have been trying to tell you how I believe things need to change in our community, but so many times I felt like you didn't hear me," I said. "It was like I didn't matter, and you only wanted me to shut up." That's when the tension started to fill the room. I felt my nerves tighten as I spoke. "And after everything I've done for you, all the end- less hours of working and volunteering, when I talked about whether I would run against Owens, it was like you didn't even know me." A lot of hurt was coming out, finally. But I had to let him know that at the end of the day, my decision wasn't personal. It was about what I knew in my heart needed to happen for the community we shared. "Look," I said. "I did not do this to hurt you. I sincerely believe I had to take a stand for the change I know is possible."

We went back and forth like that until finally he said, "I'm done with this, Charles. Let me tell you right now: Your political career is over. It's dead. It's *dead*. You messed up. If you would have waited, once Darryl Owens retired, you would have walked into that seat. But now I don't know, and I hate it because you had so much promise."

"Well," I said, my mind immediately going to losing T.J., "I've been through worse things than losing an election. I'll be okay."

"This conversation is done," he said, and he got up and gruffly left.

After he walked out, I started to think he was right. Maybe my career was dead. I questioned my future. I questioned everything. Tanesha and I put our house up for sale and I started looking for a new job, unsure of what was next for us. I knew God wasn't done with me, but whatever His plans were, I was quite certain they didn't involve me ever running for any kind of office ever again.

CHAPTER 16

THERE ARE NO MISTAKES

WATCHING THE 2016 presidential election returns come in was like living an episode of *The Twilight Zone*. We'd sold our house when my job with Seed Capital Kentucky dried up and had moved back in with my mom, again, while we waited to make our next move. Tanesha didn't want to stay up all night watching the results, so I set myself up with the TV in the kitchen to follow the news.

Throughout the whole campaign, I'd been going back and forth. In one sense, it was impossible to imagine. I had enough faith in America and in the good people I knew across the political spectrum to think, "Surely the bottom won't fall out. Surely America won't elect a known con artist to the highest office in the world."

In another sense, though, I knew what was coming. I knew because I could see Donald Trump fanning the flames of racism, bigotry, and division. Since the end of the civil rights era, most politicians, even many Republicans, had tried to tamp down or at least ignore those issues. Those who did exploit them typically did it in subtle, indirect ways. Trump was putting them at the front and center of his campaign. He was breaking every rule, violating every code, exploiting every "elephant in the room." Unlike nearly every professional pundit and strategist on cable TV, folks from the hood didn't underestimate the ability of overt hatred and fear to move people. We've never had the luxury of ignoring racism. When Trump started saying "Build the wall," we knew how powerful that would be.

I also saw what was coming because I saw the ways in which Trump, despite being a born liar, was actually telling the truth. He was telling the truth about working people's frustration with corrupt politicians and big-money interests. He was telling the truth about America's declining industries, jobs leaving communities, and the growing chasm between the wealthiest few and everyone else. Of course, he was lying when he said that "he alone could fix it." He was lying when he said he had any interest in fixing it at all; he was just exploiting people's fears and anxieties. Still, it was undeniable that he, like Bernie Sanders, was tapping into a deep well of frustration and anger with the status quo. I was holding out faith that our nation would reach for our better angels and resist the urge to give up and elect Trump, but I had a sick feeling in my stomach the whole campaign, because I knew that a lot of people were tired of the way things were.

Hell, I was tired, too.

I knew that Trump's victory meant that America wouldn't have the luxury of avoiding the unavoidable. It was the culmination of decades of ignoring our deeper problems, and now we all had no choice but to face them or succumb to them. We were headed for a reckoning.

For me, Trump changed everything and nothing. If Hillary Clinton had won, I would have been in a good position to land a job in D.C., something I was very much counting on in the wake of losing the race to Neal and losing my job at the FoodPort. That hope was gone now. But nothing about the greater arc of my journey had changed. Growing up in the hood, you become used to being deeply disappointed in government. You know not to put your faith in politicians. While I didn't want someone as dangerous and corrupt as Trump to win, the work was largely the same. My community was invisible before, and it was still invisible now. So Trump's election didn't change my goals, it only made me realize why they were more urgent than ever.

LUCKILY, AFTER MY plan to work in D.C. ran headlong into Trump's wall, Anthony Smith, one of my former colleagues in the Mayor's Office, reached out to me. He had started working as director for a national nonprofit called Cities United, which was helping cities across the country put together comprehensive plans to reduce the deaths of young Black men and boys due to gun violence, part of President Obama's overall campaign for Black male achievement. Anthony was looking for a development director and was particularly interested in someone with a policy background. As I shared my personal story of losing T.J. with Anthony, we discussed the possibility of working together. The organization was based in Louisville but had offices in Seattle and D.C., and it was the perfect opportunity for me to stay involved in policy and build national relationships, while also allowing me to keep my promise to T.J. to focus my efforts on addressing the root causes of gun violence.

The next year flew by. I did a lot of traveling, spending time in Minneapolis, Norfolk, Seattle, and D.C. We helped cities look at their programs around community safety, working with them to develop solutions in conjunction with youth leaders, the faith community, the business and philanthropic sectors, and law enforcement. I enjoyed the work, but I still couldn't ignore the drive I felt inside me to lead a new type of politics in Kentucky. I knew the way we would improve outcomes in our city was to improve leadership across the state, and I wanted to be a part of that. The sting of my loss to Senator Neal was starting to fade, and I found myself considering another run for office.

I knew if I ran again, it wouldn't be against a mentor or a strong incumbent. I would only run for the State House, and I would only do it if Rep. Owens actually retired this time. When he officially announced that he would, it was hard to ignore how well positioned I already was to make a run to replace him. The 43rd State House District fit within the 33rd Senatorial District. So while I was campaigning for State Senate, I had been covering the same ground I would need to cover to run for the State House. That experience was irreplaceable. I had just knocked on all of those doors a year before. I'd built up excellent name recognition. In addition to that, everyone who hadn't been able to publicly support me against Neal was now in position to proudly back me for the open seat.

Mom had always told me there are no mistakes. This seemed like proof.

When the filing deadline for the primary passed, seven candidates had put themselves on the ballot, but I knew I was in the front position to win. To kick off, we set up a big launch event at The Table. One of the few community restaurants in the West End, The Table was run by a church, working from a model that allowed everyone to eat and pay what they could. As the big day approached, everything was lining up for me perfectly, with the exception of one tiny detail: I was running out of insulin.

I was still working, so I had a full-time salary and benefits, but with all the extra demands of launching the campaign, my time and our household budget had been stretched thinner than usual. I try to keep two insulin pens on me at all times, one in my pocket and one in my bag. But that week I was down to carrying only one, and it was close to running out.

I'd seen a Walgreens bag in the drawer of the refrigerator and, mentally, I'd assumed there was at least one more pen inside. When I opened the bag and saw nothing there, it was like a punch in the stomach. Even with health benefits, my medication was still setting us back $500 a month. With my paycheck not arriving until the end of the week, I didn't have enough money to get my refill and groceries for the week.

At that point, it had been fifteen years since my diabetes had landed me in the hospital. I'd allowed myself to grow complacent about the risks I faced. Despite overcoming a lot of the shame of having the disease, I still had the habit of downplaying the sluggishness or pain I sometimes felt. I didn't want people to pity me or to stress out over me. Especially Tanesha. I never wanted her to worry that I wouldn't be able to protect and provide for our family. So in spite of everything my doctors had ever told me, staring down at that empty Walgreens bag in the vegetable crisper, I made a terrible decision. Instead of doing what I should have done, instead of talking things over with my wife or going to my family to ask for help, I convinced myself that I could make it a week rationing my insulin. I bought groceries so that Kaylin and Prestyn would have food for the week and figured I would just eat less, stretching out the little insulin I had left.

As the days passed, I slowly rationed my doses. I could feel the clock ticking. I knew I wouldn't make it long if I didn't get more insulin. It was a lonely, empty feeling. Between that and the stress of knowing that I needed to crush this launch event, I knew I was pushing myself too far. But I felt it was my only option.

On the way to the launch event, I was already feeling sluggish. My feet were like cinder blocks, and my eyes were heavy, but I did my best to ignore it. Then, at the traffic light around the corner from our house, I had to slam on my brakes when an ambulance sped out in front of me and I got rear-ended by a pickup truck. The impact was so abrupt that my hand flew off of the steering wheel and hit my mouth. I could taste the blood as I looked up to see smoke in my rearview.

I ended up sitting on the side of the road for nearly two hours, waiting for the police to come and file an accident report. As I sat there, every few seconds the phone would ring. It was the venue saying they hadn't received the deposit yet. Then a volunteer saying we needed more posters to put signs up. Then a call about some issue with the sound system in the room. Everything was stressing me out, and all my body wanted to do was go to sleep. I'd been a diabetic long enough to know my glucose levels had to be soaring, but I didn't have time to worry about it. I had to finish preparing for my speech, the speech that was going to set everything in motion. "I have to crush this," I kept repeating to myself.

By the time I made it to The Table, hundreds of people had packed themselves into the large meeting space in the back. Councilman Tandy and the others all took turns getting up on the stage to tell everyone why they believed I should be the next State Representative for the 43rd District. I was too disoriented to hear everything they said, but the energy in the room was electric. When the time came for me to speak, I was already growing dizzy and unsteady on my feet, but I mustered the strength to make it to that stage, and once I got up there, it didn't matter that my car was damaged and my body was weak. I was going to give it my all. As I spoke, I noticed my mouth was incredibly dry. My tongue was hardening with a white coat over it. I looked around the packed room at all the smiling faces. I could make out many of them, but my vision was blurry and my head was spinning. None of that was going to stop me, though. "God, help me through this," I said silently to myself. "I know you have work for me to do, and I need to deliver this message right."

Standing at the podium that night, I didn't just announce my run for the State House, I held it together and all but preached a sermon about how the people of Louisville and Kentucky and America had to come together. Everyone stood on their feet and cheered; I hugged Mom on the stage, and I had her lead a prayer as we ended the event. We'd kicked off exactly the way we needed to. The message was clear that I was ready to lead.

But first, I needed to sleep. Even as I savored the elation of the moment, I could feel my body shutting down. I went home, took the last little bit of insulin I had left, and crashed, thinking I'd wake up the next morning and somehow find the money or go without eating for two days until my direct deposit hit. Of course, I was only deluding myself, because that wouldn't have helped me at all. The next day, I felt worse. I got up and went to work but ended up going home early and lying down to rest. My vision was blurry. My body felt heavy.

"Something's not right, Charles," Tanesha said, standing over me. She had never seen me like this. I still wasn't being completely honest with her about how bad it was, in part because I didn't want to worry her, but also because I'd allowed myself to forget how bad it might get. It had been so long since my last episode of diabetic ketoacidosis, and I was so fixated on needing to stay strong for the race, that I actually convinced myself that I could manage it, that maybe the symptoms were the result of something bad I ate, or a cold, and not of rationing my insulin.

I started to respond to Tanesha but had to go throw up. I didn't make it to the restroom, though, and fell to the floor. Tanesha helped me get back in the bed and brought me some water. I slept through the rest of the night, waking up several times to throw up. The next morning, I finally told her that I'd run out of insulin, but I didn't tell her it had been a few days. I still thought I could make it. She was worried, but having never faced this before, she didn't fully comprehend how severe the situation was. "If you don't get any better today," she said sharply, "we're going to the hospital." Then she left to go to work.

I agreed and tried to go back to sleep. In a couple hours, though, I noticed that things were dramatically worse. I tried to get out of bed but couldn't find the strength. I had to throw up again but only had the strength to lean my head over the side of the bed to face my mouth toward the floor. I was terrified. In that moment, I realized how foolish I had been. I realized that I might die. I knew I couldn't wait anymore. I needed to get to the hospital immediately. Tanesha worked across town, but Mom was at home. I called her with the phone on my pillow and told her what was happening, and she raced over as quickly as she could.

My mom had injured her knee some years back, which made it harder for her to get up steep steps easily. I also stand about five inches taller than her. None of that mattered to her, though. She found some superhuman strength and got my shoes on and carried me down the stairs and put me in her car. I closed my eyes as she drove to Baptist East Hospital. When we arrived at the ER, I couldn't walk. A wheelchair was brought out to the car, and they rolled me to a room and checked my vitals, including my glucose. It was close to 900.

I spent the next week in the hospital. Fortunately, we'd had such a big launch to the campaign and our email program was already up and running, so we managed to keep our presence on the campaign trail felt; no one knew I was in the hospital fighting to stay alive. They ran all types of tests on me as I lay there, nearly motionless. Every twenty or thirty minutes, I would turn my head to the side of the bed and throw up bile. Mom would be there ready with a napkin to wipe my mouth. Grandad was often there, too, sitting in his wheelchair at the foot of my bed.

I couldn't keep anything down, not even water. The doctors had multiple IV needles in my arms, working hard to get medicine and fluids into my body. Nurses were in and out. I slept most of the time, opening my eyes partially to see a doctor talking to my mom or a nurse trying to clean me.

"We are going to clean you up, Charles," a group of nurses would say as they came in with cloths and foam soap. "Can you move at all?"

I was so weak I couldn't get out of the bed. For several days, all I could do was shake my head no. I was thirty-three years old and unable to wash myself. I wanted to be humiliated by it, but I was too tired. I just accepted that this was happening and closed my eyes while they rolled me around to clean me. With my head back on the pillow, I prayed silently. I didn't want to die, but I knew it was possible. I never heard the doctors say it, but they knew it was possible as well.

Because I was in intensive care, my family couldn't crowd into the room like usual, but folks still stopped by periodically. Tanesha wasn't able to take off work, so every day when she got off, she would pick up Kaylin from school and Prestyn from daycare and then come over to sit with me. Tanesha would say hi to me softly and kiss my forehead. She was always so strong. Being raised in a military family, she didn't cry often. If I wasn't feeling well, she would quietly get me some water or find my medicine and tell me, "You'll be all right."

I loved to see the girls walk in. Kaylin was a little nervous to see me. I could tell she didn't want to see me looking the way I did. She would lean in and lightly lay her head on my chest. While she did, Prestyn would run and jump on me, scaring everyone else in the room. "Hi, Daddy!" she would say with a big smile. She reached her little arms out to put them around my neck. I tried to hold back my tears. I wanted to put my arms around them and hug them. *Lift your arms up, Charles!* I was saying in my head. But I couldn't move. I didn't have the strength to hug them back. In that moment, I realized I might not get to see my daughters grow up. *Lord,* I prayed silently, *I'm sorry my body is shutting down. I only wanted to do what You have called me to do, and I know there is more for me to do, but if this is it, I just want You to know I tried my best. I tried my best to be a good dad, a loving husband, and a good son. I tried to do some good for this place.*

One morning a day or two later, my dad walked in, his long wooden staff in one hand and his Bible in the other. I knew he wouldn't stay long, uncomfortable as he is with difficult, emotional situations. But I was glad that he came. "You're going to be healed, son," he said as he opened the Bible and put it on my head and started to pray. Then I heard someone else walk into the room. I couldn't see who it was, but I felt a hand on mine and something cold being placed in my palm. I didn't even have to open my eyes. I immediately knew what it was and who was handing it to me. After T.J. was murdered, my Uncle Tyrone had a dog tag made with a picture of him and his little son. Now he was pressing that piece of cold metal into my hand, and I started sobbing. Something whispered to my spirit right then. I immediately knew my journey wasn't ending in that hospital. It was as if T.J. was there to let me know he still needed me in the fight.

Slowly my strength started to return. Soon I was able to sit up on my own and walk to the restroom. By the end of the week, I was able to consume liquids on my own. By the top of the following week, I was heading home, and doing so with a new resolve: I would never put myself in the position where something like this would happen again. I would never hide my condition from the people I needed to support me. And I haven't had a complication like that since. Leaving the hospital, I played "God's Plan" by Drake on my phone. God had work for me to do, and it started with winning this race.

THANKS TO MY run against Senator Neal two years before, I had the advantage of starting out the race with the most name recognition among voters. Still, in a seven-way primary, you have to find ways to make yourself stand above and apart, and the main thing that set me apart was my ability and deep desire to build a broad-based coalition. My goal wasn't just to appeal to 51 percent of the voters of the district. My goal, lofty as it may sound, was to transform the whole way we approached politics in the Commonwealth of Kentucky.

Because of how gerrymandered the 43rd District is and the fact that it is a majority-minority district, it's very easy for a candidate to win by only focusing on the precincts in the West End, which were majority Black. Indeed, that was how Rep. Owens had held the district for so long, and it was the strategy most of my opponents were relying on in this race. However, the 43rd District doesn't just include the West End. It stretches across Louisville to cover several wealthy zip codes in the East End as well, areas that are majority white.

My record and intentions regarding the needs of the West End were indisputable. But because of my work across the city, I also understood the power of connecting the hood and downtown to the newer, wealthier suburbs in the East End. I knew that any agenda for the Black community would benefit everyone. We needed to find ways to bring unlikely people together so that we could actually apply the pressure to lead for long-term change. Doing that required us to build relationships with people we didn't always agree with. Many in the West End looked at the fancy suburban enclaves to the East and saw diverging interests. But I saw assets where others saw deficits. I saw common bonds where others saw only hardline divisions. While all my competitors campaigned in the West End alone, I loaded up my car with yard signs and campaign literature and drove over to canvass the East End as well.

Same as I had in my State Senate race, I went to every area and walked nearly every street. It was an unorthodox strategy. I could tell that East End folks were not used to seeing people like me walking in their neighborhood; on four separate occasions, someone called the police on me while I was knocking on doors.

"You live around here?" the cops would say.

"No, sir!" I'd reply, smiling and handing them a flyer. "My name is Charles Booker, and I am running for State Representative."

"Oh," they'd say, a tad perplexed. "Okay. I apologize, Charles. Be careful around here. Good luck."

Kristal Smith, the woman who'd read my piece on T.J. in *The Courier-Journal* during the State Senate race, lived in the eastern part of the 43rd District and joined me for my canvassing. Since she was white, walking with her helped me get through the area without having more police called on me. If Kristal wasn't available, a white staffer would join me, because we knew police lights were likely to show up if I walked alone.

Uniting the East End and the West End was a matter of understanding the issues and knowing how different communities saw those issues. In the West End, I talked about how homicides were impacting our families; in the East End, I talked about their concerns for a safer city. In the West End, I talked about jobs leaving our community; in the East End, I talked about supporting local business growth. The goal was to make everyone see the ways in which our interests are aligned and not in opposition to one another.

Of the residents who opened their doors, most of them shook my hand, let me make my pitch, and cordially thanked me for coming by. But not everyone. The racism I did encounter was of the inadvertent, backhanded variety, mostly in comments about the West End. "I wish they would stop causing so much trouble." Or, "Why don't they go to school and do better?" Even to this day I hear similar statements, almost always said by a friendly face with a big smile and a positive attitude.

By and large, the way I respond has remained consistent. Generally, I don't try to expose people for having blind spots. I don't call them out or try to argue. I simply try to show them a different point of view—one that they might already agree with, although they might not have realized it before. It isn't easy. It requires me to let a lot of things roll off my back, but that's okay. It's part of reaching and connecting with people to try to bring them around to understanding your ideas, and it works. After a few months of campaigning, there were yard signs for all seven candidates across the West End. In the East End, however, there were nothing but Booker signs as far as the eye could see.

As we entered the home stretch, the seven-way race had largely boiled down to a contest between me and Pam Stevenson, an attorney and retired Air Force lieutenant colonel. I had worked with her on the FoodPort and other community projects, and she volunteered with the FoodPort Community Council. I liked and respected her immensely, but it was clear that our campaign had the momentum. The endorsements were rolling in. Labor unions got behind me. National organizations like Moms Demand Action and statewide organizations like Kentuckians for the Commonwealth all got behind me as well.

The night of the primary, my family and my team all piled into the Healthy House on Portland Avenue, a community space created by a local nonprofit focused on building green, sustainable neighborhoods. Chairs were lined up in rows facing the large projector screen where the results would be displayed, and Mom was helping the campaign staff decorate, filling pitchers of tea and water and shuffling chairs around. And that's Mom for you, always the one setting the tables and getting everyone in order. "Mom, you don't have to do that," I said as she was blowing up balloons. I could only smile, though, because nothing was going to stop her. It's her way of showing love.

Several of my cousins had made it, and my Uncle Tyrone, T.J.'s dad, showed up as well. I hugged him tight and told him I loved him. David Tandy was there, as well as Rep. Meeks. And of course Grandad was there, dressed in a brightly colored suit with a matching brim hat. Tanesha and the girls got there a little after things were set up. With everything going on that day, Tanesha had had to get the girls ready by herself. When they walked in, wearing jean jackets and black-and-white dresses, everyone clapped. Tanesha smiled shyly and handed Prestyn to me. Kaylin ran up and hugged me too.

We settled in, gathered around the screen, and waited. I was so nervous I couldn't sit down. This was just the primary, but in a district that was nearly 90 percent Democrat, everyone knew the winner of this primary would likely win the seat.

Polls in Kentucky close at 6 P.M., which in our country is incredibly early. Since our district is farthest west, it was the last to be reported. The results that started coming in first were the larger precincts in the West End. With every update, my numbers kept moving back and forth between first and second, swapping places with Pam Stevenson. Once it was clear the race would be close, I stopped watching. I got up and walked away, listening to Tandy and my staff stress over the numbers instead. It took at least two hours for the race to be called, and for those two hours, I didn't sit down once. My mind wouldn't slow down. I went around the room, hugging everyone, talking to my grandad. Every few minutes Tandy would blurt out, "We got a precinct!" and everyone would erupt into cheers.

With all the candidates splitting the vote in the West End, the numbers there didn't have me far ahead. I was neck and neck with Pam Stevenson. For the first thirty minutes of reporting, she was ahead. I wasn't worried, though. "Wait until they report the East," I kept repeating with confidence.

And that's exactly how it went down. As precinct after precinct from the East End came in, my name was at the top of virtually every single one. I'd been proven right. By investing time in the majority-white neighborhoods in the East End, by making those voters care about the issues that affected everyone in the district, Black and white, rich and poor, I'd racked up a margin that Pam Stevenson couldn't close. I was praying quietly to myself and doing my best to stay calm when I heard David Tandy say, "Charles . . . you did it. You won."

Everyone cheered.

I was the Democratic nominee for the 43rd District of Kentucky.

I stood up in front of everyone to give my speech. It's one of those things where you feel your whole body go numb, and the reason you go numb is so you can stay on your feet and not pass out from the enormity of it. As I looked out over the room, I thought about the fact that I was going to be Kentucky's youngest Black state legislator since the very first Black state legislator, Charles Anderson, was elected some ninety years before. I thought about the history of what I was doing, and my heart swelled with pride. "The people won today!" I shouted, holding up Grandma's Bible in my hand, clutching it as if I were hugging Grandma herself. "Grandma is right here with us too!" I shouted out. "We are going to finish this race, make history, and go to that Capitol building together. And when I swear in, it is going to be on this Bible!"

Everyone was on their feet by the time I finished speaking. I held up the Bible with one hand and in my other hand was T.J.'s dog tag that Uncle Tyrone had given me in the hospital. I couldn't stop thinking about where I came from, how far I'd come, and every sacrifice that was made for me to even be alive. This win was for T.J. This win was for my ancestors and my children. This win was for my mom and all her prayers. This win was for my grandparents and their sacrifice.

I stood there, scanning the audience, looking at all the people who'd come together to support me. My heart was filled with joy but also a tinge of sadness. Because I'd set out to build a political movement that united everyone from all walks of life, and as I scanned the crowd I realized that at least one person I loved had declined to join me. He had not come out to support me that night, and since that night he has never supported me again.

I'D TEXTED MY dad before the event to tell him where we would be meeting. He hadn't responded, but I still held out hope that he would be there. My dad had started acting strange after he moved to a condo in Bardstown after his divorce from his second wife. He started listening to a lot of talk radio, Rush Limbaugh, a bunch of shows that were supposedly Christian but regularly talked about hate and fear of others. From my childhood up to graduation from college, my father had never been terribly political. He'd never once talked about abortion or gay marriage. Once he started listening to these shows, it seemed like he talked about those issues more than most anything else. He had the Fox News talking points down verbatim.

Everything about him changed. To this day, I don't know how or why, but it started after Obama was elected. It was like he became another person. He grew a long beard. The way he talked was different. He joined a church where he was the only Black person. The dad I knew, the guy who was super cool and who rapped and danced and drove the Batmobile—that guy was gone. I started getting emails with links to YouTube videos and Facebook articles about weird conspiracy stuff: viruses and bioweapons, anti-Obama conspiracies, gay people corrupting children, abortion doctors committing infanticide, you name it. At first I'd look up the authors of the articles and fact-check them. I'd email my dad back, pointing out that his sources were regularly reported for publishing false and misleading articles. When I did, he ignored me. It never mattered how easily the lies were to debunk. It was what he wanted to believe, so he believed it.

I tried to talk to him in person, too, but we soon reached a point where we couldn't have a conversation that didn't turn into an argument. It felt like he had joined a cult, and it gutted me, watching that happen to him. I can't stand liars, and I especially despise the notion of exploiting someone's faith as a weapon against them. That's what I saw happening to my father, my hero. I don't know if he voted for Trump, but he would talk all the time about how Trump was going to shake things up, that God wanted someone like Trump to stop all the abortion and corruption. A bunch of political con men had used my father's faith to manipulate him into believing all sorts of conspiratorial propaganda, and there wasn't much I could do about it.

As disheartening as the political disagreements were, none ever made me want to cut him off or turn my back on him, and I never thought he would do that to me. Even if he saw things differently from me, I was still his only son. I expected him to keep sight of what mattered most. He didn't. He slowly separated from most of the family and stayed to himself. When he came to visit and prayed over me in the hospital, it was one of the few times I'd seen him in recent months. We stopped talking about politics and pretty much stopped talking altogether, and when that happened it hurt more than words can describe. He even told me that he couldn't support me in my career and asked for his past contributions to my campaign to be refunded.

I had only wanted him to be proud of me, and knowing that he was disappointed hurt more than anything I had ever felt. I still loved him the same, and I wasn't angry with him. I just needed to let him have his space to protect myself. I'd built a career on working with people who had different ideologies and beliefs. For my own father to choose politics over a relationship with me was a crushing blow. The moment I realized he wasn't coming hurt me deeply, but I didn't allow myself to dwell on it. God had opened a door for me that I never even dreamed of walking through as a child. I wasn't going to let anything make me miss the magnitude of this moment. I knew my only purpose was to be obedient to what God was leading me to do. I did the only thing I could do: I said a prayer for my dad, and then I moved on to pursue my goal of helping all of the people of Kentucky.

CHAPTER 17

THE WORK OF THE PEOPLE

"WE NEED TO get two vans!" I said to Mom as she counted heads. We were getting ready to make our trip to the State Capitol for my swearing in, and some of the family was going to join us. I was so honored to go with them, and even more privileged to know that I was going to stand in that building and speak for them. We were taking the hood to the Capitol.

As predicted, the general election had been a landslide, given that I was running in a district that was 90 percent Democratic against a guy, Everett Corley, who'd appeared on white nationalist podcasts and blamed minorities for the problems of the white working class. When the race was called on Election Night, I'd won with nearly 80 percent of the vote. Now we were headed to Frankfort, where I was going to place my hand on Grandma's Bible and make history as the youngest Black state legislator in Kentucky in over eighty years.

Once we arrived in Frankfort, I was trying to get everyone together so we could walk in the wheelchair-accessible entrance with Grandad. My cousins and aunts were scattered around the Capitol grounds, and it was beautiful to see them fanning out on the lawn. For many of my relatives, this was their first time ever at the Capitol building. Seeing their reactions reminded me of my own first visit with Senator Neal ten years before. I was running around the perimeter of the Capitol building, rounding everyone up. The walkway around the building was lined with red brick pavers, and I couldn't help but listen to my shoes clack on the bricks. The noise echoed. It sounded like I was on a mission, which I absolutely was.

Grandad stayed mostly calm, but I could tell he was as excited as everyone else. He had always told me he was proud of me ever since I was little. On this day, though, I could see it on his face. He kept smiling and nodding his head as we pushed his wheelchair up the ramp and down the grand hallways. As I pushed him in, I was wiping tears from my face. This was a building where laws had once decreed my ancestors to be property. Now, standing on their shoulders, I would be the one making the laws. The history in each step I took sent chills through my body.

On the way up to the House chambers, I took the family into the rotunda. We stopped and looked at the statue of Abraham Lincoln. "This is incredible, baby," Mom said in a low voice. I grabbed her hand as we both looked up. "You deserve this, son. God is with you. Mama is so proud." She hugged me and laid her head on my shoulder. Tanesha was quiet. She held Prestyn tightly and kept fixing Kaylin's hair. Kaylin and Prestyn were looking up at the rotunda, watching in awe as the big dome changed colors from blue to green, purple to orange. I watched Tanesha's face as she took in the marble stairs and the gold-plated doors. She didn't smile, but I could tell she was taking it all in. My heart was pounding, but looking at her and the girls settled me down. Having them with me meant everything.

Once I was sworn in, I delivered my first remarks as a state legislator. "I would like to introduce some of my family who made the trek from the West End of Louisville to be here with me today," I said. "My grandad is here, Sergeant Lindsay E. Hearn, Sr. Thank you for your service, sir." The room gave Grandad a standing ovation. As everyone clapped, I noticed Grandad fidgeting in his wheelchair. "Don't try to get up, Grandad," I quickly said into my microphone, hoping he wouldn't hurt himself. It was too late, though. Grandad rose to his feet in the chamber of the Kentucky House of Representatives. Nothing was going to keep him in his seat. I could only smile. That is exactly where I got it from.

As the day progressed with lots of handshakes and introductions, I walked down to the Senate chambers with a couple of my cousins so I could show them what it looked like. There I ran into Senator Neal, who was standing off to the side, talking to another senator. As we walked by each other, he smiled and nodded his head. "Congratulations, young man," he said. I thanked him and made my way back down to my side of the Capitol. He reached out to me and we talked again later that week. "The past is the past," he said. "We're on the same team now. It's all about working together to help the people in our districts." I was grateful to hear him say that.

Not too long after that we spoke again. He called me to talk about a hate-crime bill he wanted to introduce, and I took the opportunity to apologize to him. I apologized for not understanding that running against him was an indictment of him. I apologized for hurting him and told him that I love him. "You mean a whole lot to me, Senator," I told him.

"You mean a lot to me, too," he said. He told me he respected my determination, and I could tell he was finally beginning to see me as a peer and a colleague, and not merely his pupil. It felt, honestly, like I was reconciling with my father, which was a good thing to feel.

Once the swearing-in ceremonies concluded, it came time to settle in. I had spent plenty of time in legislative offices over the years, but to now have my own was something truly special. Whenever I moved into a new home or started a new job, my mom would take olive oil that had been prayed over and go around the place, dipping her finger in the oil and making a tiny cross at the head of every doorway. She did that for the office, praying over the room and asking God for my protection as I did the work of the people. I set Grandma's Bible on the top of my bookshelf so that I could see it every time I walked in. I hung up my degrees alongside pictures of Dr. King, Malcolm X, and Barack Obama. My mom printed out some Bible scriptures and framed them, and I placed those around the office as well. Then, once everything was in place and everyone had left, I played Kendrick Lamar's album *To Pimp a Butterfly* on my computer speakers and leaned back in my chair. When "Alright" came on, I turned it up louder. Just like the words said, I knew we were going to be alright.

THE EMOTIONAL HIGH from my swearing in quickly gave way to the speed of the session. There were one hundred of us serving in the House of Representatives, each representing a district of around forty thousand residents. The session was a short one, meaning that every decision we made to affect the lives of Kentuckians would be made over the course of thirty calendar days, every one of which would be a whirlwind.

Every member of the legislature had the chance to submit the preferences for committee selections. My choices were Judiciary, Natural Resources, and Economic Development. I wanted to serve on Judiciary because I wanted to make sure my perspective as a young Black man from a heavily criminalized area was in the initial deliberations on bills that shaped our justice system. Natural Resources I chose because of my work in Fish and Wildlife. After traveling the Commonwealth, I grew a deeper love for the work of protecting our land and rich resources. I also wanted to be a voice for communities being crushed by the declining fossil fuel industry. I knew we could fight for new industries that would help communities across Kentucky. And I wanted to be on the Economic Development Committee to have the chance to review how the state supports investment in local economies. My goal was to make sure we made the types of structural changes that would uproot poverty.

Coming into my first session, the Democratic caucus was in an extreme minority in both chambers, but there was still a great deal of collegiality between members of both parties. Most of the legislators spoke to one another and shook hands. Several of my Republican colleagues patted me on the shoulder and said, "Congratulations" and "You ran a hell of a race." There were a few legislators in the Republican caucus that seemed to keep their distance, but for the most part, everyone was cordial when we were not in session. When the bell would ring, though, and the Speaker would gavel us in for the day—that's when the cracks began to show, not just between Democrats and Republicans but within the Republican caucus as well.

By 2019, Trump and Trumpism had split the GOP in two. There were many seasoned, pragmatic legislators who seemed to avoid the overt race-baiting and conspiracy theories, representatives like Spencer County's James Tipton and David Osborne, who served as Speaker of the House. But they were clearly at odds with the wave of legislators who'd been elected alongside and because of Trump. Everett Corley may have failed to beat me in a heavily Democratic district, but plenty of other far right-wingers were winning easy victories in heavily Republican districts. Legislators like Rep. Savannah Maddox and Rep. Melinda Prunty would stand in the chamber and drone on with their Fox News talking points. On several occasions, the minority caucus would have to wait for hours while the Republicans fought among themselves over passing the kind of extremist abortion and gun legislation that typically wouldn't have seen the light of day in the past. Over time, the debates only grew more and more lopsided; the pragmatists could no longer muster the backbone to push back against the most extreme elements in their own party.

My first task in office was to try and finish the work my predecessor had started: I wanted to pass Rep. Owens's bill regarding the expungement and the automatic restoration of voting rights for Kentuckians with felony convictions who'd completed their sentences. Going into that environment, I knew it would be difficult for me to pass legislation. I had several strikes against me before I'd even filed a bill: I was in the minority, I was a new legislator, I was young, and I was Black. I tried to tackle that head-on, going out of my way to meet with the Democratic and Republican legislators in the leadership as well as the legislators who were the lead sponsors of bills I was concerned with. I spoke to every single person I saw and showed everyone respect. Even if it was a group of Republican members crowded in the hall, I would stop and greet them all. To me, everyone in the building was my family, and I treated them that way.

By taking those steps to build relationships, I was able to work myself into the middle of deliberations on several priority bills during that first session and even found myself in a position to actually pass legislation in my first session. In the House chamber, each desk had a drawer that locked. Because of my diabetes, I made sure to keep some snacks in mine so that my glucose wouldn't bottom out, usually peanut butter crackers or some peppermints. Sitting beside me in the chamber was an older gentleman from Eastern Kentucky, Rep. Danny Bentley. One day as I was putting snacks in my drawer, I noticed he was doing the same. His hand was shaking slightly, and I heard him say he needed to get his glucose up. I wondered if he was a diabetic like me, so I asked him. It turned out that he was also a type 1 diabetic. I offered him some of my snacks and told him that anything in my drawer was available for him if he needed it. He smiled and told me the same thing. The next day, I came to my desk and found some candy in my chair. It was from Rep. Bentley.

Bentley and I were from different parts of Kentucky, were registered to different parties, and voted differently on many things. If a bill was brought up for a vote, we would both get up and, typically, would argue passionately on opposite sides. But when we sat back in our chairs, he would ask me if I needed a piece of chocolate, or I would ask him if he needed a cracker. We always took care of one another. His wife learned about me and started baking me cookies. During recess, we would sit in our chairs and trade stories. As far as I was concerned, Rep. Bentley was my brother.

At the time, I had been receiving emails about the national effort to make sure people had emergency prescription refills for their insulin. The bill was named Kevin's Law, in reference to a man from Ohio named Kevin Houdeshell. In 2014, Kevin ran out of insulin over the New Year's holiday when his pharmacy was closed. Forced to ration his insulin, he died in his home from diabetic ketoacidosis. The bill would allow people to get emergency prescription refills if they were unable to get ahold of their physician. I wanted to file a version of the bill in Kentucky.

"Why don't we work together on this?" I said to Bentley. He said he was already planning on it, and he'd be happy to collaborate. So instead of filing my own version, I signed onto his as a co-sponsor. Since he was one of the Republican members with a record for getting bills heard and brought to a vote, I knew that we increased our chances if I supported his instead of pushing my own.

We formed a team, working in tandem to whip votes in both caucuses for our bill. When the bill came up for a hearing in committee, we sat at the speaker's desk together, looking very much like the odd couple: a young Black man from the hood and an older, white-haired white man from up in Appalachia. That difference didn't divide us, though. It helped us tell a broader story than either of us could have told alone. The bill passed out of committee with nearly unanimous support. As it headed to the House floor, we both felt confident that it would pass. Day after day, we checked the list for the orders of the day to see if our bill would finally be brought to the floor for a final vote. The session was moving toward an end, and we started to question whether we would get our vote. Leadership took their time in getting to it. That could have been because it just wasn't a priority, or it could have been the fact that there were so many bills being jammed through in the session. Then, finally, it happened. The bill was brought to the floor, and we both took turns getting up to speak about the terror of running out of insulin and how this bill would save lives.

Standing beside one another, we watched the board light up as our colleagues, one by one, voted to pass it. I was proud of us. I'd built a relationship with someone I never expected. We'd put our differences aside and done something that would help Kentuckians avoid going through the types of anxiety and fear that we knew all too well. When the bill passed, I put my hand on Bentley's shoulder and whispered, "We did it."

The passage of Kevin's Law helped to reinforce my faith that new coalitions were possible. Not every moment on the House floor was as uplifting. In fact, most days were outright exhausting. Hundreds of bills were filed each session. As a new legislator, I filed and co-sponsored several dozen, hoping to tell a story of the type of leadership I believed in by drawing legislation that spoke to various structural challenges in Kentucky. But my bills to both legalize and decriminalize cannabis never made it out of committee. I also co-sponsored a bill to legalize cannabis for medicinal use that passed in the House but died in the Senate thanks to conservative legislators who still felt that it's better to criminalize people than to treat them—even as other substances like bourbon and tobacco continue to be heralded as a part of the state's heritage. I also filed a bill to end the practice of cash bail that the leadership killed, despite the fact that we had bipartisan support for reforming the practice.

I faced similar frustrations when it came to the bill I'd inherited from Rep. Owens to restore voting rights for people who had felony convictions in their past. The right to vote is the foundation of our democracy. To say that people should be banned forever, even after they have served their time, is not punishment; it's suppression. It is robbing people of the chance to have a voice. I reintroduced the bill along with my co-sponsor and frat brother, Rep. George Brown out of Fayette County. The House leadership agreed to allow a hearing before the Elections and Constitutional Amendments Committee, but it was for discussion only, which meant no vote would be taken to pass the legislation. On the one hand, it was tremendous progress to even get a hearing; this was the first bill sponsored primarily by Black legislators that was given a hearing in committee that session. On the other hand, the fact that this overwhelmingly popular bill only got a discussion was a slap in the face of every organization and every Kentuckian who showed the courage to speak up for democracy.

I used the hearing to highlight what every member in that chamber knew to be true. "We know our history," I said. "We know the story of Black Codes that were used to criminalize Black people for doing things like being on the wrong side of town or standing too close together. We know that disenfranchisement was a tool used to undermine the progress made after chattel slavery was largely outlawed. We know this is tied to structural racism and inequity that blocks Kentuckians from being heard today."

My words resonated with many on both sides of the aisle. I even had a Republican, Rep. Jason Nemes from Jefferson County, join me in testifying in support of the bill. We held out hope for a couple weeks, getting signals from leadership that they would reverse course and allow a vote. We knew that if it were brought up for a vote, it would absolutely pass the House, so that was an exciting prospect. Our hopes were dashed, though, as the Speaker banged the gavel for sine die, and the session ended before a vote could be taken.

Given the extreme minority the Democrats held in the Kentucky State Legislature, I quickly realized my efforts to pass meaningful legislation were going to be severely curtailed. Indeed, there was very little I could do to stop bad legislation from becoming law at all. After a while, I accepted that even if I couldn't use my voice to change the fate of a bill, I still had a responsibility to use my voice nonetheless. I had an obligation to speak my truth on behalf of T.J. and every person whose life was not seen as valuable.

Speaking on the House floor was an art. You had to gather your words and effectively speak on a platform that would be televised for the entire Commonwealth to see. In addition, you had to quickly develop a solid grasp of Robert's Rules of Order and the House rules. This was intimidating and encouraged most new legislators to ease into standing up to speak on the Floor. No one wanted to embarrass themselves. But I felt comfortable up there. My years coming to Frankfort with Senator Neal as well as my time as an intern and then legislative analyst helped me quickly move past the jitters a lot of new legislators experience. Leadership started to look for me to stand up and speak on issues. The leadership staff would text me notes, thanking me for standing up to speak on the Floor. I was in my element, and everyone knew it. There were only a few legislators who regularly got up and gave passionate speeches; many seemed to be nervous or just going through the motions. I quickly understood the importance of my role. I was able to speak about issues and the legislative process in a compelling manner that Republicans couldn't hand-wave away, so much so that at least one of them grew frustrated enough to tell me to "sit down."

But hostility wasn't the only response I met with. One day as I was walking into the annex, I noticed a tall, balding white man in overalls walking toward me. He was walking so quickly, I actually thought he might be looking for some kind of altercation. But when he made it to me, he put both hands on my shoulders and started to cry. "Rep. Booker," he said. "Thank you for using your voice to speak up for all of us across Kentucky. When you speak, I know you're speaking for me."

I put my hand on his arm and thanked him. And the amazing thing about it was, I hadn't changed my message since the day I first stood up in the community meeting for the FoodPort. I was still speaking about the things people needed to live lives with dignity and respect in the West End. The difference was that now I had a bigger stage and a bigger megaphone, and the message I brought with me from the hood was resonating with people all over Kentucky, because people all over Kentucky were getting fed up with the same old same old.

BY THE SUMMER of 2019, a political awakening was underway in Kentucky. Down in Harlan County, a group of coal miners made national news as they rose up in protest of how their employer, Blackjewel, was treating them. Blackjewel had filed for bankruptcy, which led to the abrupt firing of over 1,700 miners across multiple states, including over 600 Kentuckians. Because of the bankruptcy, the terminated miners wouldn't be receiving their final paychecks. Their benefits were being slashed, too.

Many of these miners came from generations of Kentuckians who'd gone down into the ground to keep our Commonwealth running. They sacrificed their health, committed their entire lives to this work. Then, out of nowhere, their hours started to get irregular. Several of them noticed that their paychecks stopped coming. Checks started to bounce, a crushing blow for families who had only this one source of income.

They filed a class-action lawsuit. Nearly a month went by with no movement from Blackjewel. Then some of the miners noticed a train coming down the tracks to a mine in the Cumberland area. It was being filled up with the very coal that these miners had busted their butts to dig. They knew that once that coal was gone, so was everything they worked for. So they camped on the tracks, blocking the train from pulling out.

The miners weren't alone. Their protests were coming in the wake of one of the biggest statewide walkouts Kentucky had ever seen. Our governor, Matt Bevin, elected in 2015, was Kentucky's own version of Donald Trump. Like the president he loved to tout his relationship with, Bevin billed himself as a big-time business person when really he was more of a bull in a china shop. He was brash, said exactly what he felt, and had no qualms disrespecting anyone. More than anyone else at the state level, Bevin had given oxygen to the Fox News conspiracists and damaged the climate of political discourse.

Bevin also had a total disregard for the institutions of government. He used his time in office to take a sledgehammer to organized labor, healthcare, and above all, public education. Shortly before I was elected, during the last month of the 2018 legislative session, Bevin and the Republican leadership in the House had slashed teacher pensions, sparking an open revolt among Kentucky's educators. They organized "sickouts" all over Kentucky, and school districts in all 120 counties ended up closing as teachers called in sick and headed to Frankfort to march in protest.

When the teachers marched on the Capitol, I went and stood with them out of solidarity. Now, hearing about the Blackjewel miners, I knew I had to do the same. I got on the road and headed to eastern Kentucky to stand on the tracks with them, riding down with a couple of teachers who wanted to support the strikers as well, bringing them cases of water, boxes of chips, baby supplies, gloves, and ponchos. Driving through Pike County and Martin County, I was in awe. I saw mile after mile of rusted-out cars and crumbling houses and busted old trailer homes. I saw the Dollar Stores and McDonald's franchises that had driven out local businesses. I saw a lot of isolation, but I also saw incredible beauty. The rolling hills and tree-covered mountains made the world feel big. The sky was a perfect blue, and the sunlight kissed the mountains. Although there was poverty here, there was a natural peace that made me jealous. As a

Kentuckian, I felt pride being there, similar to the pride I felt in the hood. Both places were like the rose that grew from concrete, like Tupac talked about.

By the time I made it to Harlan County, the protests had been going on for a couple of weeks. Everyone was kind and gracious. I ended up standing on the tracks beside a man named Scott. He and his father both worked in the mines, and he was standing in solidarity with the Blackjewel miners who had lost everything. I met another man with his wife and children, and they all thanked me for coming.

"I can't believe you came all the way from Louisville," the woman said.

"I had to come be with my family," I told her.

Together we helped to unload trucks of supplies from people sending water and food from across Kentucky. The miners' spirits were strong. They were singing, playing cornhole, and telling jokes. Kids were running around, picking up rocks alongside the tracks and throwing them at the rail line. The iron would clang as the rocks skipped off of them. The miners had tents set up around the tracks with rows of chairs on the tracks as well. They were camping out, with no plans to move until Blackjewel treated them like they mattered.

"We have nowhere else to go," one man said as he wiped sweat off his brow. "We made this company millions. They owe us our pay-checks." That was the energy from everyone, including the children. Nothing was going to run them over, not even a train.

Standing on the tracks, I listened to them talk about the future of the industry. "Rep. Booker," they told me, "we would love to do other things than go down in those mines. We would love to see new industries like solar. No one ever listens to us, though. This is all we have."

I tried not to say too much. I just wanted to be there to stand with them in support. As a state representative, I saw my role as a fighter for not just my district but every single Kentuckian. I was there for them. I was there to listen, lie on the tracks, or if need be, lock arms with them to physically block the train from moving. The whole experience reaffirmed the feelings I had about my own hood: that we shouldn't be judged or dismissed because of where we live. And, just as important, that the people closest to the struggle know exactly how to change things, if only the powers that be would listen.

After sitting on the tracks for several hours, we got in the car to head home; we had a four-hour drive and wanted to get on the road before the sun started to set. "It gets pitch-black in the mountains," Scott had warned me. We shook hands and hugged and then hit the road. On the way back, we stopped at a McDonald's. There weren't many places to grab a bite, but McDonald's and the Dollar Store were open. McDonald's was also one of the few places you could go that had fairly decent internet. For the majority of the drive, we didn't even have cell coverage.

You see the world differently when you can't afford to take things for granted. I couldn't help but think of the families that had to deal with that kind of isolation and deprivation day after day. It reminded me of the same urgent desperation we felt in my own community when we gathered in the streets to protest. When I looked at those miners, I saw family. Same as those teachers outside the Capitol, on those tracks I saw Kentuckians who were willing to stand together and demand that things change. They were sacrificing for their hopes of having a future.

The faith I held in building coalitions across Kentucky burned brighter than ever. I was determined to make sure we seized this moment together. As I finished that year in the legislature, I prayed about how I could continue to help inspire this uprising of regular people. I firmly believed this was the key to transforming Kentucky for the better.

The Blackjewel protests stretched from late summer into early fall of 2019, and by the time they were finally over, two amazing things had happened. The first was that the miners got their back pay. The second was that the people of Kentucky started coming together with a singular goal in mind: kicking Matt Bevin out of the governor's mansion on the first Tuesday in November.

Kentucky still holds statewide elections in nonpresidential years, but this year's gubernatorial contest wasn't just the most important race in Kentucky. With Bevin being cut from the same cloth as Donald Trump, this election was being touted as a bellwether for the president's possible re-election in 2020.

Bevin's opponent was Andy Beshear, the state's attorney general as well as the son of Steve Beshear, the sixty-first governor of Kentucky. The Beshears were a longtime political power in the Commonwealth. Their name had been on statewide ballots for years, and Steve Beshear had gained in popularity in his last term thanks to the successful expansion of Medicaid and the implementation of Kynect, Kentucky's nation-leading health insurance marketplace under the Affordable Care Act.

Statewide elections hadn't been going well for Democrats in Kentucky for some time. Luckily, this year the teachers gave us the momentum we needed. They marched on Frankfort, thousands of them in red T-shirts on every corner of the Capitol campus, standing in the hallways and crowding in the rotunda. As the representatives walked into the chambers, we could hear the teachers singing Twisted Sister's anthem "We're Not Gonna Take It." Their protests helped galvanize the movement that would take on Bevin, and Bevin himself only made it worse. He called the teachers thugs and said they were fostering child abuse by forcing kids to be at home by coming to the Capitol to protect funding for their schools. Matt Bevin insulted teachers with so much vitriol that even his fellow Republicans were disgusted.

On Election Day, the race was too close to call. And once the race was called, it was still too close for comfort. In the end, after Bevin refused to concede and demanded a recount, Andy Beshear won the race by just over five thousand votes, a margin of exactly 0.37 points. Most people believe that Bevin likely would have won if he had only been less of a jerk to the teachers. Republicans won every other statewide constitutional office. It was almost like we traded the Governor's office for Secretary of State, Auditor, Treasurer, and Attorney General. The election cycle largely hinged on the fact that Matt Bevin was a terrible governor, and that alone was not enough to carry the other races across the finish line. There was no substitute for doing the type of deep organizing that could sustain the energy ignited by the teacher protests.

Still, slim as it was, Beshear's victory was the shot of hope that many of us needed. And two days after getting sworn in, the newly elected governor kept his word, promptly signing an executive order to restore voting rights for people with past felony convictions. There was a buzz of anticipation in the Capitol the day of the signing. Everyone was jockeying to get a good spot for the commemorative photograph. I squeezed into position as close as I could, wanting to see the exact moment when he used his thick blue pen to make democracy real for over 170,000 Kentuckians. Senator Neal and Rep. Owens were close by as well, along with several people who now had the ability to be heard at the ballot box. Because I'd been a part of bringing the issue to statewide attention, the governor handed me one of the pens he used to sign the order. Looking at that blue pen, I could feel that a new movement was growing. I wasn't exactly sure what that meant for me at the time, but something in my spirit told me that I would have a big part in whatever was going to come next.

CHAPTER 18

THE HEAD OF THE DRAGON

I HAD SOMETHING I needed to tell Tanesha. She was sitting at her desk, which we'd wedged into the only place it would fit, the little nook at the end of our upstairs hallway, right outside Prestyn's room. It's where she worked for her job processing medical claims, usually setting herself up with her earbuds in and a movie streaming on her phone to make the time pass a little quicker. If I wanted to talk to her during the day, I typically had to catch her in between claims and get her to pause the movie and take out the earbuds. Which was exactly what I did when I let her know I wasn't going to go back to Frankfort for another term.

"Tanesha," I said, tapping her on the shoulder and waiting for her to stop her movie. "I don't think I'm running for reelection to the State House."

The window by the desk cast rays of sunlight across her face, so I couldn't really see her expression, but her voice told me she wasn't exactly thrilled by the news.

"Really, Charles?" she said. "You just got to the House. You're doing great work there, and I'm just now getting used to you being a representative."

I knew Tanesha didn't love the political arena. She wasn't happy that I had to travel from Louisville to Frankfort every day, work late hours, and at times stay overnight. But she had finally come around to the idea. Or at least she wasn't complaining about it. Now, I was pulling the rug out from under her.

Her reaction was the same that I got from the political friends I'd mentioned the idea to. One of them, a former labor organizer I affectionately referred to as "Ms. Wanda," said, "*Please* tell me you aren't serious!" I could hear the dismay in her voice. "If you run for re-election," she said, "you'll more than likely be unopposed. Why would you give that up?"

I couldn't really explain it, but I was already restless. My first year in the legislature had been one of the most inspiring of my career. I felt so much purpose walking into work. I was one of three legislators representing the West End, along with Rep. Reggie Meeks and Rep. Attica Scott. Meeks loved his big pickup truck and riding his motorcycle. A kind and graceful man, he didn't speak up as often as I did, but when he did his words were always timely and clear. I loved learning from him. Scott, a longtime organizer and the only Black woman in the legislature, was maybe more outspoken than me; she always kept a bullhorn close by in case we needed to make our way to a protest. I tried to balance Meeks's poise with Scott's passion, using their positions to figure out how I wanted to address various bills coming for a vote in the House.

The three of us often rode to Frankfort together, and pulling up to the Capitol in Meeks's truck always felt right. I loved walking in with them, my chin lifted and my chest filled with righteous pride. Our presence in the Capitol was a testament to the generations of Kentuckians who had fought for justice, civil rights, and democracy. It felt like the three of us were walking onto the battlefield to stand up for the people of Kentucky. I often had a song in my head as we walked, sometimes DMX, other times the theme from *Rocky*. As we walked in, various organizations and educators would be lined up in the halls. "There's Representative Booker!" I would hear them say, followed by a cheer and applause. They knew the fights we would face and wanted us to know we weren't alone. It was all tremendously inspiring. But it didn't stop this nagging feeling.

I never questioned whether I would stay in the thick of the movement happening across Kentucky, the teachers and the unions fighting back against injustice. Still, something was telling me that my role in changing the way politics works in Kentucky was going to go to a higher level. I wanted to be more involved, not less. I just wasn't sure how.

THE DRIVING FORCE behind my discontent was not the Republican Party; it was what the Republican Party had become in the age of Trump. It was degenerating so fast that the change was noticeable even from my first year to my second. Trump showed Republicans a whole new way to build a political movement in the age of cable news soundbites and the social media rage machine. The Kentucky legislature was now filling up with people who, like the president, had zero interest in governing. They pounded their fists and spouted right-wing radio conspiracy theories and did their best to accelerate the destructive approach Trump had unleashed on political discourse.

Fueled by Trump's anti-immigrant rhetoric, they introduced a family deportation and sanctuary city bill that had nothing to do with the actual facts of immigrant populations in Kentucky. It was just red meat for their base, stoking irrational fears about people flooding across the border to cause harm and somehow ending up in Kentucky. None of it had any relevance to the issues the people of Kentucky were actually facing, even their own Republican constituents, who were dealing with the same poverty, crumbling interstate highways, and disappearing jobs that Democratic voters wanted leaders to address.

The Democratic caucus always met ahead of the House being gaveled in for session. Since Republicans were in leadership, we were forced to either pile into the minority staff office suite or find an open office the Republicans weren't using. There were about twenty-five members of the caucus, and we would join the minority leadership staff and sit and talk strategy.

In those caucus meetings before session, I typically stayed quiet as I listened to fellow legislators vent. "What are the Republicans going to try to do today?" Would they bring up legislation to cut food stamps? Try to weaken the permit process for firearms? Pass yet another total ban to abortion for the Supreme Court to strike down? Or would it be further restrictions on voting access?

All of these bills were being driven by the Republicans' broader national strategy; in the wave of abortion-related bills being filed by Republican legislatures across the country, many of them were even filed with identical language. Bills that never should have made it out of committee were now being moved up the line. Even Republican leadership in the House seemed to be frustrated, often at odds with their own caucus. It didn't matter. From Trump on down, the agenda was to focus on fear and contentious wedge issues, and Republicans in leadership appeared all but powerless to stop it.

The more pragmatic Republican leaders knew as well as we did that these pointless culture war debates were not really about protecting life or religious liberty. They were being used to target state legislative seats to drive up turnout and win big majorities to amass power. The problem was that these arguments were pulling at deeply passionate divides in our Commonwealth; they were tearing at the very fabric of the state. One man was responsible for all of this, and one man had the power to stop it, and that man was not Donald Trump.

Despite being almost wholly ignorant of Mitch McConnell when I failed to get his scholarship, I started to dig deeper on who he really was following Obama's historic election, when I heard him say that his priority was to make sure that the country's first Black president would only serve one term. Then, once I started spending time in Frankfort, it was hard to ignore his presence there. Even the Republican Party headquarters is named after him. It should be. He built it.

Mitch McConnell has never been an eloquent speaker. He's never been charismatic or even particularly likable, so it's easy to underestimate the deep impact he has had on the state. Starting in the early 1980s when the Republican Party of Kentucky was reeling, Mitch McConnell traveled the Commonwealth, gathering support for his eventual Senate run. He found and groomed candidates for local races, building a pipeline of people to run for office across Kentucky. The snowball grew over time, and each cycle saw more seats become competitive across the Commonwealth. The Democrats were caught flat-footed; secure in their hold on power, they weren't doing any-thing to build a bench for future candidates. Even as McConnell moved up to join the leadership in the U.S. Senate, he remained dedi-cated to his mission of controlling state-level politics. To this day, vir-tually every elected and appointed Republican official in the state owes their position to Mitch McConnell. His enforcers are every-where, and nobody will cross him.

For years, McConnell's power has kept Democrats scared of their own shadow, a fact that was driven home for me when I got fired over the Alison Lundergan Grimes video. As I was getting pushed out, I started to hear rumors about who was doing the pushing. There are no secrets in Frankfort. Everybody talks. The undercurrent of the ru-mors was that I'd been pushed out because McConnell's office had come down on Republican leadership to make it happen. Not because McConnell cared about me; I was nobody. It was just an opportunity to score political points by painting the Democrats and Alison Lun-dergan Grimes in a bad light.

In the days after, so many reputable people kept coming to me to tell me, "Man, it's not right what McConnell's doing to you." These were folks high up in my party's leadership telling me this. Now, was Mitch McConnell actually behind my getting fired from the LRC? I have no idea. But that's exactly the point: Even if McConnell had nothing to do with getting me fired, everyone believed that he did, so now all those people are going to think twice about crossing the man because if they do, they'll lose their paychecks. When people are scared of you because they believe you have powers that you don't ac-tually have? *That's power.*

Of course, the fact that McConnell has run Kentucky like an old-school political boss wouldn't be as much of a problem if Mitch McConnell were still the man he made himself out to be at the start of his career. Our junior senator, Rand Paul, is the worst kind of true believer; the fact that he was the only senator out of a hundred to block passage of a law making lynching a federal crime says a lot about him. McConnell, on the other hand, started as a politician who sup-ported organized labor, women's rights, and expanded access to healthcare. He was even an early advocate for civil rights. But over the years he's proved to be a chameleon of sorts. His politics changed dramatically. His interest in policy gave way to his devotion to power. He is one of the smartest politicians in our lifetime, and he understands how to seize on the current social climate to collect power for himself.

Mitch McConnell follows the money. Practically every decision he makes can be tied back to a corporate donor or big-money interest. As the Republican business establishment has adopted ever more radical, libertarian positions on gutting the tax base and passing right-to-work laws, McConnell has moved with them. As the Fox News base has grown ever hungrier for culture war confrontations over abortion and guns and immigrants, McConnell has moved with them. Over time, he's become the single greatest obstacle to anything that would help Kentuckians live a better life, consistently opposing raising wages and protecting labor unions, and he's absolutely ignored the Kentucky communities that lost jobs in the decline of the coal industry. He says he's a friend of coal, but he didn't give a damn about the miners who did the work. Although Kentucky was a shining example of how to expand healthcare following the passage of the Affordable Care Act, McConnell used his authority to fuel the ongoing fight to repeal it. While opioids were wreaking havoc on our families, McConnell took big money from the pharmaceutical industry and blocked urgently needed reform.

The moment I remember most clearly is the horrific mass shooting at Sandy Hook, where children my daughter's age lost their lives. Mitch had the ear of a cold stone, using his position as leader to block even the most basic gun reforms, even ones with overwhelming bipartisan support. He wouldn't give an inch if it meant he wasn't seen as holding absolute power. Heck, he had helped to ignite the idea of the 2nd Amendment as a wedge issue in the first place.

The thing that's most damning to me is that he knows what he's doing is wrong. He's not a true believer. He's not an ideologue. He only cares about one thing: power. Even if it comes at the cost of rampant poverty and sickness in Kentucky. This is a man who smiles when people refer to him as the Grim Reaper. As he's ascended to the heights in the U.S. Senate, the same dynamic has played out in the whole country, from the Supreme Court on down.

The election of Donald Trump proved to be the ultimate test of McConnell's chameleon nature. Trump's overt racism and cable news theatrics were the polar opposite of McConnell's quiet and stealthy approach. Yet McConnell managed to adapt and survive again, keeping Senate Republicans and Kentucky Republicans in near-total lockstep behind Trump's divisive agenda. He saw the shift in the nation's politics and found a way to make it work for him. He gave cover to the rise in conspiracy theories and fearmongering, allowing our already divided political climate to spiral downward.

I couldn't understand why the Kentucky Democratic Party was seemingly toothless in fighting back. So much of what McConnell and the Kentucky Republicans were doing was deeply unpopular, particularly their actions against the teachers and the mine workers, yet the party's power only grew over time. By 2019, Republican domination of Kentucky state politics was so complete that it's easy to forget that Democrats had only recently held majorities in both chambers. When Republicans took control of the State House in 2016, it was the first time they had done so since 1920.

I only began to understand the nature of the problem after I met a strategist by the name of Jeff Noble while I was working on Congressman Yarmuth's campaign. A longtime member of the State Central Executive Committee, the governing board for the Kentucky Democratic Party, Jeff has a brilliant understanding of Kentucky politics. The way he explained it to me, over time, the party's leadership had grown older; they had stopped recruiting new Kentuckians to serve in leadership, and everyone got comfortable with where things were and didn't think about what the future would look like. On top of that, the old-school spirit of getting out in the community and organizing all but went away. "Charles," Jeff told me. "There was a time when many people got jobs because of the party. Legislative district chairs actually had influence, and precinct captains actually organized their precincts."

All of this sounded like something out of a history book, because

I never saw it in my lifetime. Even when the party was very active, communities like mine were not at the table. So the issue was a matter of both falling asleep at the wheel and overlooking large areas of people who vote Democrat but are disconnected from political power structures, all of which was bound to catch up to the party. And it did.

Furthermore, the growing presence and weaponization of wedge issues dominated political discourse. Through Fox News and talk radio, Republicans made themselves the loudest, angriest voices in the room. When Democrats tried to develop messaging, it largely amounted to deflecting or defending themselves from the Republican talking points. Everything the party did was reactive, which frustrated Democrats who wanted to see the party fight for its values. With every election, the sense of hopelessness grew and the map shrank. Fighting for votes in Eastern Kentucky—why bother? Once Steve Beshear termed out of office, Western Kentucky was written off as well. In Democratic strongholds like Louisville, the party retreated to a get-out-the-vote strategy and nothing more, missing the chance to reach persuadable moderates and swing voters.

There were still some steadfast voices on the left, but it felt like many were on the verge of giving up. Others were getting up in age or had passed away. Some, like Jefferson County Representative Denny Butler, simply changed parties. We needed new voices, new perspectives that could stand up in leadership. I saw myself as one of those new leaders. I wanted to do my part to help folks rise up and find their voice, and as dysfunctional and broken as things in Frankfort were, I saw a path forward.

THE REALITY OF Kentucky is that its politics don't reflect its people. Our legislative districts are extremely gerrymandered, and our strict voter laws have kept Kentucky one of the most disenfranchised states in the country. Years of corruption have caused many people to give up on politics and opt for working outside of government channels.

In spite of all that, everywhere I went across Kentucky I felt energy and electricity. The teachers marching on the Capitol and the Black-jewel miners standing up for their families—I knew they were just the tip of the iceberg. The biggest problem in the Kentucky Democratic Party was that regular people were disconnected from it. I believed that if we could encourage more regular people to have faith in and get involved in the democratic process, we could give ourselves a chance of actually changing things for our families. We could build power across Kentucky and fight back. For me, the only option was to organize, to build a new statewide coalition across every county in Kentucky. It was either do that or give up, and I hadn't come this far to give up.

I envisioned two possible paths toward this goal. One was a twelve-year plan that would have me staying in the legislature, working my way into leadership, and then using that platform to open the door for more new leaders across the board. This path was long but realistic. I was already gaining support from the caucus, I had proven I could pass bipartisan legislation, and I was building a contingent of support across Kentucky. We were undergoing some leadership changes, with Rocky Adkins not seeking re-election as House minority leader, and I knew that more retirements were likely in the next couple years. I could have stayed in what would most likely be a safe seat and built out this longer plan.

The other path I could see would require me doing something big, taking a bold step that would immediately catalyze the growing unrest and urgency that had fueled the teachers flooding into the Capitol. The teachers had been a huge factor in my believing big change was possible. They had coordinated across all of Kentucky's 120 counties. They had created a network to communicate with educators who were not in formal leadership. They developed a way to quickly mobilize actions across Kentucky. Most importantly, they were not a strictly partisan movement. The teachers were from all ends of the political spectrum. They found a common bond and used that to bridge divides of party, geography, and economic status.

That was the magic I believed we needed more of to transform Kentucky. If we could capture that energy while it was growing, we could possibly fast-track building up the new infrastructure that would allow more Kentuckians to step into leadership at the local and state levels. To make that happen, I'd have to do something big enough to gain everyone's attention, something that would cause shock waves, something that would bring Black, white, and brown Kentuckians together and halt the free fall of political dysfunction and division.

Once I began thinking about the two paths I could take, I immediately knew there was only one real option. I had to go big. Pacing back and forth outside of Quills Coffee on East Main Street, I called my oldest and most trusted advisor to get her opinion. "Real change is possible in Kentucky," I said once my mom picked up. "I can see it in the eyes of those teachers. I can see it in the eyes of those coal miners. I can see it in the eyes of those students organizing across the Commonwealth. I don't want to leave the legislature too soon, but I just keep feeling like there's more I need to do."

"Son, I know your heart is in the right place," she said. "Whatever you decide to do, you know I got your back."

That was all I needed to hear. "I knew you'd understand," I said, "and I know this seat doesn't belong to me. It's the people's seat. My job isn't to keep it but to do right by it. That's what Grandad taught me: If you see a problem, you don't look around and wait for someone to step up, you run to it. So that's what I'm going to do. I'm going to go for the head of the dragon, Mama. I'm going to beat Mitch McConnell."

CHAPTER 19

THE SMOKETOWN COLLECTIVE

"MY NAME IS Charles Booker," I said, standing onstage in front of the roaring crowd, "and I am running for United States Senate."

The room erupted with applause. It was January 5, 2020, and I was standing onstage at Manhattan, a Black-owned event space on the eastern edge of downtown Louisville. It felt like the place was shaking. The energy was electric. Mom, Tanesha, and the girls stood onstage behind me, and my Pastor, Dr. F. Bruce Williams, who'd just introduced me, stood off to the side. They all joined in as the crowd shouted, "Booker! Booker! Booker!"

There were easily 250 people crammed into that room, but the doors were open and supporters were crowded outside as well. I looked out and saw faces that I'd met on my exploratory listening tour, including the folks I'd met in Paducah who'd driven over three hours to be there. We'd decorated the room with gold balloons, and the crowd was batting them back and forth over their heads like beach balls. The sight was absolutely amazing. I could only smile. I reached into my pocket, grabbed T.J.'s dog tag, and squeezed it tight in my hand. Looking up to the sky, I nodded my head at the two people who couldn't be there, Grandma and Grandad.

We'd lost Grandad to a stroke only a few months before. The last time I saw him was a few days before he passed, at church. We'd just celebrated his ninetieth birthday, and his spirits were as strong as ever. I walked over to where he was sitting in his wheelchair, put my hand on his shoulder, and reached out to shake his hand like I always did. At that point, I'd launched my exploratory committee but hadn't yet committed to formally enter the race. Grandad looked up at me, smiled, and asked, "Have you decided to run for Senate yet?"

At that point, I still wasn't 100 percent sure. From the moment I'd called my mom telling her I wanted to run, the first thing I had to do was convince myself I wasn't crazy. I'd been in politics long enough to know any campaign I ran would be the longest of long shots. I had no money. No Black Kentuckian had ever been elected to federal office. The national Democratic Party had already coalesced behind a favored candidate, Amy McGrath, who'd raised close to $30 million. Beyond that, we were talking about Mitch McConnell, one of the most powerful politicians in the country, a man who could grind the Senate to a halt and crush anyone standing in his way. But the crazy thing was, once I started talking to people about it, nobody thought I was crazy.

To test the viability of a run, the first thing I did was spend a week in D.C. talking to anyone who would listen: polling specialists, communications experts, labor leaders, congressional staff. In every meeting, I told my story and presented my vision of how we could build a new coalition among poor white, Black, and brown communities rooted in the common bonds I'd learned about during my time working across Kentucky. How we could train a new wave of organizers and political leaders in communities that have typically been written off. How I would leverage my extensive relationships to build the kind of grassroots movement that could overpower a big-money campaign. In every single meeting, the response was the same. Everyone doubted that anyone could beat McConnell, but they all acknowledged that the idea was compelling. Most importantly, nobody laughed me out of the room, and nobody told me not to run.

Back in Kentucky, after putting together a bare-bones staff, I launched my exploratory committee and went on a listening tour, going deep into the reddest parts of the state, from Covington in the northeast to Paducah out west. I was testing my theory that people, regardless of race and regardless of party, were open to a message that brought Kentuckians together. We made nearly a dozen stops over three weeks. The rooms were always packed; every event was at stand-ing capacity. Forty people crammed into a deli in Whitesburg; nearly seventy people in a restaurant in Bowling Green; forty people stand-ing shoulder to shoulder in a smoothie and tea shop in Paducah. It felt like a concert tour or a revival. Time and again I found myself in rooms of folding chairs filled with retired miners, exhausted moms, and frustrated young people. A truck driver would jump up and talk about how sick and tired he was of the attacks on labor unions. A woman would talk about her bout with cancer and plead for universal healthcare. Every time I shared my story of battling type 1 diabetes, someone would come up to me and tell me their own story, thanking me for letting them know that they mattered.

Across the state, with every place that I went and every person I spoke to, the energy I felt confirmed for me that Kentucky needed precisely the type of movement I was trying to build. Still, the ques-tion remained: Was I the right person to build it? I'd be lying if I didn't say I was intimidated by how daunting the task would be. Part of me was actively looking for reasons not to do it. I'd be opening my family up to political attacks. I'd have to raise millions of dollars. I'd have to ask dozens of people to commit a year of their lives to helping me. What if I let all those people down? As the months passed, I went back and forth. I was searching for a sign from God to tell me I was going down the wrong path, that it was a mistake, that I was simply pursuing blind ambition. Then, one morning as I was getting dressed for a meeting, I got the call from Mom.

"C.J.," she said, "I need you to meet me at the hospital."

"What is it?"

"It's your grandad."

"What's wrong?" I asked, alarmed and confused. "Why are you sending me to the hospital?"

She wouldn't answer. She just kept repeating, "C.J., just get to the hospital."

I walked into Kaylin's room and paced around, pressing the phone to my ear. Mom's voice was stern and shaking. Fear started to set in, but I wasn't going to assume the worst. "Mom, if you're saying what I think you might be saying, you're going to have to tell me." I got stern myself. I wasn't being disrespectful, but I knew there was something she didn't want to tell me. This was about to become one of the most serious conversations of my life.

"Mom?" I repeated, waiting for her to respond.

"C.J. . . . He's gone."

I heard the words, but I couldn't take them in at first. Then, when I finally understood what she told me, I fell to my knees and screamed at the top of my lungs, "No, no, no, no!"

Grandad had always been my rock and my inspiration. Growing up, I revered him and wanted to be just like him. For years, every proud moment of my life had been followed by a handshake from that man, a handshake that made me feel like I wasn't invisible. Grandad's commitment to family shaped how I looked at my own daughters. This man had seen his classmates kidnapped and forced to work on farms for free in Mississippi; he'd had to count the number of beans in a jar in order to vote; he'd spent his whole life fighting for better lives and working conditions for the people of Louisville.

Sgt. Lindsay E. Hearn Sr. was the reason I had made history as the youngest Black state legislator in Kentucky in nearly ninety years. Seeing him stand up out of his wheelchair in the Kentucky House of Representatives on the day of my swearing-in had been one of the greatest moments of my life. Losing him was paralyzing. I was crushed.

I gathered myself and drove to the hospital in a daze. When I pulled into the ER parking lot, some of my cousins were standing outside crying. I did my best to pull it together. I walked inside, found my mom, and we walked into the room where his body lay in rest, and I shook his hand for the last time.

Still, even though I felt alone, I knew that he was with me. He had taught me so much, and now I knew it was my turn to carry the torch. Walking out of the hospital, I couldn't shake the memory of the last time I'd seen him alive, sitting in his wheelchair, looking up at me, and asking if I'd decided to run. Now I knew the answer.

"Yes, Grandad. I have."

THE COMMONWEALTH OF Kentucky has over three million registered voters, but even before I launched my exploratory committee, I knew there was one vote I had to win just to get started: Tanesha's.

When I first stood in the doorway of our bathroom, leaning on the frame and pitching her the idea of running, she looked up from across the room with genuine concern. "Mitch McConnell is so dirty," she said, "and he'll do everything he can to drag you through the mud. How will we stay safe if people start attacking you?"

"Well, I can handle that," I said. "The most important thing for me is that we have a plan to keep you and the girls safe."

She still looked skeptical. Up to that point, Tanesha had already accommodated my passion for politics more than I had any right to expect. The long days in Frankfort, the public-facing nature of the work—she didn't love it, but she understood that it was my mission. I wouldn't say she was excited about my taking on Mitch McConnell, but her concern this time around wasn't about me running. Rather, it was about my plan to stay safe given the high profile of the race.

"I'll put together a plan," I said. "I'll build a real team and protect us, and if I can't do that, I won't run. Okay?"

"Okay, Charles," she said calmly.

The first step to launching a campaign was putting together the right team, and that team started with Taylor Coots. I'd first met Taylor back in 2008 when we were both working on the Louisville mayoral race, me for Councilman Tandy and Taylor for Councilman Jim King. Taylor was a longtime political operative who'd worked on several statewide races and even worked on presidential campaigns. His wife, Kelsey, was a teacher from Owensboro who had spent time in the Deep South with Teach For America before coming back to teach in Louisville.

Our paths crossed again when we both took staffing positions at Metro Council and then again as staffers in the state legislature. We would often meet up for lunch in the Capitol Annex cafeteria and talk shop, and the two of us just clicked. We were like an odd couple:

a tall, white guy with sandy brown hair swooped back like JFK, and a young Black guy from the hood. What we had in common was a passion to transform Kentucky politics. By the time the U.S. Senate campaign came around, Jacie and Perry had both moved away from Louisville, so I wasn't in as close communication with them as during my previous runs. More and more, when I needed a sounding board and advice, I was turning to Taylor. His insights into Kentucky politics were nearly unmatched, and I trusted him to give me clear-eyed and honest advice.

Now, when I say nobody thought that taking on Mitch McConnell was crazy, that's not entirely true. Taylor absolutely thought I was crazy. "It's a suicide mission!" he said, the first time he heard me explain my whole plan. But Taylor was there with me for every step of my listening tour across Kentucky, and he'd come away a true believer.

In the beginning, our team was small. It was me and Taylor and Kelsey and my friend LaShea Burt, who basically wound up being asked to do everything administrative. Eventually we were able to hire someone to manage the finances and take over more of the campaign management so that LaShea could do more political work.

We didn't have a lot of money, but we had enough to hire a couple staff. Taylor recommended two guys, Colin Lauderdale and Will Carle. A tall, skinny guy with long, flowing hair, Colin was meticulous and detail-oriented. He was also the son of Burt Lauderdale, the executive director of Kentucky's largest grassroots organization, Kentuckians for the Commonwealth, or KFTC. Colin had also worked extensively with the Mountain Association for Community Economic Development, or MACED, which supports development projects in Appalachia. Will, the oldest guy on our team, was short in stature, with short brown hair and a scruffy voice. A seasoned political strategist, he'd worked for State Auditor Adam Edelen and built good relationships with many labor leaders. Colin and Will both seemed intrigued by the challenge of helping me. Neither of them really believed I would win, but they believed in what I was fighting for. I was grateful for the help.

We couldn't afford to rent a large space, but one of my supporters, a local attorney named Ben Carter who was known for fighting for housing rights, stepped in to help. Ben owned an office space in Smoketown, one of Louisville's historically Black neighborhoods, and he'd set up the space as something he called the Smoketown Collective, built to house artists, small businesses, and activist groups. Ben carved out a part of the space for us to rent.

Running the campaign from Smoketown made me feel steeped in a particularly powerful piece of Louisville's history. In the late 1800s, freed slaves migrated there in large numbers, and the area took on its name from the massive kilns in the brick-making factories that used to billow thick clouds of smoke out over the small shotgun houses that sprang up around the area. In the early years of urban renewal, the homes were cleared out and a segregated public housing project called Sheppard Square was built. Like most public housing projects, Sheppard Square became a hub for poverty, segregation, and violence. But at the center of it all the story of Black perseverance and community continued: Smoketown's Presbyterian Community Center is where Muhammad Ali learned how to box. With the implementation of the HOPE VI federal program under Obama, these distressed housing projects were being torn down to be replaced by upgraded single-family and multi-unit housing, and the area was becoming more contemporary.

Going to our Smoketown campaign office each day, I felt all of the tension, uncertainty, frustration, and hope of this changing neighborhood. Many families in the area were still struggling to get by. The corner outside our office was littered with trash. The curb was crumbling. The light pole at the corner was leaning to one side, mostly because several cars had smashed into it over the years. The street corner outside our office always had people wandering around, many of whom seemed to have fallen on hard times. Our windows were so thin we could hear everything: a man groaning as he walked by, looking in the trash can; the tire screech of a car swerving to avoid an accident. More than a few times, someone would come up to the door asking for help. I tried to keep some snacks available in case someone needed it.

Inside, our tiny office was just large enough for a table on one side and two cubby-sized desk areas on the other. A gap under the front door let cold air in. Ben put a small heater in the room, but it was on the wall near the ceiling. The heat didn't reach the floor. Most days we froze in there while I made donor calls or gave phone interviews. But none of that mattered. It didn't matter that it was small and cold. It didn't matter that people would regularly try to walk through the office to get to the rest of the building, even barging in while I was making national donor calls. The only thing that mattered is that we had stepped out on faith and found a space that was just for the campaign. We put up some of our rally signs in those thin, rattling windows. The journey was starting in earnest. I was ready to take on the most powerful Republican in the U.S. Senate. But first, all I had to do was beat one of the most well-funded primary candidates in the history of Kentucky politics.

IN 2020, Amy McGrath was the anointed candidate of the national Democratic Party. She'd become a media fixture overnight thanks to a very well-made ad that went viral during her 2018 race against Andy Barr for the 6th Congressional District in Lexington, which covers Frankfort and Lexington. McGrath had a compelling story. She was a working mom and a former Marine fighter pilot taking on a Republican incumbent in the wake of the #MeToo movement. When her campaign took off, she'd raised a huge amount of money. But in the end, even with the midterm backlash against Trump, she'd lost. It was hard to believe she would defeat McConnell this time around. But she was tapped into the big-money machine and had already raised close to $30 million.

It was easy to see where she was spending the money. It seemed as if every minute there was an ad on TV for Amy McGrath. They were polished and well produced but uninspiring. The words felt like empty phrases meant to check off a political box of some sort. It felt robotic. "On paper, she's perfect," one media consultant told me, but what looked good on paper didn't resonate the same with Kentuckians. There was no message, no vision about us and how things could be better.

If you spent one minute on the ground in Kentucky, though, you knew that she had very little support. People in Lexington still had tough feelings about her for squandering a congressional race against Andy Barr. Despite being born and raised here, she'd spent her adult life elsewhere, as a career military officer. She was an unknown quantity to the labor unions, the grassroots organizations, and most of our elected officials. Of those who did know her, virtually no one was excited about her. In her rollout on *Morning Joe* she'd said she would look for ways to work with Trump, and that pissed everyone off. It was a complete slap in the face. We were desperate for change, and McGrath sent the message that nothing was really going to change. At every campaign stop, at least one person would share why they were disappointed with her. "What is a pro-Trump Democrat?" people would ask.

Democratic leaders in Washington, D.C., namely the Democratic Senatorial Campaign Committee, threw their weight behind McGrath from the beginning. Considering her lack of support on the ground, this move sent a signal that national leaders were counting Kentucky out. It was an admission that they had no confidence that a campaign that ran boldly on Democratic values could actually win in Kentucky. They were ignoring the growing energy on the ground for real change, ignoring the discontent and desperation that helped to elect Trump—which was exactly how we ended up with Trump in the first place. And given Amy's anointed status as the DSCC pick, the national media talked about the Senate race as if she were already the nominee. It was virtually impossible for us to get any major outlets to pay attention to our campaign.

There was a third candidate in the race as well, a farmer from Eastern Kentucky named Mike Broihier. Mike was a retired Marine, just like Amy. He was from Wisconsin and had moved to Kentucky to start his own farm. He was a nice guy when I met him, but no one knew much about him. He had a platform similar to my own. We both supported universal basic income and criminal justice reform.

His launch video focused on getting rid of labels, a nod to the idea of people coming together. However, very few people knew him, as it was his first time running for office.

Ultimately, Mike's message was a troubling one. He started wearing a cowboy hat and he kept saying over and over again that Kentuckians needed to support someone who could actually win. Mike never mentioned the color of my skin, but his campaign supporters often did. A number of national progressive groups that I had worked with in the past got behind Mike, and some of their members and supporters were on social media being perfectly candid about why they were doing it. I would hear phrases like, "We need someone who actually understands all of Kentucky." Or "We like Charles, but we need someone who will win in rural parts of Kentucky." Or "We need a candidate every Kentuckian can support." Since Mike's platform was so similar to mine, at times it felt like his primary pitch to voters was simply that he was electable because he wasn't Black.

In the 2020 Democratic primary for the U.S. Senate, I was the only candidate on the ballot with actual government and policy experience in the Commonwealth of Kentucky, yet there was a deep cynicism among some Democrats that only a certain type of person could win, and that type of person didn't include me. Ironically, while the Democratic establishment tried to dismiss me and some progressive groups failed to see past my race, the one person who immediately realized just how much potential I had was Mitch McConnell himself.

Mitch McConnell knows the Kentucky electorate like the back of his hand. He knew he could easily beat the national Democrats' big-money candidate, but his campaign saw the movement I was building as the very real threat that it was. From the moment I announced, if someone googled my name, an ad from Mitch McConnell would pop up attacking me. McConnell's people came for me, too, calling me radical and buying ads to compare me to Alexandria Ocasio-Cortez, the progressive New Yorker who'd replaced Nancy Pelosi as Fox News's favorite bogeywoman. His Team Mitch social media team regularly attacked me as well.

To get the chance to take on McConnell, I first had to get past Mike and Amy. I knew Mike had very little chance to compete statewide, but Amy's financial and institutional support were almost insurmountable. I essentially had to run against the Democratic big-money machine in the primary just to get the chance to run against the Republican big-money machine in the general. I was going to have to do it from my tiny, drafty one-room campaign office in Smoketown, and the one thing I needed was the one thing I didn't have: money. It doesn't matter how much money you raise if you don't inspire people; if you can't do that, money's just a ticket to an expensive defeat. But campaigns cost money, and at the end of the day you can only go so far without it.

Going all the way back to my first campaign for State Senate, I had never liked fundraising. I don't come from money, and when you don't come from money you're used to everyone around you being broke. You might ask for their help, but you don't ever ask them for money because you respect the fact that they don't have it. So calling people as a candidate to ask for money never felt right. Up against McGrath's $30 million war chest, I had to get over that mentality fast.

As the campaign took off, I would have to hole up in my kitchen or at the office for four or five hours straight, calling and calling. It was brutal. Every minute I spent on the phone asking for money was time I couldn't spend meeting Kentuckians and helping them feel the power of this message. I needed to be in front of people so they could know the momentum was real.

I called everyone: former classmates and colleagues, frat brothers, Democratic leaders across Kentucky. I would do calls every weekday between the hours of 10 A.M. and 6 P.M. On Saturdays we would call until 4 P.M., and on Sundays we could call between 1 P.M. and 5 P.M., being careful not to upset people coming home from church or preparing for Sunday dinner. LaShea would sit with me most days, reading the numbers to me and telling me who I was about to call before they picked up the phone.

Many of the calls were positive, and it was clear that most of the

Kentuckians I spoke to were happy that there was going to be a primary. However, for every word of encouragement I received, I'd run into someone reminding me that I was Black.

"Charles, it's going to be tough for you running as a Black man," one might say. Or "I support you, but I don't know if Kentucky will support a Black person." Over and over. One older legislator erupted in laughter when I called. "Charles," he said, still chuckling. "I hope you win. But if these folks in Kentucky vote for a Black man to beat McConnell, I'll run through the streets naked!"

He didn't mean me any harm—he even made a contribution—but his cynicism was a part of the bigger obstacle I had to get over. Some Democrats that naturally aligned with me were hesitant to help me because of the color of my skin. That hurt, but I understood. They were acknowledging their fears of being unable to overcome the weight of Kentucky's history, and I knew I needed to prove them wrong.

One phone call stayed with me more than any other. It wasn't a phone call that I made; it was one that I got. I was sitting outside the Pizza Hut on West Broadway, getting ready to head in and get some dinner for the girls, when my phone rang. It was the Louisville journalist Phillip Bailey, the same reporter who'd written the piece on me over the video for Alison Lundergan Grimes that got me fired from the LRC.

We talked for a few minutes. He seemed generally skeptical of our campaign and raised a few points about Republican dominance in Kentucky politics. I pushed back, telling him all the stories of the people I'd met across the state that I thought proved him wrong. Then he asked the question everyone had been asking for months and would keep asking for the rest of the campaign: Will Kentucky—especially white, rural Kentucky—vote for a Black person?

"Well," I said, "they at least deserve the chance to choose. So I guess we'll find out."

CHAPTER 20

HOOD TO THE HOLLER

COLIN'S ADVICE RUNG in my ears as I stood over my suitcase, deciding what to pack. "Charles," he said, "it's going to be cold. Appalachian winters are a different type of cold. Make sure you bring layers."

It was the last week of February, and Colin and I were getting ready for a four-day road trip east. I shoved in a few extra sweaters and made sure to grab Grandad's black leather gloves. Next to my suitcase on the bed sat one of our organizer travel kits: a box with clipboards, voter registration cards, stickers, campaign literature, rally signs, markers, flip chart paper, and Post-it Notes.

"Can I go?" Prestyn asked, hugging my leg as I zipped up my bag.

"Not this time, but soon!"

"I'm going, too!" Kaylin yelled from down the hallway.

I hugged them all and grabbed Tanesha's hand to pray. I prayed that the Lord would keep them safe while I was gone and that he would place angels around me as I stepped out on faith to take my message deep into the heart of Trump Country. Tanesha didn't say she was worried, but she kept asking questions about where I was going and who would be with me. "I'll be fine," I told her reassuringly.

Just then, Colin knocked on the door. I gave the girls one last hug, hustled out to the street, and threw my bags in the back of his Subaru SUV. Idling behind Colin was a small sedan. At the wheel was Travis Waldron, a journalist with *The Huffington Post* and a native Kentuckian who was going to be joining us for the trip. I nodded to Travis and hopped into the SUV with Colin. It was toasty inside.

"Let's hit the road!" I said, and we were off.

The drive from Louisville to our first stop in Pikeville took a little over three hours. The first time I'd gone out to Eastern Kentucky, driving down to Harlan County the previous July to take part in the Blackjewel miner protests, the trees along the mountains had been full and green, and the valleys were covered with beautiful grass that swayed with the warm summer breeze. Now, in the dead of winter, many of the trees were bare. There was a constant dusting of frost on the mountains, giving them a beautiful light-gray shadow, and the air was so cold and crisp it made my face tingle.

We were taking this drive so that we could put to rest the one question that our skeptics refused to let go: Could a Black man really win in the mountains of Eastern Kentucky? By this time the question did more than annoy me. It offended me. Because I remembered walking into those commission meetings as a director at Fish and Wildlife, standing before a crowd as the only Black person there. I remembered how the stereotypes and misconceptions melted away once you actually sat down and talked to the person you'd pre-judged. I remembered how my own eyes were opened when I saw how families in Appalachia experience so many of the same things I experience in the hood.

Virtually no one who was following or writing about this race could see it the way I did. None of them were talking about the real chance to bring struggling white, Black, and brown communities together, but I knew if I gave them a glimpse of what it looked like, our campaign would catch fire.

"We need to tell the story!" I'd told the team as we were planning the trip. "We need to make people see the coalition we can build. If people can see what we see, we can win this race. So let's show it to them. Let's go to Eastern Kentucky." So here we were, on a big tour across Eastern Kentucky. We even decided to call it a "Green New Deal Tour" just to make sure the doubters paid attention.

Colin was a big help in planning the trip because he knew a lot of

organizers and party leaders in the area from working with Kentuckians for the Commonwealth. Meanwhile, Will knew the counties and
their vote history like the back of his hand. Together, we pulled out
the map and circled every county people had written off as Republican strongholds and told us we couldn't win—that's where we were
going. I wanted to sit down with miners and their families. I wanted
to meet with people in Appalachia who were running solar farms and
trying to increase sustainable energy. I wanted to meet with real people who weren't typically involved in politics. I wanted to meet with
people who had voted for Trump—or had never voted at all.

"Let's go to Martin County," I said, pointing to the map. A major
water crisis there had recently made the national news; their water
treatment facilities were in severe need of repair, and their water was
largely undrinkable. In addition, their utility rates were astronomical,
which meant they were paying a lot of money for water they couldn't
drink. We knew all about high utility costs in the West End, and I
wanted to make that connection. Will took out a marker, circled Martin County, and started listing off other counties and precincts for us
to hit on what would become a four-day trip.

With Travis following behind, Colin and I pulled into Pikeville
late in the afternoon for the first event of our tour at the local university. Colin knew an instructor at the University of Pikeville who supported our campaign, and since we wanted to organize student leaders
at all of the colleges and universities across Kentucky, this would give
us the chance to meet with some students there.

We arrived on a quiet evening. The roads were clear, except for a
few students crossing back and forth between buildings and the husky
that charged at me as soon as I got out of the car. A nurse was walking
the dog past Colin and me, and the dog lunged at us for no reason.
"She doesn't bite!" the nurse yelled out. I have never understood why
people say that; the dog was clearly capable of biting. Luckily, the
woman caught the dog's leash right in time. I quietly hoped that the
dog's attitude wasn't an omen of the reception that was waiting for us.

Colin's friend had arranged for us to use a community meeting
room on campus. As our event began, the room quickly filled up with

current and retired miners, students, and educators. In the front of the class was an organ. I pulled the bench out from it and sat on it in front of the room. This moment was going to be the big test. As much as I believed in my theory of what a winning campaign would look like, I was about to find out if that theory was true. I knew I was stepping out on faith and the whole thing might blow up in my face. Still, I wasn't nervous, because I knew I was going to give it my all. Even if the people of Kentucky ultimately chose differently, I was serving my purpose by making sure they had a clear choice.

"I'm State Representative Charles Booker," I said, introducing myself, "and I represent the 43rd Legislative District. Although you don't live in the 43rd District, I need you to know that every time I walk into that Capitol building, I am representing you. It is the privilege of my life to go into that crazy place and be a voice for regular people fighting to survive."

I saw heads nod. I wanted them to know who I was so that they could trust the conversation we were about to have. So just like I did when I worked at Fish and Wildlife, I told them my story. I shared about the time I learned Mom was going without food so that I could eat. I saw their heads nod again when I talked about my faith, my mother's conviction that we are more than conquerors. When I explained how jobs left my neighborhood and never returned, I could see a young man shaking his head in frustration. "It's not right," he blurted out. "That is exactly what's happening here!"

From there the conversation shifted to drug addiction and the opioid epidemic, and more people started speaking up. "People in my family went to the doctor for an injury, and ended up becoming addicted to painkillers," one lady said, reminding me of stories I heard back home.

After opening up to them, I shared that we were going to talk about a Green New Deal. Given how badly the name had been demonized in right-wing media, I scanned the room, curious to see their response. I saw a few smiles, many excited nods of approval, and a couple of blank faces. I was honestly surprised how many were immediately excited. I asked the room what they knew about the premise of a Green New Deal. The first hand that shot up was from a retired miner, a middle-aged white man wearing a United Mine Workers of America shirt. He started out by saying that a lot of people don't know what the Green New Deal is about, but that he knew it wasn't about taking away hamburgers. I smiled in agreement.

"You're right," I said, "a lot of people don't really know what it is. So let's have a real conversation. What do clean water, lower utility costs, and good-paying jobs that don't require black lung mean to you?"

Hands flew up around the room. One miner said his family had gone into the mines for generations because it was the only thing they could do. "We don't have the chance to do other things," he said. "I would love to work in solar or do a trade like carpentry. But there's no opportunities for us."

I told him that's exactly how people in my hood feel. "Forget the name," I said. "Call it a Green New Deal or don't call it a Green New Deal. But let's get the solutions we need. For me, I want us to own our future. I love you—that's why I am here with you. I am locking arms with you in this work. Because I love you, I am going to tell you the truth. The fossil fuel industry has been in decline, and coal jobs are leaving."

"They're already gone," another retired miner interrupted, and the whole room erupted in agreement. They knew that the idea of saving coal jobs was an empty promise made by politicians who just wanted their vote, and the fact that I was there to actually listen to them and tell the truth meant a lot.

One young mother stood up to thank me. "I've never been excited about a politician before," she said. "You're a real person. You actually understand what we are going through. I never thought I would meet a politician that made me believe things can change."

The discussion kept going, and it was incredible. Miners shared their stories about battling black lung disease when they couldn't get health coverage or compensation for their injuries. We talked about high utility bills, dirty water, crappy or nonexistent internet. A lot of what we talked about was the pointless divisions in our politics. I quickly learned that everyone in the room was sick of the partisan divisions. Mostly, everyone was just worn out. "No one cares about us!" one lady shouted out.

By that point, the energy in the room was electric. A middle-aged Black man in a University of Louisville hoodie stood up and took the floor. His name was Sam, and he was a miner, too. "We're tired of things being this way," he said, emphatically pounding his fist in the air, "and you're the man to get rid of Mitch and turn this thing around. You came here to fight for us, so we're gonna fight for you." Everyone looked at him, and then the whole room broke out in applause.

Over the next few days, as we drove up and down US 23 and the Mountain Parkway, we spent time stopping in diners and visiting community resource centers. I saw a lot of UK hats and hoodies and sat down to a lot of tasty meals. At the Farmhouse Diner in Salyersville, all the tables had those red-and-white checkered tablecloths on them, and the servings were huge. I ordered a chicken salad that was big enough to eat on for a couple days. "This is poor man's cuisine," the waiter said with a smile as he set down my plate.

We went to all the places most politicians don't bother to go. We went to Ashland and Prestonsburg, to Whitesburg and Inez. As we drove, I regularly smelled the smoke from a controlled fire in the mountains nearby. We stopped to look at abandoned mines. I had never really seen the mines up close before and I wanted to learn more about them. I saw where the tops of mountains had been cleared away in mountaintop removal. I saw the rusted pipes and broken-down equipment that had been left to decay.

Colin was trying to take me to spots from his memory of organizing in Appalachia, and he wanted to show me the streams that had turned orange from the acid mine drainage. After hunting for a bit, we found one. Colin parked, and we got out and slowly walked down to get close to the creek, and that's when I saw it. The water that should have been clear and pure was a neon-looking reddish orange. We both watched in silence as it trickled over the rocks on its way downstream. I thought about the families who could be getting sick from it—and about the companies who'd done this with little to no consequence.

One afternoon we were driving outside of Isom, a small town in Letcher County, on our way to Whitesburg. We'd just finished up a visit to the Isom IGA. The IGA was the only grocery store in a ten-mile radius, proving yet again that this area faced the same challenges we faced in the West End. But the IGA was unique in more ways than one. It was owned by Ms. Gwen, a Black woman. She'd started at the store as a clerk, eventually coming to an arrangement with the previous owners to take it over—and since taking it over, she'd worked with the Mountain Association to put all energy-efficient lighting in the store and solar panels on the roof. In the heart of coal country, a Black woman was using renewable energy to find enough savings to hire more staff and bring healthy food to a deep red, Trump-voting county. I wanted to visit the store and talk to Ms. Gwen, because they're shining examples of what's possible, and proof that we should not count out or stereotype people in places like Appalachia.

As we were driving, Colin started talking to me about the hollers. A holler, for anyone who's not from Kentucky, is a "hollow." It's the valley or ravine between the mountains that is habitable to live on where there's often tillable land that runs along a creek. Colin pointed out the window at a dotted row of houses in between the hills in one of the hollers we passed. There was only one road in. The homes were old and in need of repair. Some of the roofs were caving in. Several of them had old rickety front porches, maybe a barbecue grill out in the yard. Other than the beautiful hills around us, it all felt familiar. These were the same houses I'd grown up with in the West End. I even saw one house with the same plastic lawn chairs my mom had in our backyard.

"Some folks in Eastern Kentucky live in hollers like this," Colin said, brushing his hair out of his face and pointing into the distance. "It's rough. There aren't a lot of jobs. The utility bills are sky-high, and that's if they have utilities cut on at all. People take internet access for granted these days, but in a lot of places like this it's still impossible to get."

"I know all about that," I responded. "If we do have internet in the West End, it is crap."

Colin nodded and shrugged, then slightly lowered his tone. "Folks in the hollers get counted out, but there's a lot of hardworking people around here, people who'll take care of one another, even if they don't have a lot."

"That sounds like the hood!" I told him. "That is exactly how it is where I'm from. We may not have a lot, but we work hard, and we take care of family. The folks in these hollers are just as much my family as those I live with in the West End. That's why I am fighting, man. We are going to bring change for all of us, from the hood to the holler."

As I said it, we looked at one another and sat quietly. I could tell he felt the same reverence that I did. We were on the verge of something powerful. "From the hood to the holler" conjured up my memories of praise services growing up in church, how the pastor would use rhymes and alliteration to drive home a message. It felt like something I would hear in a powerful sermon, something Dr. King would say.

"That's it, man!" I told Colin. "From the hood to the holler. That's going to be our rallying cry." I imagined Black, white, and brown Kentuckians standing together to say these words in solidarity. No one would be invisible anymore. We were going to take our power together.

We were bursting with excitement about our new slogan. Somewhere between Isom and Whitesburg, Colin pointed to a cluster of houses nestled in the hills and said, "Let's get out here and knock on some doors." So we grabbed our stacks of campaign literature and decided to do just that. I didn't really care where we went; I just wanted to talk to people. I wanted to connect with Kentuckians wherever they were.

We jumped out of the car, me in my blue sweater and big gray wool coat, and braced ourselves against the cold. Despite the temperature it was a clear, beautiful day, and the sun was bright. Strolling down the narrow road, we passed homes that were near collapse. Several of them flew Confederate flags and Trump flags. In a few yards, I even saw small statues of Black lawn jockeys.

My personal safety had crossed my mind. I was very aware of the fact that there weren't many people who looked like me in the area. I was also aware of the history of overt racism across Kentucky; I'd read aloud the list of lynchings for Kentucky counties from the Equal Justice Initiative records on the floor of the House of Representatives. I wasn't fazed, though. I shook it off. Even as I realized what we were about to do might be dangerous, I knew God had me on this journey, and I believed I was protected.

"Let's knock on this door," I said, pointing to a trailer with a huge Confederate flag waving in the front yard. No one answered, but I left my card with a note.

The next few homes we walked up to, residents opened their doors cautiously but respectfully. When I asked about their utility costs, several of them told me they hadn't had utilities for months. "There's no point," one woman said. "I can't afford it, and even if I could, the water would probably be brown."

I responded with my own story, about my mom struggling to pay the bills and those brown LG&E envelopes that always came right before the power got shut off. Then I explained that that is why I was fighting for a Green New Deal, fighting to help her lower her utilities and get access to clean water.

"Well, hell," she said. "I want a Green New Deal, too. You have my support." I handed her my literature and thanked her for her time. She had a big smile on her face as she closed the door.

We walked a bit farther, tried a few more houses to find nobody home. By that point we'd walked a fair bit; most of the houses were pretty far apart, and there was one more house up the road before it wound around the hill and out of view. I walked up to the door and knocked hard. The woman who answered actually welcomed us into her home and offered us some food. She took us in through the side door facing her gravel driveway, through her narrow kitchen with a small round table and an old gas stove, and into her living room. There were pictures of her family on all the walls, and a shelf with University of Kentucky memorabilia. She had a poster on her closet door signed by the 1996 championship basketball team. I pointed out to her that my cousin Winston was on that poster, and she lit up with excitement.

Then, as we talked, she started on about how glad she was to see a Black man doing some good. She then proceeded to tell me about some young Black men she knew growing up, about how nice they were and that I reminded her of them. "I am so proud of you, young man. I believe you can win this, even if you are Black."

I looked at Colin and Travis. They cringed. As awkward as it was, I kept my composure. This woman was so happy and excited, she had no idea she was insulting me. It wasn't the first or the last time I experienced something like that on the campaign. So many people across Kentucky would earnestly try to compliment me while inadvertently letting on that they thought someone like me would never do something like run for U.S. Senate.

Still, I couldn't deny the woman's hospitality. UK was about to play that day. She had her old floor TV with the big metal knobs on the front, and she was ready to have us stay over to watch with her. We thanked her for the invitation and told her we had to keep moving.

On our last day, after attending a church service in Lynch, Kentucky, once the largest company-owned coal town in Kentucky, we stopped by a community center before hitting the road to head back to Louisville. The building was right off the road and backed up against a wooded hill. It looked like a gym and had a stage outside of it with an old mine cart in the front where people could pose for pictures. We parked in a large parking lot and waited for the center's director to meet us. The air was sharp, so I had my collar up on my jacket.

The center was run by a woman, along with her son. "Thank you so much for coming to see us, Representative Booker," she said as she walked up to the car, extending her hand. The lady was short, and her brown hair blew in the cold breeze. Despite her soft voice, you could tell she was the person that kept everything running on time. As she told me more about the history of mining in the area. I could tell she was proud of her home and the people there, but I could see the stress in her eyes. "A lot of people are facing real hard times," she said as we started to walk toward the building.

She welcomed me in and showed me around, telling me about the

meeting room for residents and the services for people who were battling opioid addiction or trying to get back on their feet after serving
time. "We help people here," she told me. "Miners who lost work,
people who fell on hard times. If they need some food, a pair of socks,
a tube of toothpaste, or somewhere to warm up, that's what we give
them."

I nodded my head with deep appreciation. "My grandma did the
same thing in our neighborhood," I said.

We sat down at the table with her, and I told her how much I appreciated what they did. I shared my story with her and let her know
that she was helping people like my own family.

She nodded along. Then she sort of lowered her head and said, "I
am ashamed to tell you this, but I voted for Trump. I was sick and
tired, like you, and I was willing to vote for anything that could change
things for us here. I didn't feel like Hillary really cared about us. I felt
like she looked down on us. When Trump said he was going to bring
our jobs back, all I could think about was the people who come to our
center looking for help. No one ever cares about us, and at least Trump
was talking about us like we existed. I didn't like the other things he
said, but I just wanted things to get better here." She looked up at me
with hurt in her eyes and kept talking. "I am ashamed that I voted for
him. He wasn't really interested in helping us. My mother would be
upset if she knew I felt this way, but the next time I won't be voting for
him."

As she spoke, I heard the desperation in her voice. She cared so
much about her community. Everything she saw people going
through—fighting just to eat and stay in their homes and get basic
toiletries to clean themselves—all of it weighed on her. I realized she
had blind spots to the depths of the racism that Trump was stirring
up, but I understood her painful choice. It was the same reason a lot
of people in this area were fans of Bernie Sanders, too. They were
looking for anyone who was going to help them survive and live a little better. But I also knew that every Kentuckian deserved to have
leadership that lifted up love and healing instead of hate and vitriol.
As we got up to go, I hugged her and promised to keep fighting for her

and the people in Lynch, and she told me that she would do whatever she could to help me, too.

The drive back home was a heavy one. The entire trip had surpassed all my expectations. So many people were worried about me being a Black man going out to Eastern Kentucky, but pretty much everyone I met had a warm smile and an open heart. A handful of times I saw people closing their doors as they saw me walking up the street, and I'd have a laugh about it with Colin and Travis. "They must not want me to knock on their door!" But other than that, everyone was kind. The stereotypes you hear about Eastern Kentucky are no different than the ones about the West End. People say it's dangerous, and filled with crime, but that is far from the truth. If you need help in the hood, someone will look out for you. We show love. We help one another. I expected that same experience in Appalachia, and with every encounter I was proven right.

What made the drive home a heavy one was processing all the pain and the frustration that I'd witnessed, and it only reaffirmed my faith in what we needed to do to win this campaign: We needed to connect with people, the way I'd connected with the people I'd met in Eastern Kentucky. We needed to bring people together. We needed to raise an army of volunteers to canvass the state, to go door to door, to talk to their fellow Kentuckians, to listen to their fellow Kentuckians, to shake hands, to build trust, and to build a movement for a new kind of politics for the future.

And that's when we got the news.

CHAPTER 21

SAFE AT HOME

EARLY THAT FEBRUARY, I started to notice news coverage about this virus that was spreading across the world. I was still in legislative session at the time, so I didn't really have the time to fully digest it. I couldn't really wrap my mind around it, either. I wanted to believe that whatever this was would never get bad enough to hit us at home, and I just couldn't imagine it would change our lives.

"I hope this doesn't get as bad as it could," I said to Taylor as we were discussing the campaign.

"I think it might," he replied.

With each passing day, the news got worse, with cases spiking around the world. What really had me worried was President Trump telling the country not to worry. If Trump was anything, he was a liar who sought to avoid responsibility. Hearing him downplay this was confirmation that things would surely get worse.

Even so, I held out hope. We kept moving forward with our plans, reaching out for volunteers to go door to door and pass out literature and talk to voters as a part of our first statewide canvasses at the end of February; our plan was to get a head start on things, because most campaigns in Kentucky don't really kick into gear until close to the Kentucky Derby in early May. The canvasses went forward without a hitch. The crowds were huge. We passed out hand sanitizer and encouraged everyone to keep their hands washed. Based on our success, we planned to start holding them at least three days a week.

That canvass, however, would be our first and our last.

I got my first sign that normal life would be going away for the foreseeable future when the local news notified us that stores were running out of toilet paper. I rushed over to Family Dollar to make sure we had a few packs, and it all felt too surreal to be true.

From that moment on, the cases were rising in the United States, and it was becoming clearer that this wasn't just going to go away. The news started to recommend that we wear masks. In Frankfort, we were hearing rumblings that the governor was going to announce school closings and close down the Capitol to the public. Once that happened, for the safety of ourselves and the voters, it was clear what our campaign was going to have to do. "We have to shut it down," Taylor said. We put a pause on public events and canvasses and closed the office for all staff. We moved all of our operations online, and everyone started working from home.

I knew I was making the right decision. Still, it was a gut-wrenching one. We knew that our first signs of momentum would be all but wiped out. While Amy McGrath could fall back on her $30 million war chest, we had predicated our campaign on the kind of grassroots relational organizing that brought thousands of teachers together in Frankfort. Our whole philosophy was built on reaching out and connecting people who had been alienated from each other by a lack of communication and divided by years of fearmongering from politicians like Mitch McConnell. How were we supposed to pursue that strategy in a time of "social distancing"? We had always planned to leverage social media as part of our efforts to reach more people. Now that in-person events were halted, it was one of the few tools we had left. COVID felt like a knockout blow. I didn't consider giving up, but our chances felt grim.

From then on, our office was a ghost town. I went home and, for the most part, stayed there. As a type 1 diabetic, I took every precaution I could. I knew that I was at high risk of being infected, and I didn't want to do that to my girls. I needed to stay healthy for them. I was worried, because I loved to hug everyone. I figured it was just a matter of time before I got sick. It felt paralyzing. For the next few months, I didn't really see anyone other than Tanesha, the girls, and my mom. Mom stayed home. Her church closed in-person service, and she cut down her contact with others. I checked on her daily, and her spirits stayed high. I didn't get to see her often, but I did drive by her house a couple times a week. I would call when I was outside, and Mom would come out and wave. I would yell out to her that I loved her. It was the first time in our lives that we went weeks without hugging one another.

My campaign staff and I spent the next few months like everyone else: in front of a computer. We would email or text, talk on the phone or Google Meet. For media interviews over Zoom and Skype, I would still go into the office where our staffer, Edwin, a local DJ and artist who knew how to rig audio equipment, had built a backdrop for me. He tacked my banner to the wall, found a purple glow light to put on the floor, and brought two ferns to put on each side. The setup was perfect, but we still had trouble because the internet wasn't stable at our office, just like in many parts of Kentucky. Several times my screen froze in the middle of TV interviews.

I would also use the empty office for my fundraising calls. It broke my heart asking for money during this time, especially as the weeks rolled on and things got worse. Asking for donations is hard enough in regular times. Now I found myself calling up people who had lost their jobs, their businesses, and their loved ones. Eventually, I stopped calling to ask for money. I just called people to check on them and see how they were doing.

Making all those calls, I realized we couldn't just let COVID-19 shut us and the whole country down. I saw it as a chance to help people see why we needed to make investments that help families prepare for these types of crises. I knew my campaign needed to show leadership in this moment.

I called the team together and said, "Let's release a statement. Let's take this time to explain the types of policies we believe are critical to help Kentuckians get through this." So we did. We called for financial protections for workers forced to take leave from their jobs as well as support for small businesses struggling to stay afloat. We called for a moratorium on evictions, the cancellation of credit card and student debt, and the immediate implementation of a universal basic income. We also called for the immediate implementation of Medicare for All, making the point that Kentucky was disproportionately vulnerable to this virus because of the glaring health challenges that keep us near the bottom in national rankings on health outcomes, including often leading the nation in deaths from cancer. Realizing that this shutdown could lead to dramatic changes in our voting procedures, we also called for universal mail-in voting. We even turned our campaign into a public health resource, deploying our social media to share information on COVID-19, setting up coordinated volunteer check-in calls across Kentucky, and placing information about COVID-19 in people's doors.

Saving lives was our biggest concern. At the same time, while we focused on helping the people of Kentucky, we all began to realize that the pandemic was causing more people to take my policy platform seriously. Communities that were in the greatest need of quality healthcare were being hit the hardest. People didn't have the financial freedom to stay home, which caused more people in low-wage positions to get sick. We were seeing the results of not investing in people. As a society, we were not prepared for the bottom to fall out. Now it was gone, and things were about to get worse.

ONE AFTERNOON AS the lockdowns were beginning, I was heading into the Capitol building for that day's legislative session, where we would do our best to conduct business as usual under these strange new COVID-19 protocols. That was the moment I got an alert on my phone about the death of a woman named Breonna Taylor.

I paused midstep because I knew Breonna. She was my cousin T.J.'s friend. When he was wrongly arrested, she had been a steady source of support for him. When we had the funeral for T.J. after he was murdered, she was there as well. I didn't know her beyond seeing her in passing, but like T.J., hers was another senseless death that hit too close to home. I stopped and said a prayer for her, like I always do, and continued into the Capitol building.

At the time there wasn't much else to do. The details around her death were vague, and I was not yet aware of any suggestions of foul play. Over the weeks that followed, more and more people started posting about Breonna on social media, saying that she'd been murdered by the police. Absent any kind of official statement or report, I was unsure of what to believe, but the deafening silence from the Mayor's Office meant that we didn't have much to go on. There was talk about a drug raid gone bad, a warrant that had been wrongly obtained, but it was all very vague. I kept looking for some report from the city to drop, but nothing came.

Something about it wasn't right. I asked Tanesha if she was hearing anything I wasn't, but she just shook her head no. Meanwhile, nobody in the media was really paying attention either. A week after the news first broke, there was a small gathering in her honor. I got stuck in the legislative session and couldn't go, and the local media didn't appear to report anything about it. Everyone was going into lockdown, and the flood of stories about COVID-19 made it all but impossible for anyone to pay attention to anything else. I asked Taylor Coots to keep an eye on the situation and let me know if he heard anything, but there was no new information for him to report. Other than a few updates in *The Courier-Journal,* the story seemed to go dark.

Then, on May 25, came the murder of George Floyd in Minneapolis. The nine-minute video of his death at the hands of police officer Derek Chauvin was so brutal, so shocking, the world had no choice but to stop and pay attention. The scourge of state-sanctioned violence in Black communities has always waxed and waned in the media spotlight while never actually abating for the people who live with it day in and day out. The killing of Michael Brown in Ferguson, Missouri, had set off a wave of national attention in 2014, bringing the nation to a boiling point and launching what would become the Black Lives Matter movement. In the years that followed, America witnessed the killings of Walter Scott in South Carolina and Sandra Bland in Texas and Alton Sterling in Louisiana and Philando Castile in Minnesota, along with so many others.

I felt deep trauma with every new hashtag, a burning pain with each breaking news alert. In Louisville, we have plenty of other names we can add to that list, names that never gave rise to a national outcry but are well known in every home in the West End. James Taylor, a Black man who was shot by police while in handcuffs in 2003. Michael Newby, a Black teenager who was shot and killed by police in 2004. And every one of those killings brought home a truth that people in my hood know all too well: If you come from an area like mine, if you look like I look, you will be seen as a deadly weapon before you are seen as a human being.

At first I couldn't bring myself to watch the George Floyd video; I didn't want to see what they'd done to him. But so many people were sharing it on social media I felt I had no choice. I sat down on the steps by the front room, staring at my phone in silence. The video seemed to go on forever. I couldn't help but stare at Chauvin's face as he casually killed this man. I felt like Chauvin was staring at me, letting me know he would do the same thing to me if he could. Even after all the violence and suffering I'd witnessed in my life, the video still took my breath away. "Why?" I asked out loud. I said it over and over, even though I already knew the answer.

The reawakened awareness of police shootings, coupled with the mass protests gathering nationwide, made people in Kentucky take another look at Breonna's case. It was like a light switch came on; all the details of her story spilled out and fell into place, and we all collectively realized what had happened. Shortly after midnight on March 13, plainclothes officers used a battering ram to bust down the door to Breonna Taylor's apartment. They had obtained a no-knock warrant based on disputed information claiming that Breonna's ex was moving suspicious packages out of the apartment. Upon hearing the door being busted in, Kenneth Walker, Breonna's current boyfriend, later reported that he fired one warning shot into the darkness. After that, a hail of gunfire rained down on the two of them: Thirty-two shots hit every room in their apartment, including neighboring apartments. Kenneth and Breonna never saw who was shooting at them. She was hit six times. She died at 12:48 A.M. It was a betrayal of justice in the deepest sense of the word, and the moment those officers busted down Breonna's door, they busted open the floodgates.

The uprising that was taking place took on a special resonance in Louisville, as Breonna's name joined George Floyd's in the calls for accountability and justice. A number of local groups started calling for an organized protest downtown. Chanelle Helm, one of the leading Black Lives Matter organizers in Louisville, started reaching out to help people set parameters and a plan, and other organizations chimed in as well. But their efforts at organizing were quickly overwhelmed by the raw emotions that everyone felt. Driven by the outrage on social media, people just started flooding downtown. The prevailing sentiment was desperation. People were taking to the streets with a look in their eyes that said they didn't know what else to do, that there was nowhere else they could be other than right there. What was manifesting was more than a tactical movement for civil unrest. It was a collective gathering of people from all backgrounds, mourning and grieving in the streets.

As the protests downtown swelled on Friday afternoon, I was pacing back and forth in my front room, searching Facebook and Twitter for updates. Outside of our window, I could see groups of people walking past our house toward Metro Hall. It was like there was a fire downtown, and everyone was dropping whatever they were doing to run and help put it out. I felt sick to my stomach. I wanted to be helpful. I wanted my title as a state representative to mean something for my community. I felt an immense responsibility to stand in solidarity with the community as we all grieved. I ran upstairs, grabbed some old tennis shoes, and called Taylor. "Taylor," I said, lacing up the shoes. "I'm going downtown."

"Charles, I know you want to go down there, but you can't, man. It is too risky."

I started to get agitated with him. "I'm not asking you for permission."

"Charles, if you go down there, you can kiss our chances of winning goodbye."

I paused when he said that. I knew he was trying to protect me. He understood that if violence broke out and I was caught in the middle, it would define my candidacy in a way that might make Kentuckians afraid of supporting me. Worse than that, he knew that a possible arrest would dominate our race and make it hard for me to garner support. Ultimately, he knew that I wouldn't be afforded the same grace as my white counterparts. If I made a mistake going into an environment that I couldn't control, it could lead to me being hurt physically as well as politically. I realized the risks, too, but my mind was made up.

"I trust God, Taylor," I said. "I have to follow my heart here. I need to be with my people." Taylor kept pushing back, but I stopped listening. People were running down the street at this point, and I had to go. "I'll call you back when I get home. I'm heading out."

"Okay," he said. "Stay safe."

I jumped into my old Ford Taurus, put the windows down, and pulled out, passing the crowds of people making their way downtown on foot. I parked a couple blocks west of the city jail, just in case traffic got too congested, and when I got out there was an eerie calm in the air, the type of feeling you get when there is a death in the family—which there had been. I fell in with the crowds marching east and made my way to where everyone was gathering.

Jefferson Square Park is a small city park surrounded by the Mayor's Office, Metro City Hall, the Hall of Justice, Metro Corrections, and other government buildings. All of which are in the center of the downtown business district, several blocks south of the Ohio River. Walking up, I saw people standing on the steps of the Hall of Justice and on the steps of the Mayor's Office across the street, but most were standing in the park itself. The police had gathered at the northeast corner of 6th and Jefferson, and they stood there, waiting. The crowd was in pain but peaceful. People were singing songs like "We Shall Overcome." They were hugging and crying on one another. Some were kneeling to pray.

Slowly, I noticed the police starting to line up in the middle of Jefferson Street in front of the Mayor's Office, facing west. The hour was getting late, and they were looking to disperse the crowd. The tension was heavy in the air, and watching the officers line up with their weapons in hand was deeply troubling. It looked like they were preparing for combat.

Then came the order. I could hear the officers yelling out. "Stand down!" they cried, and "Please disperse!" The crowd started scrambling around in confusion and fear. A few people started to yell back at the officers, "What's wrong with y'all?" and "Why are you doing this?" There was a lot of commotion as people jostled around, trying to figure out what the officers were planning to do. I stood in the middle of it all, frozen in my tracks. I kept thinking, *I know they see me. I know some of the officers know I'm an elected official here in my official capacity. I don't want to run. I shouldn't have to run.*

Then, out of the corner of my eye, I saw a couple of water bottles being thrown in the direction of the officers, and people started screaming, "Don't do that! They'll shoot us!" The officers started walking forward toward us, marching in lockstep and giving warnings that they would use force to disperse us all if we didn't leave. The problem, however, was there was no easy way for people to leave without crossing the path of the officers. I scanned around the crowd, looking to see what was going on, and that's when I heard the first *pop!* The officers were shooting rubber bullets into the crowd, and canisters of gas came rolling down the street. I have no idea what triggered the first shot, but now it was coming down.

At the sound of the gunshots, people started running in every direction. For a moment I stood motionless, in a daze at what was happening, then I snapped out of it and started running with the crowd as it moved west on Jefferson Street. People were screaming and crying. I had no idea what was going on. I was scared. I had to get out of there before I got hit with a stray bullet. I had to get home to my daughters.

As always, the crackdown from the police had the opposite of its intended effect. It only stiffened the resolve of the people, and the following morning and for the rest of the last weekend in May, the peaceful vigil and protest resumed its place in Jefferson Square Park, which residents had started referring to as "Injustice Square" or "Breeway" in tribute to the ongoing work to honor Breonna's life.

I went downtown again the very next day, this time with a greater sense of clarity and purpose. The night before, I hadn't known what to expect or really what to do. I'd simply been responding out of the natural impulse to be with family in a time of crisis. Now I was going down as a state representative to aid and serve the people I represented. I walked around with the energy and poise of a local elected official. I wasn't trying to blend in. I announced myself to law enforcement. I walked around checking on everyone, asking, "Are you okay? Do you need any help?"

Around 8:30 that night, as the evening curfew approached, I was standing on West Liberty Street, about fifty yards from the square, and I noticed some high school students standing on the sidewalk by the jail. One of them called out my name, and I recognized him as one of the students who helped at Kaylin's old elementary school in their after-school program. I stopped to ask him if he was okay, and we chatted for a moment and then, out of nowhere, dozens of people started running past us at full speed. "Rep. Booker," one lady screamed as she ran by. "They're about to throw tear gas!"

I looked up, confused. "Why would they throw tear gas?" I said to myself. There was no altercation going on. It was just me and a couple of students standing alone on a street corner, and it wasn't even past curfew. I looked back up West Liberty Street and saw the officers. They were standing by themselves, no one threatening them or even close to them. I started walking toward them calmly, planning to ask what was going on. I got about twenty yards away from them and they turned in my direction and threw three canisters of tear gas at me. I made eye contact with one of the officers, and he just stared at me. He looked like he was testing out a new toy.

The green smoke billowed out, filling the street. The few people still on that side of the street ran. As the gas wrapped around me, all I could think was that it didn't matter to them who I was. I was a state representative, but in that moment, my title was irrelevant. My heart broke. I couldn't believe they were doing this. I didn't want to run away; I just wanted them to stop. It was like time slowed down. I felt my eyes starting to burn and my throat getting itchy. I knew it was about to choke me out, so I hung my head and turned to run away.

THE MORNING OF Monday, June 1, the protests were still going downtown, and I was preparing to leave the house and head to the office to prepare for that night's big event: the debate in the race between myself, Amy McGrath, and Mike Broihier at the KET studios in Lexington. It would finally be my chance to draw a stark contrast between my vision for Kentucky and theirs. I hadn't even stepped out the door when I got a news alert on my phone: Another shooting had taken place.

At first glance, I was prepared to open up the story and see that the police or the National Guard had shot someone in the protests downtown, even though the governor had declared that the National Guard would only be used as additional support for police as needed. Once I opened up the story, however, I saw that was not the case at all. The shooting hadn't taken place where the protests were happening. It had happened in the West End, just blocks from my home. One of the community's most cherished men had been gunned down.

Most people in the hood knew David McAtee as YaYa or the Barbecue Man. He owned a popular place, YaYa's BBQ Shack, near 26th and Broadway. Because of the protests outside Metro Hall, the city had a 9 P.M. curfew in effect, and the police had implemented a crowd dispersal policy downtown to break up groups of protestors. There was no one protesting at YaYa's BBQ Shack, which was miles away from Metro Hall, but there was a crowd of people there just because most nights there was a crowd of people there. YaYa's BBQ Shack was a regular hang-out spot for people looking to grab some food before heading home after a night of partying.

According to the published reports, the police were called to address a complaint, and the National Guard accompanied them. As the military vehicles pulled up, armed officers jumped out to disperse a crowd that was in no way a part of any protest. The officers started shooting pepper bullets to disperse the crowd, and people started to run. Mr. McAtee came out of the shack to see what was going on and noticed that some of his relatives were running as well. As the peacemaker for the area, worried there was some sort of threat, Mr. McAtee was said to have fired a warning shot into the air outside the doorway of his restaurant to urge whatever threat there was to stay away. Then, supposedly, the National Guard and the police rushed toward his restaurant and shot him.

None of it made any sense. There was no need for the National Guard to rush into a residential area at night. Mr. McAtee was a well-loved man, known to feed everybody; it was very common to see police officers in his place getting a bite to eat. I flipped over to Facebook to see what people in the community were saying about the shooting, and I saw, to my horror, that his body was still lying in the street, nearly thirteen hours after he'd been shot.

I immediately called my team. "They killed him," I said. "They killed the Barbecue Man. I have to go down there to see how I can help make sure no one else gets killed today. I have to be with the people." Taylor and Will immediately understood that there was nothing they could say that would persuade me to stay home. "Please stay safe, Charles," Taylor responded. "I know the community needs you, just be careful."

I feared that this was going to explode into a war. The police were already trying to spin the shooting as part of the National Guard regulating the protests. That was a lie, and that lie, coupled with the fact that his body had been left out for so long, coming so soon on the heels of Breonna Taylor's and George Floyd's murders, was simply going to be too much for people to bear. I threw on my clothes and jumped in my car.

Broadway is the West End's main business corridor; it spans the entire West End, running from the central business district through to Shawnee Park. It is where our Kroger's is located, along with the few fast-food restaurants in the area. YaYa's BBQ Shack was in the parking lot of a larger bar and grill, across the street from Dino's Food Mart.

When I made it to 26th & Broadway, I could see Mr. McAtee's body still lying behind the tape. Crowds had formed along the south side of Broadway, and they cried in agony as they stood staring at the lifeless body across the street. Nearly everyone had masks on. Some had bandannas over their mouths. A lot of people had on goggles as well, but that was because of the threat of tear gas. I had a mask and gloves on with my black jacket zipped up. I was ready for COVID-19—and anything else.

Between us and Mr. McAtee stood a long row of officers lining the sidewalk on the north side; they were holding their weapons as if prepared to use force. The crowd was growing, and people were getting increasingly frustrated with the posture of the officers. Observing the officers, I sensed that they were just there to protect Mr. McAtee's body from anyone who might try to disturb the scene. The residents were there to do the same thing. There was no reason for the officers to have an adversarial posture, since they were tasked with doing the same thing the community wanted done. That fact was not apparent to the increasingly agitated mourners, though, and I could tell that one false move could end in disaster.

I immediately called Governor Beshear to tell him that the residents were terrified and that the National Guard presence was only making things worse. "If you want to keep people safe," I said, "please call them off." Governor Beshear said he agreed the National Guard shouldn't be in the West End and that he would call them off right away.

I ran over to the residents to share the news with them. They were getting angrier by the minute, looking across the street at Mr. McAtee's body still lying there, but the news that the Guard would be leaving eased their anger. Then, shuttling back and forth from one side of Broadway to the other, pulling my mask up to keep it from falling off my face, I walked over to the police officers who were lined up with their weapons in hand. I identified myself to them, and I could tell that a few of them recognized me. I had worked with many of them through my time in Metro Council, and they were relieved to see me;

they didn't want this turning into a violent altercation, either. I started peppering them with questions. "Why is Mr. McAtee still in the street? What is the timeline for getting him up?"

The officers confirmed that they were only there to protect the scene so that Mr. McAtee could be removed safely. They also informed me that because a federal agency was involved in the shooting, additional investigations still had to be completed. I appreciated their calm demeanor, and through the simple act of communicating clearly and respectfully, I helped to ratchet the tension down. We all wanted the same thing, and we knew we could get there peacefully.

"Well, if you're here to protect Mr. McAtee, why do you need to hold these weapons as if you're ready to go to war with residents? They're here to protect Mr. McAtee, too." I pleaded with them: "Please, put your weapons down so that the residents know you're not looking to hurt them. It would help calm things down so that we can all be safe."

As tense as the officers were, they understood what I was saying. One of them pointed me to the major in charge. "Representative Booker," he said, "we can't put our weapons down. That would need to come from an order from Mayor Fischer. It's above my pay grade."

I pulled my phone out of my back pocket and called Greg Fischer, the mayor. "Mayor, we have a problem on our hands that will get worse any minute without your help. These officers are standing in a combative posture with the community, and it's antagonizing them. I've asked the officers to put their weapons down to show the residents that they don't intend to hurt anyone. They say they'll do it if you give the order. I need you to give the order." The mayor quickly assured me that he would.

In the background, I could hear more and more people gathering across the street. There were elders in wheelchairs, students, veterans, ministers, youth activists, and various community leaders. Everyone was walking back and forth, growing angrier the longer Mr. McAtee lay in the street. You could feel that things might explode at any moment. My anxiety was running high, too, but I was able to step back and observe everything that was going on. I knew this could be a defining moment for our city, and I didn't want that moment to be a deadly brawl between citizens and the agency that was supposed to protect us. I immediately knew what I had to do. It was the same feeling I had when I spoke up at the community meeting for the Food-Port. I ran over to the crowd and grabbed a bullhorn from a friend of mine, Hannah, who was among those who'd shown up to protest.

"Everyone," I said, my voice echoing down the street, "hear me out. I know you're upset. I am, too. What happened to Mr. McAtee was unspeakable. I know you're here because you love him and want to protect him. These officers are here because they've been ordered to protect the scene while a federal review takes place. I've asked them to put their weapons down, and the mayor has agreed to give the order."

By that time, the officers had put their weapons down, but people were too agitated to notice. I pushed the button on the bullhorn and spoke again.

"Everyone, please look at the officers right now. They have put their weapons down. We just need to allow the federal review to finish so the family can see the body. Now look, if you've had enough and want to run across the street at these officers, I understand. But if you run, let me go first. And know that if we do that, more people will get hurt and someone could get killed. I know you're upset, but let's show support for Mr. McAtee and his family and keep the scene clear so they can get his body off the ground."

As I finished speaking, I saw a calm come over the crowd. The officers stood quietly, with their weapons put away. A space opened up in the crowd. It was Mr. McAtee's family coming to view his body. Tears were falling, but we stood in complete silence as they walked across the street. You could hear a pin drop. Slowly, everyone started to hold hands. As we held one another, Pat Mathison, a noted singer in our community, began to sing.

Her voice rumbled through the streets, deep and strong, and the words of "Amazing Grace" sent a wave of peace through the crowd. You could feel the anointing. We raised our fists as Mr. McAtee was finally lifted from the ground and taken away. The officers quietly walked to their cars and drove off. I could only thank God. One of my younger cousins, TreVonte, whom we all call Tre', was in the crowd. He hugged me tight, and we both cried.

AFTER SEEING THE tension in the streets between the police and the community, I knew I couldn't just go back to my office to prep for the debate. I needed to be at Metro Hall. We couldn't afford for more violence to erupt. I drove downtown and stayed there all day, doing exactly what I'd been doing all weekend, talking to people, listening to them, making sure everyone was okay. As the hours passed, we prayed, we sang songs of justice, we raised our fists, and we screamed out Breonna's name. The world's eyes were upon us. On social media, in the national media, and even in the international media, the story of Louisville was blowing up, and Breonna Taylor's name had joined George Floyd and all the others on the memorial wall of Black lives taken too soon.

I tried to work as a diplomat between the protesters and the police, going over to police and asking them about their plans for the evening. "I want everyone to be safe," I told the officers. "People are here in pain. My hope is that you will protect them." Several of the officers nodded. Some ignored me. Others responded saying they wanted the same thing I did.

As nightfall approached, the police looked like they were once again preparing to go to combat, but nothing had happened yet. I kept looking at my phone, checking the time, agonizing over whether I should leave to go to the debate. My suit was pressed and hanging in our campaign truck a few blocks away, ready to go, but I told my team I was only going to leave if things remained peaceful. Taylor and I stayed in constant contact on the phone as I walked around the square. As the hour for the debate got closer, he kept saying, "We gotta go."

"I'm not worried about a debate right now," I barked back.

"If you want to stay, Charles, I understand. We really need to do this debate if you're going to win this race. But I understand."

I stood in the street and closed my eyes. I didn't want to get in the truck and drive off if I was still needed here. Ultimately, I realized that out of everyone in that park crying out, I was the only one who could take that cry into the televised debate for one of the biggest U.S. Senate races in the country, which meant I had an obligation to go. This was my state. These were my people. The pain that filled my heart was lighting a fire in me to stand. It was on me. At times I had questioned why God charged me to run in this race, but at that very moment, I understood clearly. I needed to do my part, and I could do that better onstage than I could in a crowd.

"Okay," I told Taylor. "Let's go."

We barely made it to the KET studios in Lexington on time, and before I even walked through the door I was completely exhausted. Just inside there was a woman waiting to check our temperature. Then, as she signed us in, she told us the producers were already getting ready to start the debate without me because they didn't know if I was going to make it. I had no time to gather my thoughts. We took off running and made it to the soundstage right as the opening music was starting to play. I was briskly escorted around the cameras to my seat. Because of COVID-19, they had spaced the three of us out. Mike was in the middle, and Amy and I were basically on opposite sides of the room. I didn't have a chance to speak to either of them. We all simply nodded at one another as the moderator, KET's director of public affairs, Renee Shaw, prepared to give her opening remarks.

I was still in a state of shock. The hours that had passed from my standing in the street crying out for YaYa and the moment I sat down on that stage felt like months. Time had lost all meaning. I did my best to breathe and relax and collect my thoughts for the questions that were about to come my way.

Amy seemed nervous the entire debate. She was tripping over her words and doing her best to repeat her résumé as a fighter pilot, which was actually to her detriment. As compelling as that part of her biography was, she failed to show that she had any lived experience that was relevant to the present moment. The pandemic and the Breonna Taylor protests had rendered her message of cooperation with Trump obsolete, and she had nothing meaningful to say.

At one point, Renee Shaw asked each of us about going down to the protests. Leadership is about showing up when you are needed most. In that moment, I knew this question was one that only I could answer. My life's journey had prepared me for it. I sat back and waited as Amy fumbled over her words, struggling to explain why she didn't go. Mike was more forceful, explaining that he didn't go because he didn't want to be a political prop. Then, when the camera panned to me, I gathered myself and explained that the people in my community were not props. I spoke to the grief that filled the streets and how I felt compelled to be with my family in that moment of impossible pain. Taylor had been so worried that my going to the protests would hurt me politically. But the protests were the only political story that mattered in Kentucky that day, and the fact that I'd gone while Amy and Mike hadn't told voters everything they needed to know about who was actually fighting for the issues that mattered.

Before the debate ended, I was asked the question that seemed to be reserved for me throughout the entire election cycle. Renee looked at me and asked me the question that Mike and Amy never had to answer: Why is it I felt I could connect with voters in rural parts of Kentucky?

The persistent assumption that I couldn't relate to people outside my hood had been looming over me the whole campaign, so I knew I had to crush the answer once and for all. So I took a breath and just told the truth: It doesn't matter where you're from or what you look like, the struggles of working people in Kentucky are more alike than they are different.

"I know what it means to feel invisible," I said, "to feel like no one listens to you or cares about you. And the reason I have to answer this question so much is because no one pays attention to my neighborhood in the West End of Louisville. With roughly seventy-five thousand people, we have just a couple grocery stores, a handful of dollar stores because they prey on us, and if you need to use public transportation to get to the hospital, it can take you a couple hours. Jobs have left. Unemployment was around 30 percent for years in the neighborhood I've lived in. People in Eastern Kentucky know that struggle: access to clean water, high utility bills, they know what that's about. That's why my campaign is building momentum, from the mountains all the way to the four rivers. And we're going to build the movement to win this race."

Walking off of that stage, I could hear my team whooping and cheering down the hall. Every cylinder was clicking. The whole world was watching.

The only thing left to do was win.

CHAPTER 22

CAN YOU SEE US NOW?

DURING MY FIRST campaign against Senator Neal, I suffered one of the greatest losses in my life. Losing my cousin T.J. hurt me in ways I am still learning about to this day. Losing him also helped me find my voice. It pushed me to have the courage to stand on my convictions and not cower from the magnitude of what I was taking on. It also forced people to pay attention to what I was saying. When I spoke, people were hearing the words that he was unable to say.

T.J.'s murder was a tragedy, but the bigger tragedy was that it took his death for people to finally stop and pay attention to the plight of young people in the West End. Now, four years later, it had once again taken the needless deaths of innocent people for the world to sit up and pay attention, to hear the voices of the unheard and see the lives of the unseen. Breonna Taylor and George Floyd and David McAtee shouldn't have had to die for people to finally pay attention to the scourge of state-sanctioned violence in our cities. Thousands of vulnerable Americans shouldn't have had to die from COVID-19 for people to finally pay attention to the gross inequities of our broken healthcare system.

It shouldn't have happened that way, but it did happen that way. The world was finally paying attention. Their eyes had turned to Kentucky. They were watching us grieve in real time, hearing our collective cries for justice and seeing my campaign's push to turn that protest into meaningful political power. Just like with T.J., I felt a responsibility to use my voice and my spotlight to make sure that the tragedy of the moment was not spent in vain.

With the June 23 primary closing in, the Sunrise Movement helped us put together an incredible ad for the campaign's final push. It reached over two million views, showing the world the movement we'd been building all over Kentucky—a movement of everyday people coming together across the dividing lines of race, religion, and class and standing up for change. The words I spoke were addressed directly to the Grim Reaper and all the politicians like him who had refused to see us for so long. I spoke about our hopes and dreams that have gone unmet year after year and why we weren't going to sit back and take it anymore. And in the final shot I looked right through the camera and stared Mitch McConnell dead in the eye and asked him the one question I knew he was terrified to hear.

"Can you see us now?"

Because I knew that he could.

UP TO THAT moment, we'd had some minor interest from the national print media, but we couldn't get any coverage whatsoever on national television. Joy Reid from MSNBC had shown some interest, but we kept getting bumped every time a bigger story came along, which was pretty much every week. It became a running theme in the campaign. "This week, Joy Reid's going to call us back for an interview," we'd say with hopeful optimism. But as time passed and the phone didn't ring, it seemed like she never would.

Then she did. So did Chris Hayes, and CNN, and ABC, and the BBC. Most of the major national newspapers and magazines reached out as well. It got to the point where I was getting double-booked and had to start turning people down. Before, on the rare occasions I managed to get an interview, the questions were always some variation on, "How do you feel you can relate to rural voters?" Now, the questions were, "How does it feel to have all of this support?" and "Do you think McConnell is afraid of facing you?"

To which I looked at the camera calmly and said, "Yes."

With all of the newfound attention coming from outside of the state, my following on social media exploded. On Twitter, the numbers more than tripled in the course of two or three days, going from 30,000 to 100,000. I kept refreshing my pages to see the increase, and there were times when, with a single click, I'd add another hundred followers from one second to the next. To me, it wasn't about being popular but about being able to help more people see what we were building in Kentucky and, ultimately, support us in doing it. As 100,000 followers ticked up to 200,000 and 300,000, I kept reminding myself that it wasn't about me. It was about doing the work, and while I was glad the whole country was finally paying attention, the support that mattered most to me was right here in Kentucky.

When I went through my interviews with the two largest newspapers in Kentucky, *The Courier-Journal* for Louisville and the *Herald-Leader* from Lexington, I knew the odds for getting their endorsements were still against me. Like the labor unions, it was unusual for these major papers to support a candidate other than the DSCC's endorsed candidate. I did the interviews remotely due to COVID-19 and sat at the boardroom table on Shelby Street so that I could use the nice backdrop Edwin had set up for my interviews. The editors of both papers asked a wide range of questions about my policies and priorities. They asked whether I believed I could win against McConnell's big money, to which I explained that you can't beat someone like Mitch McConnell by outspending him. It didn't matter how much money you had if you didn't have a vision that inspired people to believe things could actually be different. "I realize that the big-money interests are behind my primary opponent," I said, "but the people of Kentucky are behind me."

I saw a room full of nodding heads as I spoke, but I had to wait several days before hearing their answer. I finally got it on the day of all news days. I'd been waiting for Bernie Sanders's endorsement for months, and the morning I finally got it I was actually on the phone with Alexandria Ocasio-Cortez, the New York progressive who'd shocked the nation with her own surprise primary win in 2018. She congratulated me and informed me of her decision to endorse me as well, and then as soon as I hung up the phone to turn around and tell Taylor, he was hanging up his phone and turning around to talk to me. "Charles," he said, "you got both of 'em! You're being endorsed by not only *The Courier-Journal* but the *Herald-Leader* too."

I jumped up and cheered and ran around the house. It was huge on so many levels. The *Herald-Leader* is the Lexington paper. That's in Amy's backyard. It was one thing for the Louisville paper to endorse me—I was an elected official from Louisville. But for her paper to endorse me, too? That was unheard of. I also landed endorsements from the former attorney general and Speaker of the Kentucky House Greg Stumbo, as well as the former secretary of state Alison Lundergan Grimes. We announced all the major endorsements on one day, making sure to bookend the day with *The Courier-Journal* and the *Herald-Leader* so that people wouldn't only talk about the national endorsements. By putting all of that out at one time, we made our point clear: We appreciated the national support, but this campaign was about Kentucky. No one could deny us now. The wind was at our back. We had built so much momentum, you could feel it in the air.

"We've already won," I told Taylor. "When you see Kentuckians believing again, that's the win. This race is ours. The people of Kentucky are ready. Now we just need to show it at the ballot box."

BEFORE OUR CAMPAIGN began to surge, there were some polls that showed I was down fifty points to Amy McGrath. Taylor had even tried to hide the numbers from me, showing them to me only begrudgingly. "I didn't want you to worry," he said.

If I'd been worried before, I wasn't now. With two weeks left to go before Election Day, the momentum and excitement was clearly on our side. "The question," one local reporter said in an interview, "is whether Charles will run out of time." Everyone felt the same way. We were barreling toward the finish line, and there was nothing McGrath's campaign could do about it. Their only hope was that we wouldn't close the gap in time. Because not only did we have the momentum to close the gap; we had the means to do it as well.

During the early days of the campaign, with me dialing for dollars every night at my kitchen table, it took us three months to raise our first $300,000. Now we were raising that much in a day. By those last two weeks, we'd raised enough money to go dollar for dollar with one of the best-funded Senate campaigns in the country. We also had the ability to use it. During the days running a shoestring campaign, we had made a plan for how we would run once we became the kind of operation we knew we could be. We recorded ads before we had enough money to put them on the air. We trained volunteers and organizers before we had the money to send them out into the field, hoping all the time that the money would come in. When it finally did, we knew exactly what we needed to do. We put all that money to work. We blanketed the airwaves with moving and powerful messages. We sent forth an army of volunteers to knock on doors all over the state.

Taylor and I had started this campaign driving our own worn-down used cars everywhere we went; the radio in my Taurus didn't always work—it still doesn't—and Taylor had to start his car with a wrench. Now, parked outside my house on Chestnut Street was what we called "The Booker Bus"—a mega-bus with beds and TVs and a big banner with my face on the outside of it. My head looked huge! I had never seen anything like that up close. It was hard to believe. The first night Taylor pulled up with it out front it was raining, but we didn't care. We all ran outside to gawk at it. "Wow!" Tanesha said, laughing. "That's definitely your face on the bus. Do you think this is a bit much?" The girls screamed with excitement and ran to the bus. "Hop on!" I told them. I wanted them to see what this was and know that it was real. The girls laughed as they rolled around in the beds on the bus. We turned on the radio and cranked it up and soon had Jack Harlow's "Heavy Hitter" blasting through the speakers.

"You want to take a ride?" Taylor asked.

"Yep."

"Just tell the driver where to go."

"Let's take a ride through the hood."

We opened the windows and took off. As we pulled onto Muhammad Ali Boulevard we had the driver blow the horn. People outside waved and put their fists in the air. I stuck my fist out the window.

The driver craned his head back. "Where do you need me to turn?" he said.

"Let's go back to where it all started," I said. "Take us to 35th and Market."

We turned onto Mom's street, and I felt myself starting to cry as we pulled up in front of my old house, the same house where the lights were always getting cut off and those LG&E bills would always show up, the same house that nearly burned down because of a busted old space heater, the same house where my mother used to go without food just so I would have enough.

"Mama!" I called with excitement. "Come outside!"

She opened her door and saw this gigantic bus with her son's face on it, and seeing her joy was pure magic. "Wow, son!" she said in shock. "You're doing it, baby!" She hopped on the bus, climbed into one of the big leather chairs, reclined it all the way back, and smiled with pride.

The bus was a tight fit on our narrow street, and the driver had to go slow, but I wanted to make sure the rest of my family got to see it, so we took a tour past several of my cousins' houses, too. As we drove past, they ran out, pointing and yelling, "That's C.J.!" I told them all to hop on the bus. "This is your bus!" I told them. Riding around the West End, I felt like we were taking a victory lap. Regardless of what happened at the ballot box, this was a win for the West End.

Now that we had the money to travel, we took the Booker Bus everywhere. We pulled out our map of counties and precincts and sketched out routes to hit as many places as we could in a day, finding outdoor venues where people could gather and still safely distance due to COVID-19. We took the bus to every corner of Kentucky, sleeping on the bus whenever we weren't crashing at some small hotel. We hit Richmond and Morehead and Ashland and Prestonsburg and Corbin and Owensboro and Hopkinsville and Paducah and everywhere in between. We had our local organizers gather folks outside in a field or in a parking lot, and we would pull the bus right up to the crowd. Everyone would have their masks on, and they'd all be six feet apart, but it still felt like a rock concert.

Getting off the bus, I could hear everyone outside yelling and clapping just at the sight of the bus. I would hype myself up and then hop off, and my security guard Chuck would usher me through the crowd. A fist bump here, an elbow there, and a selfie over there. The energy was palpable.

Matt Jones, a good friend and host of the biggest sports radio show in Kentucky, joined me for the tour. Matt represented Eastern Kentucky, so the two of us together definitely showcased the spirit of "Hood to the Holler." We were like a tag team, traveling to different parts of Kentucky to tell everyone that this was our time to stand and fight together. Having his endorsement was huge. It helped more people in rural areas know that I was the real deal. I could see it in their eyes and hear it in their voices.

In Ashland, we pulled up to an open lot outside of a train station, where we were joined by Rep. Terri Branham Clark, a conservative Democrat whose support was a powerful sign of the broad coalition we were building. In Henderson, we hopped out to a huge crowd standing in the pouring rain on the steps of the county courthouse. They didn't care. They were fired up anyway. I hopped out and bumped elbows with everyone there, soaked to the bone and skipping over puddles along the way. In the tiny Eastern Kentucky town of Corbin, we pulled up to see a roaring crowd outside. Looking out his window, Taylor said, "Charles, did you know that Corbin is nearly 99 percent white? I would have never expected to see something like this."

In Paducah, we had another big crowd waiting for a march we'd planned, but just as we were about to get on the road to drive down there we learned that a white supremacist group was planning to crash the event. "Do you want to figure out a different location?" one of the local organizers asked us.

"No way," I said, without even hesitating. "We're standing with a message of love. If white supremacists want to see what that looks like, they can come on. But we'll be there."

The crowd was ready to go as soon as we pulled up. From young Black men that looked like my cousins to elderly white Kentuckians on canes and walkers, they were there to stand together. "You all ready to march?" I asked. They cheered. "I hear some people don't want us here, but we're here. And we're standing together as family!" They hollered even louder and started clapping as we lined up to march down the middle of the street. As we walked, some of our local supporters pointed out some known white supremacists who were just about thirty yards away, leaning up against a tree. They were watching us. I was glad they were. I lifted my fist in the air, and one by one, the rest of the crowd did, too.

It was such a whirlwind. We had everything on our side except the clock. I was numb the whole time. There were moments on the road when I couldn't tell what day it was and only knew what town I was in because the staff told me as I was getting off the bus. I didn't sleep much at all. The anxiety of getting this far and not winning made me lose my appetite, and I had to force myself to stay on my regular eating schedule. I didn't want to let down all the tear-filled faces I saw across Kentucky. I was meeting people who'd never voted before, people who started organizing with my campaign because they believed. I didn't want them to feel like they'd done that for nothing. I felt like I was carrying the hope of so many, and as each day brought us closer to Election Day, the load only got heavier.

With every roaring crowd and every endorsement, all I could do was pray that it was going to be enough. Each week, we heard reports of internal polls showing us cutting into McGrath's lead, ultimately getting it down to single digits. But we were down to the wire. Early voting had already started, and several people we met on the trail had voted for McGrath before finding out about me. One little old lady actually came up to me and said, "I didn't know who you were, and I wish I had. I voted for her, but I hope you win." I heard that so many times, and I appreciated the words, but it hurt. I had the right message, but with so many people I just couldn't get to them in time.

I told the team over and over again, "There's no way we can lose." In reality, there was no telling which way it was going to go. The race was neck and neck between McGrath and me. Mike Broihier was polling in the single digits, but it looked like most of his support might break to me. It was a straight toss-up.

The night before the election, on our way back to Louisville, we stopped the Booker Bus in Lexington one last time. Kaylin had joined me on the bus for this leg of the tour. It meant so much to me that she could see this in person. Honestly, I just wanted someone else in my family to be there, so they could see the magic that I was seeing all over Kentucky and know that it was real.

We met a crowd of a couple hundred people spread apart outside at Cheapside Park. Today, it's the park that hosts Lexington's local farmer's market, but long ago it had been one of the largest slave marketplaces in the Commonwealth of Kentucky. As Chuck guided us off the bus and over to the space, I leaned over and whispered to Kaylin, "Cheapside Park is where enslaved people were sold. Now we are walking here, as the descendants of those enslaved Kentuckians, and your dad is about to win a primary election for U.S. Senate." Kaylin smiled quietly and looked at the cheering crowd. I can't fully imagine how she felt to see all of this, but as a parent I was deeply grateful to share this moment with her.

With Kaylin beside me, I poured my heart out one last time. "This is our moment!" I belted out to the crowd. We were outside but under a sheltered area, so when I spoke, my voice filled the space. "We have a chance to prove the doubters wrong. We have a chance to show that when regular people come together, we can beat big money and we can beat a Grim Reaper. If you've ever felt like nothing would change, I understand. I've felt that way, too. But that's why we're standing right now. We are the change. Let's win this race and do the bigger work of transforming Kentucky!"

I put my fist in the air and told the crowd that I loved them. The applause echoed throughout Cheapside Park, filling up the pavilion that stood where my ancestors had once been bought and sold, a symbolic moment that will always stay with me.

After spending thirty minutes in the selfie line with every person there, we filed onto the bus to head back. Adrian Wallace, a Black minister and veteran from the area, jumped on real quick to say good-bye. "You're going to win this, Charles," he said, pumping his fist. He hopped off, we opened up our windows, and we waved to the crowd one last time. Then we lay back on the beds and reclined in our big chairs, turned up the music, and headed home.

ON THE MORNING of Election Day, time stood still. As I ironed my clothes, I kept envisioning what it would feel like to win, what it would mean to my family, to the people of Kentucky. I did my best to put all those thoughts out of my mind, because the anxiety and the emotions were overwhelming me.

As I picked out which of Grandad's ties I was going to wear, Tane-sha quickly walked past, rushing to get the girls dressed. I grabbed her hand as she slid by. I didn't say anything. I looked at her, taking a moment to remember our run in Cherokee Park, all the galas and events she'd endured when she didn't feel she belonged. She took a moment herself, but then said, calm and cool, "We need to hurry up so you aren't late." Then she moved on down the hallway to help the girls. That was Tanesha: keeping the train moving and keeping my feet on the ground.

I grabbed Grandma's Bible to carry with me and joined Tanesha and the girls and my mom and my cousin Kim as we all loaded up on the Booker Bus to go vote. Because of COVID-19's devastating effect on Kentucky, the governor and the secretary of state had worked to-gether to propose changes to the election process. In addition to the early voting period, Kentucky had implemented no-excuse absentee voting for the first time. However, with these changes happening in such a short amount of time, there was a lot of confusion. Our cam-paign had shuttles running in cities around Kentucky, helping to con-duct a statewide ride-to-the-polls effort. Our volunteers were working nonstop, sending out texts, DMs, and phone calls.

It was a full-court effort from corner to corner. In the West End, churches were going block to block checking on whether people voted or if they needed a ride. Volunteers from the Louisville Urban

League and other organizations were helping elderly Kentuckians get to the polls. In Eastern Kentucky, volunteers were doing check-in calls to their neighbors. Meanwhile, we had legal teams at the ready in every part of the Commonwealth, volunteer attorneys and political figures who could help us make sure that everyone was being allowed to vote fairly. We were prepared to challenge voting conditions in every county if we had to.

Despite the reforms that had made voting easier in certain areas, up in Louisville the state had shut down all the polling locations across Jefferson County. Instead of going to their local school or community center, in the sixteenth-largest city in the nation, the tens of thousands of people voting in person all had to converge in one place: the Kentucky Exposition Center at the fairgrounds. The idea was that this location was large enough to accommodate everyone and keep COVID requirements in place. However, it's hard to believe that this was truly proposed as a way to help everyone vote. We immediately knew the inconvenience would keep a lot of people from voting, especially people who didn't have adequate transportation to get across town.

As our bus made its way through the traffic and up to the front of the large parking lot, my stomach was in knots. There was construction going on along the main road leading to the fairgrounds, and cars were severely backed up, wrapped around the loop that entered into the Expo Center. The clouds had grown a bit gloomy, too, and as raindrops began to streak across the windshield, I started to get nervous.

On the one hand, the pileup of cars was exciting. It showed that people were adamant about being heard at the ballot box. When folks saw our bus, they'd beep their horns and roll down their windows and yell, "I'm voting for you!" On the other hand, it was infuriating. The fact that one location was set up in the middle of the city, where traffic is generally slow, felt like the last obstacle to keep us from winning what we had worked so hard for. Volunteers were all over the parking lot trying to make sure people got where they were trying to go.

Once we hit the parking lot, we circled around a few times before pulling into a parking space, just to make sure everyone saw that we were there to finish the job. Mom and Cousin Kim were both sitting calmly. Prestyn was standing up trying to look out the window. "Look, Daddy!" she called out. "Your name is on a poster!" When we parked, I made sure to go take a picture with the young people holding that poster.

I came back to help Mom off the bus. As always, I took her purse so she could grab the rail and hold my hand coming down the stairs. Pretty much everyone who'd come had umbrellas out and ponchos on. Mom had insisted on wearing her Sunday best, including her high heels. Cousin Kim, on the other hand, had come in tennis shoes, prepared to stand in a long line.

"Don't wait for me," Mom said, once we were out. "Y'all go ahead, and I'll catch up." As stern as she was, I wasn't hearing it. I wanted to take these steps with her by my side and would rather wait than leave her behind.

Once we got to the entrance to the Expo Center, all the news stations were camped out ready to snag their interview. I stopped and spoke to all of them, explaining the historical significance of what I was seeking to do. "I know Kentucky has never nominated someone who looks like me to serve in the U.S. Senate. But I am proud to stand here today as a testament to those who blazed the trail for me like my grandad. I want the West End, the city of Louisville, and the entire Commonwealth to be proud of this moment."

As I spoke, my voice shook with emotion. It was all starting to sink in. I was on the precipice of making history. I felt chains breaking with every step. My ancestors were with me, and I realized I was bending the moral arc that Dr. King spoke of. As we walked into the voting area, Tanesha held one hand and my mom held the other, and with every step, I heard the echo of history. I tried hard, but I couldn't hide my tears. I stepped into the booth, filled out my ballot, then we made our way back through the cheering crowds and back to the Booker Bus. The next stop was our campaign war room at the AC Hotel, where we would watch the votes come in, monitor voting access and challenges across Kentucky, and, God willing, celebrate my victory as the Democratic nominee for the United States Senate from the Commonwealth of Kentucky.

As the day wore on, we stayed in constant contact with our campaign staff across the state, doing everything we could to assess the state of the race. We knew we needed to run up big leads in Louisville and Lexington to win. In Lexington, we feared our lead wouldn't be big enough, which meant we needed Louisville's margin to come in as big as possible. So all afternoon, as we watched the traffic steadily pile up outside the fairgrounds, the agonizing question on everyone's mind was, "Will they get to vote in time?'"

The law stated that anyone in line at 6 P.M. would be allowed to vote. But with only one polling location and road construction snarling up the roads all around it and all the confusion around COVID-19, it was looking like the law wouldn't be honored. If you were stuck in traffic trying to vote after work, would that count as "being in line"? Even the lawyers didn't know.

Sure enough, 6 P.M. came, and thousands of people still hadn't been able to vote, and the police stepped in and locked the doors at the Expo Center. Thousands of people were stranded outside, in the parking lot, in their cars, unable to get inside. I sat watching footage of Louisvillians banging on the doors and windows, demanding their right to vote. Worse still, the police had positioned themselves outside the locked doors, which provided a visual and physical deterrent to people trying to stand their ground and hold their place in line. All I could do was shake my head. Our chances of winning were slipping away. Seeing the long lines, I knew that every voter being blocked from the ballot box was a lost vote for me. I was numb, but my team was in a frenzy.

Taylor immediately jumped on the phone with our election attorney, my dear friend Dave Suetholz. We requested that the police be pulled back to a less intimidating position, and they complied. Then we filed a last-minute injunction to try to keep the polls open. We asked that the polls stay open until nine, noting the fact that people had been waiting in line in traffic for over an hour before they could even get out of their car to wait in the standing line. We knew it was a long shot, but we had to try. For the next few minutes, we waited anxiously to hear back from the judge. Will was pacing the hotel room, and Colin was on his phone barking directions to our attorneys. Meanwhile, I jumped online, posting videos to social media, urging everyone who was in line to stay in line. Some of our celebrity friends, like Jennifer Lawrence, boosted the signal by sharing the info as well. I laid my head against the wall as we waited, hoping we would be surprised with good news, and not long after I heard Colin yell out, "We did it!" Judge Annie O'Connell had reviewed our request and granted some relief. It was only thirty extra minutes, but it was thirty minutes we didn't have before. With the election so close, everything made a difference. The room erupted in celebration. The temporary injection offered a shot of hope.

The rest of the evening was one long, agonizing anticlimax. The race was too close to call. We had a large lead in the counted ballots, but our margin in Lexington wasn't as big as we knew we needed it to be, and there were still thousands of mail-in and absentee ballots to be counted. It would be another long, agonizing week before we learned the final results. I went out and spoke to the crowd gathered at our event and thanked the people of Kentucky for believing in me and standing by my side. Then we went back home to wait.

HEADING INTO ELECTION DAY, Taylor had sat down and crunched the polling data and given me his final prediction. "We're either going to win by three or lose by three," he said. In the end, he was right on the money, just not the way I'd hoped.

The day the final numbers were supposed to come out, we all gathered at the hotel war room again. It was crowded, and the staff were running back and forth while I sat on a stool, my eyes glued to the computer screen. Then the results were confirmed. With the final tally, McGrath had won 247,037 votes, and I had won 231,888—a margin of 2.8 percentage points. Mike Broihier had played the spoiler with 27,175 votes, around 5 percent. In Jefferson County, I'd run up the highest voter turnout for a primary candidate in the county's history—even more than President Obama. But there was no path for me to catch up.

I immediately got up and left the room. "I'm going home to lie on my couch," I said. There was dead silence as I walked out. Later, I was still lying on that couch when Taylor called. I told him I didn't want to concede. There had been so much confusion with the mail-in ballots, and we'd learned that votes were being discarded in some counties for not having proper signatures. We were hearing stories from people about thousands of votes being improperly thrown out, but we didn't have any hard facts to prove it, and we certainly didn't have anything to indicate that the irregularities were enough to overcome the 15,000-vote margin. Still, so many people were begging me to challenge the results and keep fighting.

"Taylor," I said. "I'm not a quitter. If votes were thrown out, we should fight for them. That's the point of all of this!"

"I want to fight like hell, too. I don't want you to concede, either," he said. "But there's just not a path, man. And if you contest the results and even ask for a recount, you could damage your relationships with the Party and hurt Amy as the nominee. This is not where your journey ends, Charles. You need to concede." I fussed a bit more, but eventually I relented and accepted that I would not be the Democratic nominee.

I called Amy McGrath and congratulated her on her win. It was a strange call to make, because we both knew that the deeper victory, the moral victory, belonged to me. My campaign had proved every doubter wrong. We'd shown that it's possible to build a movement for a new kind of politics in Kentucky. We'd lit a match to spark a movement for our future, and that fire was only going to burn brighter with each passing day.

It was also strange to congratulate her on her victory because I knew she'd already lost. Everyone on the ground in Kentucky knew she didn't have the deep support that would help her turn out enough voters to defeat the most powerful Republican in the country. I tried to hold out hope and worked across Kentucky to help the best I could, but ultimately I knew it wouldn't be enough. After the primary, I received passionate pleas from people across Kentucky who did not want me to endorse Amy. However, I wanted to find a way to help beat McConnell without selling out. Though I was not out on the trail with Amy, that summer I made a public endorsement alongside Congressman Yarmuth, calling on Kentuckians to focus on the greater good of getting Mitch out of office.

That November, Mitch McConnell beat Amy McGrath by double digits, and as I watched those results come in, it killed me knowing that I could have beaten him but never got the chance to prove it.

I sat on that couch for the rest of the day, 2.8 points short of making history. The texts and calls coming in all said the same thing: "If you'd had a couple more days, you would have won." It's a refrain I still hear across Kentucky today, but it was of little comfort at the time. I felt empty. My spirits were crushed.

As the sun went down, I finally began to accept that the day was going to be what it was, and there was nothing more to do. I slowly trudged my way up the stairs. I hadn't taken a shower, and I was still wearing my shirt and suit pants from the day before. Tanesha, meanwhile, was already back to work, pecking away at her keyboard, processing medical claims and keeping the family moving forward. She had her earbuds in, streaming a movie on her phone while staring at her computer monitor, as she often did. I stopped and leaned on the wall by the desk. Seeing me standing there with my sad-sack expression, Tanesha stopped typing and took out her headphones.

"Well," I said, shrugging my shoulders. "I guess we'll see what God has for us next, huh?" Then I turned and looked in Prestyn's room, growing silent again.

Tanesha, already fed up with my moping, wasn't having it. As usual, I was riding the roller coaster of public life, and behind her shyness was the steady resolve that kept our family on the rails. "Charles," she said, as clear and direct as I'd ever heard her, "this just set the stage for you. The work was always bigger than Mitch McConnell."

As she spoke, time seemed to slow down. Tanesha didn't voluntarily talk about politics. I had an idea of what she was about to say next, but I wasn't going to assume anything. I was going to wait for her to make it plain. And she did.

"You just need to get ready to run against Rand Paul," she said.

When she said it, my jaw dropped a bit. I couldn't believe that those words had actually come out of her mouth. With me losing this race, she finally had her chance to be done with the public arena. But she and I both knew the same truth: God was setting the stage for me to continue the work. My campaign had started to tell a new story for Kentucky, but now the people had to finish it. Still, even though that was what I believed, I was in so much shock that she believed it, too. I didn't know how to respond except to say, "Really? Take on Rand Paul? Are you serious?"

"Yes. I think you should."

Having set me straight, she turned back to her computer and went right back to work. A smile crept into the corner of her mouth. "Besides," she said, "you know you're gonna do it anyway."

ACKNOWLEDGMENTS

I am so thankful to share my story, our story, with the world.

I want to start by thanking Kevin Doughten, for hearing my story, seeing my vision, and believing that a message of healing like this can only come from a place like Kentucky.

Thank you to my agent, Melissa Flashman, for sharing my pride in our great Commonwealth and fighting to get this story told. Your faith and constant encouragement have meant everything.

Thank you to Tanner Colby, for your brilliance, patience, clarity, and passion. You saw the story I wanted to present and helped to orchestrate something I truly believe will inspire more regular people to find their voices and seize the power to lead for real change.

Thank you to the team at Crown: David Drake, Gillian Blake, Annsley Rosner, Dyana Messina, Dan Novak, Julie Cepler, Lydia Morgan, Alonzo Vereen, Emily Hotaling, Gwyneth Stansfield, Christopher Brand. Thank you to Isabel Cristo for helping to cross every T. Thanks to Mason Colby, and everyone else who committed time and treasure to bring the words and images on these pages to life.

I want to thank everyone that poured into me and helped me to find my purpose. Thank you to those Hill staffers who took me in: Bianca, Keidra, Mike, Brandon, and everyone who read my email, took a meeting, and made a call. Thank you to Robert Jenkins for letting me bug him for years in search of an opportunity to work for Kentucky. Thank you to Mr. Yancey, Ms. Jackie, Ms. Myra, Ms. Bonnie, and every elder who took me under their wing. Thank you to

Christa Robinson for believing in me and pushing me to run for office. Thank you to Elizabeth, Jacie, Perry, Jeff, Taylor, Kelsey, Will, Colin, LaShea, and every person who hired me, worked with me, or worked for me on a campaign.

Thank you to my big brother in politics, David Tandy. You and Ms. Carolyn helped give me a personal example of what is possible. Thank you for your counsel and prayers. Thank you for giving me a chance to help the people of the 4th District.

Congressman John Yarmuth, thank you for all you have done for me and our Commonwealth. You inspire me more than I can say.

From the bottom of my heart, I want to thank Senator Gerald Neal for the irreplaceable role he has played in my political journey and growth as a man. I learned from you, challenged you, and, in the end, have a deep and profound respect for what you have done for the Commonwealth of Kentucky. I am honored to be a part of your legacy.

There is no way I can thank my entire family without filling another couple hundred pages, and I apologize in advance for any name that is not expressly listed here. Please know that I love you, and I dedicate this work to you. To my Mama, Evangelist Earletta Hearn, thank you for being my angel. Thank you for the impossible sacrifices. Thank you for your unbreakable strength. I am so proud to be your son. Dad, thank you for being the best dad in the world. I miss you dearly, but you are still my Batman. To B.B., thank you for coming into my life as the sister I always needed. To my Grandad, Lindsay E. Hearn, Sr., thank you for teaching me about where I come from. Thank you for teaching me how to be a good father. I hope this makes you proud, sir. To Grandma, Maw Maw, and Paw Paw, thank you for giving me the best grandparents a Black kid with big dreams could ever ask for. To Latarius, Ta'Neka, Mikey, Lindsay, Clay, Tanya, Mesia, Erica, Brittany, Lonzo, Tre, Junior, Antoinette, Tonesha, Lex, Mariah (strawberry head), and every single one of my many cousins, I love you and hope this makes you proud. Geno, forgive me for sharing the roach story. All of my aunties and uncles, thank you for always having my back. I love y'all.

Kentucky, thank you for the inspiration and all the love. You are my home, and you forever have my heart. To the West End of Louisville, every neighborhood and every block, thank you for teaching me the power of community and reinforcing a sense of pride that drives me to this day. To my family in Appalachia and across Kentucky, thank you for helping me see the power of standing together from the hood to the holler. This book is my love story to you.

Tanesha, thank you for holding my hand and believing in me. Thank you for being my partner on this remarkable journey. I love you.

To Kaylin, Prestyn, and Justyce, please know that you are my reason. You are my greatest inspiration. Thank you for giving me the honor of being your dad. Hopefully this doesn't embarrass you too much.

ABOUT THE AUTHOR

CHARLES BOOKER represented the 43rd District in the Kentucky House of Representatives. A graduate of the University of Louisville and its Brandeis School of Law, Booker is a Bingham fellow and a Bloomberg Innovation Delivery Team Fellow. He is the founder of the advocacy group Hood to the Holler, which continues the work of his campaign, building bridges between previously siloed communities.

charlesbooker.org
Twitter: @Booker4KY

ABOUT THE TYPE

This book was set in Garamond, a typeface originally designed by the Parisian type cutter Claude Garamond (c. 1500–61). This version of Garamond was modeled on a 1592 specimen sheet from the Egenolff-Berner foundry, which was produced from types assumed to have been brought to Frankfurt by the punch cutter Jacques Sabon (c. 1520–80).

Claude Garamond's distinguished romans and italics first appeared in *Opera Ciceronis* in 1543–44. The Garamond types are clear, open, and elegant.